GRADES 4—5

Beyond the
BUBBLE

GRADES 4–5

Beyond the B U B B L E

How to Use Multiple-Choice Tests to Improve Math Instruction

Maryann **Wickett** and Eunice **Hendrix-Martin**

S **Stenhouse**
PUBLISHERS

www.stenhouse.com

Stenhouse Publishers
www.stenhouse.com

Library of Congress Cataloging-in-Publication Data
Wickett, Maryann.
  Beyond the bubble : how to use multiple-choice tests to improve math instruction, grades 4-5 / Maryann Wickett and Eunice Hendrix-Martin.
     p. cm.
  ISBN 978-1-57110-818-0 (alk. paper) -- ISBN 978-1-57110-899-9
  1. Arithmetic--Study and teaching (Elementary) 2. Multiple-choice examinations. I. Hendrix-Martin, Eunice, 1957- II. Title.
  QA135.6.W532 2011
  372.7--dc22
                        2010043468

Cover design, interior design, and typesetting by designboy Creative Group

Manufactured in the United States of America

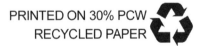
PRINTED ON 30% PCW
RECYCLED PAPER

17 16 15 14 13 12 11   9 8 7 6 5 4 3 2 1

We wish to thank our families for their support
during all the endless weekends it took to create this book.

Contents

Acknowledgments

We wish to thank all of the students at Carrillo Elementary School in Carlsbad, California, for sharing their learning and thinking with their teachers and with us. Your sharing has helped us to learn and grow. Thank you to the following teachers for their insights and assistance with this project: Jennifer Woods, Lisa Lancon, Cris Dorsey, Viki Stewart, Lisa Mariano, and Gina Duke. Without you, this book would not have been possible.

Date _____

Introduction

ng.

n addition problem.

multiplication problem.

ded and multiplied

r and found out

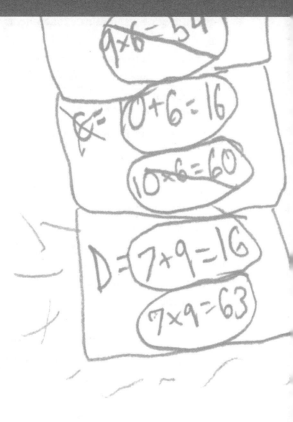

Multiple-choice testing is an educational reality for students and teachers. Rather than continue to complain about how these tests can adversely affect teaching and learning, we thought it better to turn the testing situation on its head—that is, to take full advantage of all that multiple-choice testing can offer. The purpose of *Beyond the Bubble* is to do just that: show teachers how to get more from multiple-choice tests. By asking students just a few carefully chosen questions, teachers can gain valuable insight into students' mathematical thinking.

Many schools and districts rely on multiple-choice testing to assess students' math progress. The assumption is that if a student marks a correct answer—if he or she fills in the *right* bubble—that student is proficient in the corresponding skill or objective. However, a correct answer can often mask fragile knowledge or misconceptions, or it may have been just a lucky guess. (There are many examples of this throughout the book.) The inverse is also true. If a student marks an incorrect answer—if he or she fills in the *wrong* bubble—that student is considered to be in need of remediation. But the student may have just misread the problem or made a mistake when selecting an answer. Both "correct" and "incorrect" answers reveal little about what a student truly does or doesn't understand. Consequently, instructional decisions based on this testing information may be misguided. Again, taking just a few moments to probe students' thinking can provide valuable insight leading to more effective instruction for all students.

Using typical multiple-choice questions often found on fourth- and fifth-grade assessments and in test-prep materials, we asked hundreds of students to explain their answer choices in writing and verbally. We found that both correct and incorrect multiple-choice responses often painted an inaccurate or incomplete picture of students' mathematical understanding. For example, we assumed students who answered questions correctly would consistently show strong understanding and demonstrate logical thinking, but they just as often showed partial understanding, confusion, or no understanding at all. We were surprised to find the same was also true for students who marked incorrect responses. But using these test questions and probing with a few additional questions allowed us to get "beyond the bubble"—suddenly we were using the questions to our (and our students') advantage, uncovering understanding and misconceptions, which, in turn, allowed us to make more effective instructional decisions as we considered what our students needed next.

Beyond the Bubble is divided into five strands: number, measurement, algebra, geometry, and probability. There are six problems per strand. Each problem begins with a brief overview of the test question's objective, followed by the sample test question, typical student strategies used to solve the problem, conversation starters, actual student work, student-teacher conversations along with teacher insights, and suggestions for instructional strategies that should help advance individual students' learning. Many of the "Informed Instructional Suggestions" sections include ideas for differentiating instruction and grouping students with similar needs. Reassessment questions are also provided.

At the end of the book there is a general list of questions for you to use to start conversations with your students. We've found that posting these questions on the back wall of your classroom provides a quick and easy way to use them with students when having conversations throughout the school day. Also included are reproducibles of all sample questions and a general list of teaching resources.

You may notice that some students' work appears more frequently throughout the book. These students include Penny, Lilli, Suri, Kylie, Darren, and Eddie. You may find it worthwhile to study the work of each of these students and discuss your insights with colleagues. What questions would you ask the student?

What do you think the student knows? Where do you think gaps might be? How do you know? How could you find out? Such reflection will help you prepare for having meaningful conversations with your students that you can use to inform your instruction.

Some Dos and Don'ts

o   Do take the time to ask questions and listen carefully to students' responses. They will provide you with valuable opportunities to understand and appreciate your students' strengths and weaknesses.

o   Don't rely on a single multiple-choice response alone. It may mask true understanding or misunderstanding, making purposeful instruction difficult.

o   Do discuss what you find out with colleagues. Talk about surprises, victories, and methods to engage students and help them move forward with understanding.

o   Don't be afraid to follow a child's lead. You may not understand his or her thinking initially, but by listening carefully with an open mind, you may discover brilliance in ways you've never before considered.

o   Do reflect on our examples and see if you can find similar outcomes in your class. The more connections you make to your children, the more comfortable you will be with engaging students in meaningful mathematical conversations, ultimately improving your instruction and children's learning.

o   Do keep asking good questions that uncover students' learning and understanding, providing you with valuable insights. Children deserve our attention and our best instructional decisions.

As educators, the more information we can gather, the better pedagogical decisions we can make for our students. We wrote *Beyond the Bubble* for all educators who want better, more focused mathematics instruction for their students. This includes teachers, administrators, and preservice teachers. The results of our work with students provide the basis for excellent inservice discussions or professional learning community (PLC) planning and conversations. When instructional decision makers, both teachers and administrators, examine students' written and verbal explanations, differentiation becomes quicker, easier, and more targeted. It is our hope that *Beyond the Bubble* will be used as a tool for insightful, engaging mathematics instruction for you and your students.

Number

Number: Problem One
Date
A
x B
ox C
ox D
n your thinking.
It is counting up by 20's
Every line is a 10.
160 170 180 190 200
a
b
C
d

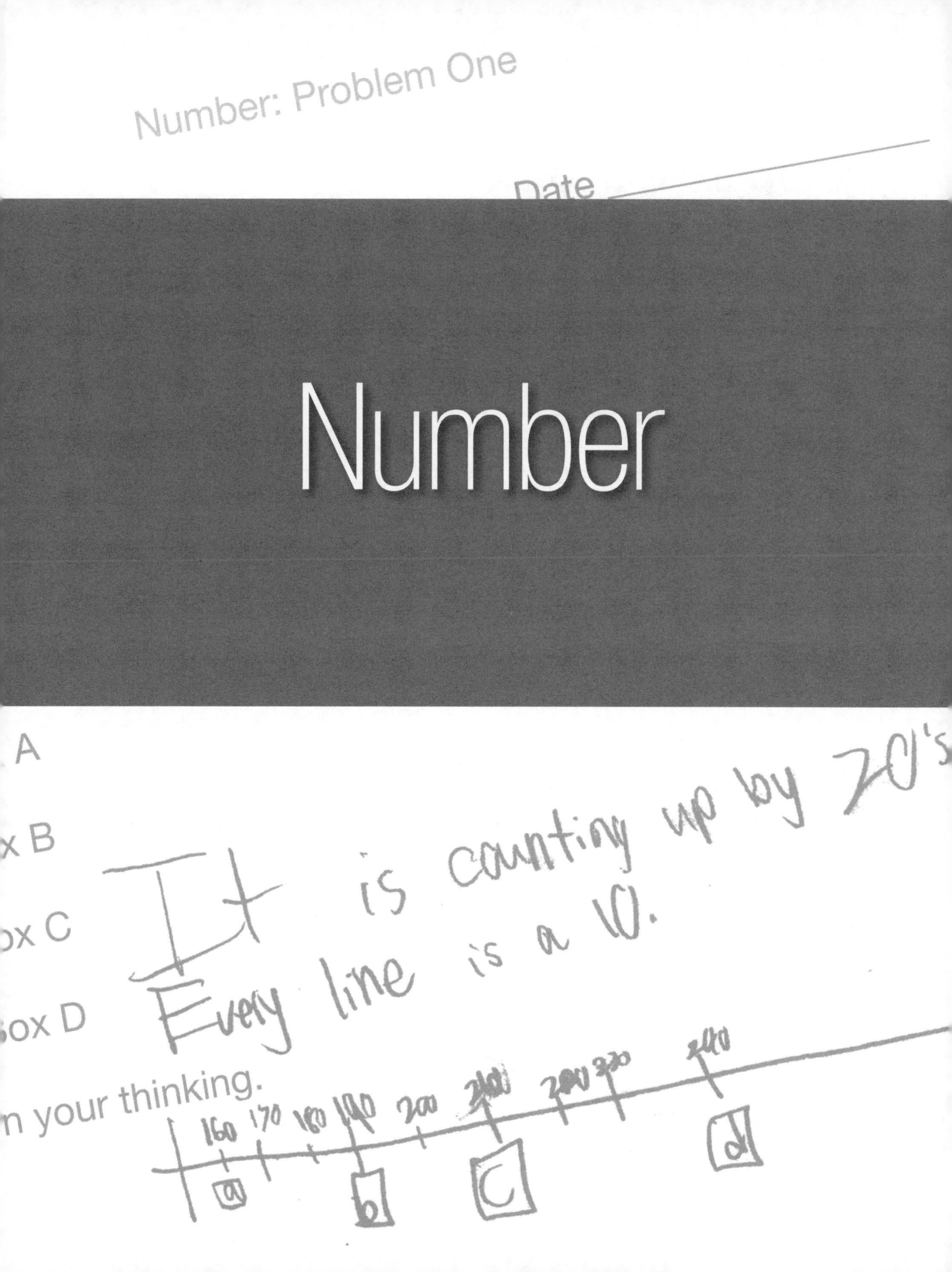

PROBLEM ONE

Overview

Students must apply their number sense, their ability to count by tens, and their understanding of place value and of number lines to answer this typical multiple-choice question.

Sample Problem

In which box on the number line does the number 190 belong?

A. Box A
B. Box B
C. Box C
D. Box D

Explain your thinking.

Possible Student Solution Strategies

o   Students use the numbers provided to find a pattern of counting by tens and use this information to locate where 190 belongs.
o   Students count by an incorrect interval.
o   Students fail to use the provided numbers correctly to determine where 190 belongs.

Conversation Starters

o   How did the information provided help you solve this problem?
o   What is another way you could solve this problem?
o   How do you know your answer is reasonable?
o   How can you prove your answer?
o   What pattern did you see that helped you solve this problem? Describe it.

Student Work Sample: Preston

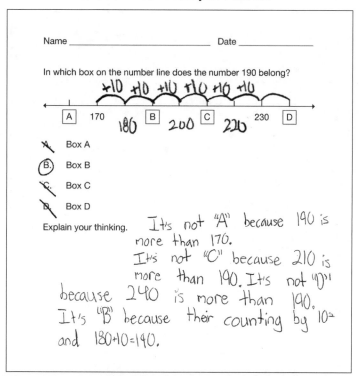

Name _____ Date _____

In which box on the number line does the number 190 belong?

A. Box A
B. Box B (circled)
C. Box C
D. Box D

Explain your thinking. It's not "A" because 190 is more than 170.
It's not "C" because 210 is more than 190. It's not "D" because 240 is more than 190.
It's "B" because their counting by 10s and 180+10=190.

A Conversation with Preston	Teacher Insights
T: How did the information provided help you solve this problem? **Preston:** I noticed that the number 170 was the first number there. I also saw that 230 was there and a bunch of lines. I knew that the lines couldn't be counting by ones because there were not enough lines between 170 and 230, so I tried counting by tens and it worked! So then I filled in the missing numbers. That made it pretty easy to find out where 190 was supposed to go. **T:** I appreciate your clear written explanation and how you were able to explain your thinking aloud as well.	**T:** *Preston was able to apply his understanding and reasoning to efficiently solve this problem.*

Informed Instructional Suggestions

Preston is ready to explore number lines with more complex patterns and larger numbers. As Preston becomes increasingly adept, he can work with number lines that include fractions, decimals, percents, and negative numbers. It would also be appropriate to have Preston create his own number lines with missing numbers for other students to complete.

Student Work Sample: Sumita

Name _____ Date _____

In which box on the number line does the number 190 belong?

A.   Box A

B.   Box B

C.   Box C

D.   Box D

Explain your thinking.

it is B because I started from 230 and counted backwards and at B I got 190.

A Conversation with Sumita	Teacher Insights
T: I see that you were able to select an answer. What could you have included on your paper to prove your answer makes sense? **Sumita:** What I did was start at 230 and I guessed and counted backward by tens until I got to 190, which was B. Then I started with 170 and counted up by tens and landed on B again. I was pretty sure I was right. But I guess I could have written the numbers on the number line, but I did it two ways, so I know I'm right. **T:** I am curious about why you decided to count backward first. **Sumita:** It's more interesting to me to do it that way. Then I can count the other way to make sure the backwards way works.	**T:** *Sumita is fluent with the skills involved in solving this problem. She was able to explain why her solution made sense in two ways.*

Informed Instructional Suggestions

Like Preston, Sumita is able to easily make sense of problems at this level. Sumita is ready for the same activities we suggested for Preston.

Student Work Samples: Tony, Danny, and Traci

Name _____ Date _____

In which box on the number line does the number 190 belong?

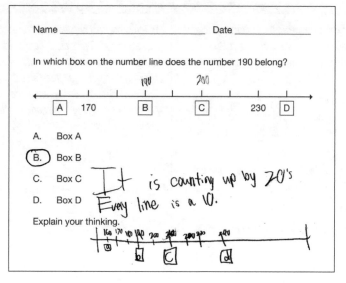

A. Box A

(B.) Box B

C. Box C

D. Box D

Explain your thinking.

It is counting up by 20's
Every line is a 10.

Name _____ Date _____

In which box on the number line does the number 190 belong?

A. Box A

(B) Box B

C. Box C

D. Box D

Explain your thinking.

Each I stands for 10. 170, 180, 190,

Name _____ Date _____

In which box on the number line does the number 190 belong?

A. Box A

(B.) Box B

C. Box C

D. Box D

Explain your thinking.

I picked B becase it going by 20 so if it's goes by 20 it has to be 190 se 170, 180, 190

A Conversation with Tony, Danny, and Traci	Teacher Insights
T: I would like the three of you to share with each other your solutions. I noticed that each of you used patterns to help you solve this problem. How are your patterns and solutions similar and different? **Danny:** I noticed that each line stands for ten. I counted by tens and got my answer. So did Tony. We did the same thing. But Traci counted by twenties and she got the same answer as us. **Traci:** But so has Tony. He counted two different ways and got the same answer. How come that worked? **Danny:** Huh? That's weird! **Tony:** No it's not. The lines count by tens and the boxes count by twenty. **Danny:** Wait a minute. Let me think about that. I think I disagree just a little bit with that. Box A is really 160, right? **Tony:** Yes. **Traci:** But 160 and 20 is 180, and Box B is really 190. **Tony:** Hmm . . . darn, I think you're right. But I still got the right answer. **Danny:** Well, Box B and Box C are twenty apart. And I agree that the lines are all ten apart. **Tony:** You know what? Box D doesn't quite follow what I said either. So I guess Traci and I are both a little bit wrong, but just a little. I guess we should check more carefully next time to be sure our patterns work everywhere. **T:** It is important that the three of you could look carefully at each other's work and see what is the same and what is different and to learn from each other respectfully.	**T:** *Tony and Traci applied an incorrect pattern but found the correct answer. In Tony's case, he also identified a correct pattern, applied it, and found the correct answer in that way as well. Through discussion, all three students discovered the error in Tony's and Traci's thinking and were able to recognize the importance of checking to be sure a pattern works in all instances within a problem.*

Informed Instructional Suggestions

These three students are prime examples of the importance of differentiated instruction. Danny is ready to take the same next steps we recommended for Sumita and Preston. On the other hand, Tony and Traci need additional experiences similar to this problem to reinforce the key idea that a pattern must be consistent within a problem.

Student Work Sample: Cassidy

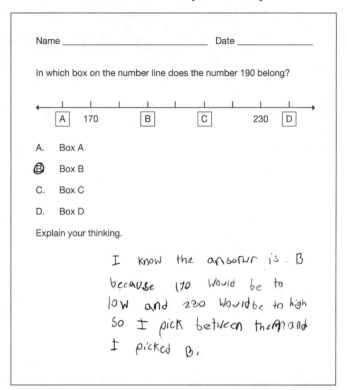

Name _____ Date _____

In which box on the number line does the number 190 belong?

A   170   B   C   230   D

A.   Box A

B.   Box B

C.   Box C

D.   Box D

Explain your thinking.

I know the ansorur is B because 170 Would be to low and 230 Wouldbe to high So I pick between them and I picked B.

A Conversation with Cassidy	Teacher Insights
T: I see that you used 170 and 230 to help you solve this problem. Beyond that, how can you prove your answer? **Cassidy:** Boxes B and C are between those two numbers. I know that 190 is between those two numbers too. **T:** Why did you pick Box B rather than Box C? **Cassidy:** It seems like 190 might be closer to 170 than to 230. Box B is closer to 170 and Box C is closer to 230. I picked B. Am I right?	**T:** *Cassidy selected the right answer, but her understanding appeared to be weak. She was able to use her number sense to help her make a reasonable and, in this case, correct answer choice. But when I challenged her thinking, she exhibited uncertainty.*

Informed Instructional Suggestions

It is important for Cassidy to have additional experiences with number lines. She should start with simpler number lines than the one presented in this problem and then build on from there. It would also be helpful to give Cassidy opportunities to use concrete methods to verify her predictions about missing numbers. One way to do this would be to have her compare her predictions with a completed number line.

Student Work Sample: Jimmy

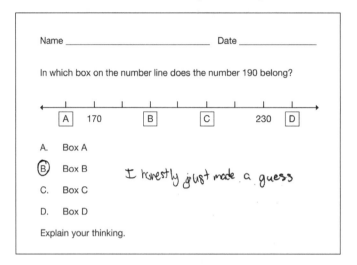

Name _____ Date _____

In which box on the number line does the number 190 belong?

A   170   B   C   230   D

A.   Box A

(B) Box B   *I honestly just made a guess*

C.   Box C

D.   Box D

Explain your thinking.

A Conversation with Jimmy	Teacher Insights
T: Jimmy, I appreciate your honesty. Why did you choose B over the other choices? **Jimmy:** It looked right and I am reading a really good mystery and I wanted to find out what happened next, so I made a guess. **T:** Do you think your guess is correct? **Jimmy:** I don't know. Maybe. **T:** How could you find out? **Jimmy:** I could put numbers where the boxes are. But I don't know what numbers to put. **T:** Use the numbers that are already on the number line to help you. **Jimmy:** [Pausing and then pointing to 170 and then moving his finger to Box B and then Box C] One hundred seventy, 180, 190 . . . oh! I should have chosen choice C!	*T: Jimmy showed little understanding of the skills needed to solve this problem. During the discussion, he tried to make sense of the situation but was unable to do so, ultimately leading him to want to change his selection to an incorrect answer.*

Informed Instructional Suggestions

Jimmy's initial correct answer choice revealed little about his true level of understanding, which is minimal. His verbal explanation indicated confusion. He is in need of experiences with basic skills involving number lines and patterns. He should begin with smaller numbers at first and then move to larger numbers. Had we relied solely on his multiple-choice response, we would have missed an important gap in his understanding and he would have missed essential, needed instruction.

Student Work Sample: Konrad

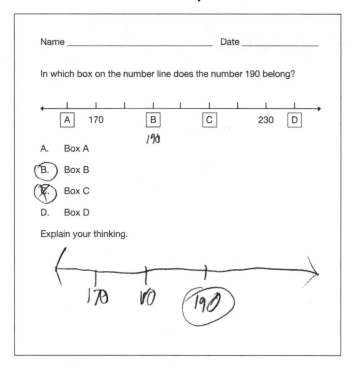

A Conversation with Konrad	Teacher Insights
T: I notice that on the number line you labeled Box B with 190, but you circled choice C, which is for Box C. Tell me more about that. **Konrad:** I did? Oh man! I hate when my pencil makes mistakes. Can I change my answer to choice B? [Konrad does so.] See, I even drew the number line and proved it that way. The lines are counting up by tens.	**T:** *Konrad understood the problem, as shown by his written and verbal explanations.*

Informed Instructional Suggestions

Konrad marked an incorrect answer but understood how to solve the question. If we had relied only on the multiple-choice response, we would have spent unnecessary time and energy reteaching him what he already knew. Konrad is ready for experiences such as those we suggested for Preston and Sumita.

Student Work Sample: Josie

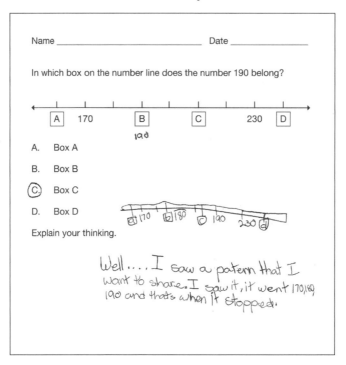

Name _____ Date _____

In which box on the number line does the number 190 belong?

A.   Box A

B.   Box B

C.   Box C

D.   Box D

Explain your thinking.

Well....I saw a pattern that I want to share. I saw it, it went 170,180 190 and that's when it stopped.

A Conversation with Josie	Teacher Insights
T: Why do you think your answer makes sense? **Josie:** I saw a pattern that is counting up by tens. I started with 170, then Box B is 180 and Box C is 190. So I chose Box C for my answer. **T:** What does each of the lines mean on the number line? **Josie:** They stand for five. **T:** Let's continue your pattern starting with Box C, or 190. What does the next line stand for? **Josie:** One hundred ninety-five. Oh, look—they made a mistake. The line after that says 230 and it should really be 200.	**T:** *Josie found an incorrect pattern. She firmly believed that each line represented a difference of five and used this incorrect pattern to arrive at her answer. She believed this so strongly that when she bumped into a challenge to her idea, she assumed there was an error in the question rather than in her thinking.*

Informed Instructional Suggestions

Josie knew to look for a pattern to help her solve this problem, which is a good start. Now she needs help with building on this skill by finding strategies for proving or disproving the accuracy of patterns she applies.

Reassessment

1. Use a similar problem at the same level of difficulty.

    In which box on the number line does the number 210 belong?

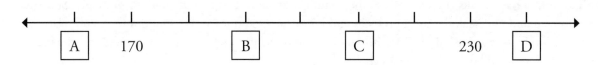

    A. Box A
    B. Box B
    C. Box C
    D. Box D

    Explain your thinking.

2. Choose a problem that is similar but slightly more challenging.

    What number goes in Box A?

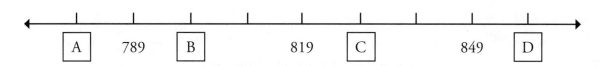

    A. 759
    B. 774
    C. 788
    D. 779

    Explain your thinking.

ⓅⓇⓄⒷⓁⒺⓂ ⓉⓌⓄ

Overview

This sample question asks students to use their number sense to compare three-digit numbers. Students need to read and understand a story problem and know how to represent it using numbers and relational symbols. Students who have difficulty with reading comprehension or who do not understand the use of relational symbols will find this problem challenging.

Sample Problem

Sarah collected 337 baseball cards. Tamika collected fewer baseball cards than Sarah. Which number sentence shows a possible comparison between the number of baseball cards that Sarah collected and the number that Tamika collected?

A. 337 < 325
B. 340 < 337
C. 301 < 337
D. 337 > 350

Explain your thinking.

Possible Student Solution Strategies

o Students are able to apply their understanding of relational symbols and their number sense to find the correct number comparison.
o Students confuse the relational symbols.
o Students misunderstand the problem.

Conversation Starters

o Put the problem into your own words.
o What do you know about this problem? What do you need to find out?
o Is there more than one possible correct answer? Explain.
o How did you think about this problem?
o How could you explain your thinking to another person?

Student Work Sample: Gary

Name _____   Date _____

Sarah collected 337 baseball cards. Tamika collected fewer baseball cards than Sarah. Which number sentence shows a possible comparison between the number of baseball cards that Sarah collected and the number that Tamika collected?

A.   337 < 325

B.   340 < 337

C.   301 < 337

D.   337 > 350

Explain your thinking.

A is wrong because 325 is not greater than 337. It is 12 smaller. B is wrong because 337 is not greater than 340. It is 3 smaller. C is right because Sarah collected 337 baseball cards, and Tamika could have collected 301 and 337 is greater than 301. D is wrong because 337 is not greater than 380. It is 13 smaller.

A Conversation with Gary	Teacher Insights
T: Gary, your answer is very clear and very complete. It helps me better understand how deeply you are thinking. Thank you for your detailed work. Is there anything else you would like to add? **Gary:** Well, we don't really know if Tamika collected 301 baseball cards, but it is the only number that makes sense. She really could have collected any number less than 337. Like, she could have even collected 336. And the problem was tricky because the story starts with 337, and in the number sentence it's the second number instead of the first! Tricky!	**T:** *Gary fully understood the problem and was able to explain his thinking very clearly both in writing and verbally. He was even able to articulate some of the nuances that make this problem challenging for many students.*

Informed Instructional Suggestions

Gary might find it interesting and challenging to develop similar problems with varying degrees of difficulty for his classmates to solve. When other students grow their understanding to the level of Gary's, they can write problems for Gary to solve. Gary would also benefit from solving similar but more complex story problems (e.g., those with bigger or more numbers).

Student Work Sample: Cali

Name _____ Date _____

Sarah collected 337 baseball cards. Tamika collected fewer baseball cards than Sarah. Which number sentence shows a possible comparison between the number of baseball cards that Sarah collected and the number that Tamika collected?

✗ 337 < 325 — it is eating the little number

✗ 340 < 337 — higher than 37

Ⓒ 301 < 337 — it eating the bigger number

✗ 337 > 350 — higher than 37

Explain your thinking.

A Conversation with Cali	Teacher Insights
T: I noticed in your explanation that bigger numbers are eating smaller numbers. I didn't know that numbers were "carnumberous." Please tell me more. **Cali:** I learned that the alligator always eats the big number because he wants the most. **T:** Alligators? How did alligators get into this problem? **Cali:** Oh, the little signs look like alligator mouths. The alligator opens its mouth wide to eat the bigger number. **T:** How would you read this number sentence [pointing to choice C]? **Cali:** The alligator ate 337.	*T: Cali has learned a mnemonic device that will generate a correct answer. However, she was unable to read the number sentence of her correct response in a mathematically correct manner. Additionally, as Cali applied the mnemonic device of the alligator eating the larger number, she completely disregarded the hundreds involved in these numbers and focused only on the ones and tens.*

Informed Instructional Suggestions

Cali needs to learn to read number sentences such as those presented in this question in a mathematically correct manner. She needs to learn to use appropriate phrases such as *greater than* and *less than* and know that these words are represented by the symbols > and <. She would also benefit from learning to consider the importance of all digits when comparing numbers. Using base ten blocks to build the numbers being compared would provide concrete experiences.

Student Work Sample: Ferguson

Name _____ Date _____

Sarah collected 337 baseball cards. Tamika collected fewer baseball cards than Sarah. Which number sentence shows a possible comparison between the number of baseball cards that Sarah collected and the number that Tamika collected?

A. 337 < 325

B. 340 < 337

Ⓒ 301 < 337

D. 337 > 350

Explain your thinking.

I. Know that its C because the los number is in the frut of the bigger number.

A Conversation with Ferguson	Teacher Insights
T: Please put this problem into your own words. **Ferguson:** It's about two girls who collect baseball cards. One of them has 337 and the other one has fewer. So, I have to figure out which number sentence matches the story. It was easy. I chose choice C because 301 comes before 337 and it's in the front of the two numbers. **T:** [Pointing to the "less than" sign in choice C] Why do you think this is here? **Ferguson:** I don't know. I've seen it before, but I can't remember.	**T:** *Ferguson saw the relational symbols in this problem as irrelevant. Although he marked the correct answer, he used faulty logic. He relied on the order of counting numbers to determine his answer, paying no regard to the relational symbols.*

Informed Instructional Suggestions

Although Ferguson marked the correct answer, his thinking was misguided and his correct answer was essentially a coincidence. If he had not provided his explanations, which revealed his misconception, both we and Ferguson would have believed he understood this type of problem, when in fact he does not. Because Ferguson did explain his thinking, we can make appropriate instructional decisions and create important opportunities for him to learn about relational symbols. Ferguson, like Cali, would benefit from concrete experiences using base ten block to build and compare numbers.

Student Work Sample: Charlie

Name _____ Date _____

Sarah collected 337 baseball cards. Tamika collected fewer baseball cards than Sarah. Which number sentence shows a possible comparison between the number of baseball cards that Sarah collected and the number that Tamika collected?

A.   337 < 325

B.   340 < 337

C.   301 < 337

D.   337 > 350

Explain your thinking.

My thinking of all four choices is Ⓒ because 337 is less than 301 so you take away the big number but not the little one.

Example

↓

951 ⊵ 890

A Conversation with Charlie	Teacher Insights
T: How did you think about this problem? **Charlie:** I know that 337 is less than 301. That's what choice C says. **T:** When you are counting, do you think you would say 337 before 301? **Charlie:** Yes.	*T: Charlie seems to have difficulty on a couple of levels. First, he seems not to understand or apply the order of numbers or number sense. Second, he seems to lack understanding of what the number sentence in choice C represents. Charlie's paper showed an example that was correct, but the written explanation made little sense.*

Informed Instructional Suggestions

Charlie selected the correct answer but seems to know little about the skills actually being tested. He needs practice with counting numbers in the hundreds. Examining patterns on a one-to-100 chart would help Charlie conceptualize counting patterns. Once he has discovered these patterns on the 1-to-100 chart, he should extend the chart to 500 by incorporating patterns he found. After he has mastered counting, he can work on appropriately applying relational symbols.

Student Work Sample: Stephen

Name _____   Date _____

Sarah collected 337 baseball cards. Tamika collected fewer baseball cards than Sarah. Which number sentence shows a possible comparison between the number of baseball cards that Sarah collected and the number that Tamika collected?

A.   337 < 325

B.   340 < 337

C.   301 < 337

D.   337 > 350

Explain your thinking.

It is hone of these because the problem didn't say how many Baseball cards Tamika had. A, B, and D are still wrong even if they said how many Baseball cards Tamika had. C would have been right, but the problem still didn't say how many cards did Tamika get.

A Conversation with Stephen	Teacher Insights
T: Stephen, please reread the problem carefully and tell me what it says in your own words. **Stephen:** The problem says there are these girls and they are collecting baseball cards. Tamika has fewer than Sarah. **T:** How many baseball cards does Sarah have? **Stephen:** Three hundred thirty-seven. **T:** Does the problem give you a specific number of cards that Tamika has? **Stephen:** No. I think that's why there isn't a right answer. Who knows how many cards Tamika has? She could have a million or so! **T:** I agree that the problem does not give you a specific number of cards for Tamika, but I disagree that Tamika could have a million or so. The problem gives you a clue. Please reread the second sentence. **Stephen:** [Rereads the sentence.] Oh, I think I get it. A million is bigger than 337 and Tamika has less than 337. It couldn't be a million! **T:** What is a number Tamika could have? **Stephen:** Pretty much anything less than 337. She could have 336 or maybe even only 1. She couldn't have a negative number or fraction, I don't think. **T:** Now that you understand that, what answer would you choose? **Stephen:** Choice C because 301 is less than 337.	*T: Stephen had difficulty with this problem because he did not fully understand what he was being asked to consider. With a few carefully chosen questions, he was able to make better sense of the situation and select the correct answer with understanding. Stephen understands numbers and relational symbols and demonstrated this in both his written and verbal explanations.*

Informed Instructional Suggestions

Stephen's failure to circle a correct multiple-choice answer indicated a lack of understanding or competence. However, his written explanation showed that this was not the case. With a few guiding questions, we were able to gain a more accurate picture of Stephen's understanding. As a result, we can make more accurate, focused instructional decisions. Stephen understands the skills tested by this question. More work in these areas would not be a good use of Stephen's time. His area of difficulty was in reading and comprehending the problem. Stephen would benefit from solving similar problems. Once he is familiar and comfortable with problems such as this one, he will be ready for activities like those we suggested for Gary.

Student Work Sample: Raynaldo

Name _____ Date _____

Sarah collected 337 baseball cards. Tamika collected fewer baseball cards than Sarah. Which number sentence shows a possible comparison between the number of baseball cards that Sarah collected and the number that Tamika collected?

A. $337 < 325$

B. $340 < 337$

C. $301 < 337$

D. $337 > 350$

Explain your thinking.

I know Sarah collected more baseball cards than Tamika so there has to be a greater sign which 337 is greater. there is two left C and D but the greater sign always has to be to the left. So it has to be D.

A Conversation with Raynaldo	Teacher Insights
T: On your paper, you said that the "greater than" sign always has to be to the left. Please tell me more about that.	*T: Raynaldo's written and verbal explanations indicated confusion. He does understand that 337 is larger than 301, but he believes that the larger number should appear on the left of an inequality.*
Raynaldo: The open side of the "greater than" sign has to be on the left. Otherwise it's wrong. Choice D is the only one that is going left, so it has to be right.	
T: [Pointing to the "less than" sign in choice C] What does this sign mean?	
Raynaldo: It's a trick. There is no such sign. Well, maybe it means less than. It's true that 301 is less than 337, but it's backwards, so it's wrong. The bigger number has to be on the left.	

Informed Instructional Suggestions

Raynaldo needs experiences that will help him develop understanding of the meaning of relational symbols and how they are used.

Reassessment

1. Use a similar problem at the same level of difficulty.

   Peter collected 414 stickers. Jasper collected more stickers than Peter. Which number sentence shows a possible comparison between the number of stickers that Peter collected and the number that Jasper collected?

   A. $417 < 414$
   B. $414 > 441$
   C. $567 > 414$
   D. $621 < 414$

   Explain your thinking.

2. Choose a problem that is similar but more challenging.

   Melissa collected 875 marbles. Trevor collected 467 fewer marbles than Melissa. Which number sentence represents the comparison between the number of marbles that Melissa collected and the number that Trevor collected?

   A. $875 > 467$
   B. $408 < 875$
   C. $875 > 412$
   D. $467 > 875$

   Explain your thinking.

PROBLEM THREE

Overview

This problem requires students to use their place-value understanding to add decimal numbers in the tenths and hundredths. Typical mistakes are often the result of students' failure to apply correct place-value understandings, leading to misalignment of the addends.

Sample Problem

Tyler added 6 tenths and 3 hundredths to 26.78. What was the sum?

A. 27.41
B. 26.89
C. 27.68
D. 386.78

Explain your thinking.

Possible Student Solution Strategies

o   Students use their knowledge of place value to correctly find the sum by either first combining 0.6 and 0.03 to get 0.63 and then adding that to 26.78 or by correctly aligning all three addends and then adding.
o   Students misalign the addends, resulting in an incorrect sum.

Conversation Starters

o   How did you decide where to begin solving this problem?
o   Which answer choices are reasonable? Which are unreasonable? How do you know?
o   Please tell me a story problem using these numbers.

Student Work Sample: Bobby

Name _____ Date _____

Tyler added 6 tenths and 3 hundredths to 26.78. What was the sum?

A. 27.41

B. 26.89

C. 27.68

D. 386.78

Explain your thinking.

[Handwritten:] I added because it says

$$\begin{array}{r} 26.78 \\ + .63 \\ \hline 27.41 \end{array}$$

0.63

tyler added. So I added 26.78 + 0.63 and I got my anweser.

A Conversation with Bobby	Teacher Insights
T: I am wondering where the sixty-three–hundredths came from. Please tell me more about that, Bobby. **Bobby:** The problem says that Tyler added 6 tenths and 3 hundredths. So I just put those two together to get 0.63. Then I added 0.63 to 26.78.	**T:** *Bobby was able to use the correct words to represent the decimals involved in this problem. Often, students will read 26.78 as "twenty-six point seventy-eight." Not only is this incorrect, but students miss a chance to realize and state the place value involved. The correct way to read this decimal is "twenty-six and seventy-eight–hundredths." Also, Bobby was easily able to correctly combine six-tenths with three-hundredths.*
T: Bobby, your explanation makes sense to me. What story problem could you create that uses these numbers? **Bobby:** I can think of one about money: Tyler earned six-tenths of a dollar and then found three-hundredths of a dollar. He already had $26.78. How much money will he have altogether now? He would have $27.41. **T:** When we talk about dollars and decimals, how is a cent represented in decimals? **Bobby:** A cent is one-hundredth of a dollar.	**T:** *Bobby demonstrated strong understanding of tenths and hundredths and correctly applied this understanding to money.*

Informed Instructional Suggestions

Bobby was confident and accurate in his application of decimals to addition and money. It would now be appropriate for Bobby to explore thousandths and how they relate to whole numbers, tenths, and hundredths. Students who understand that it takes 1,000 thousandths to equal one, or 100 thousandths to equal one-tenth, or 10 thousandths to equal one-hundredth have powerful, useful understanding of our base ten number system. Base ten materials are very effective tools for helping students understand this relationship.

Student Work Sample: Vicki

Name _____ Date _____

Tyler added 6 tenths and 3 hundredths to 26.78. What was the sum?

(A.) 27.41

B. 26.89

C. 27.68

D. 386.78

$$\begin{array}{r} 26.78 \\ 0.6 \\ +00.03 \\ \hline 27.41 \end{array}$$

Explain your thinking.

(27.41) is my answer

I added 6 tenths to 26.78 then three hundredths and I got 27.41.

A Conversation with Vicki	Teacher Insights
T: How did you know where to start when you solved this problem? **Vicki:** Well, first I saw that there were three numbers: six-tenths, three-hundredths, and twenty-six point seventy-eight. **T:** What is the correct way to say twenty-six point seventy-eight? **Vicki:** Oops, that should be twenty-six and seventy-eight–hundredths. **T:** That's right. What did you do next? **Vicki:** I added them up. **T:** Why did you write the numbers the way you did? **Vicki:** I wanted to keep numbers of the same type together. I wanted the hundredths in a line, the tenths in a line, the ones in a line, and the tens in a line. You have to do it that way or else it's wrong. It's like if you are counting dogs and as you are counting, you count a chicken as if it were a dog. It would give you the wrong number of dogs because you counted a chicken. That's how I think about it.	**T:** *Vicki has a clear understanding of how to solve this type of problem. She was able to explain her understanding in a very unique way through her example about counting dogs.*

Informed Instructional Suggestions

Vicki is ready to explore thousandths. She would benefit from the same types of activities that would be appropriate for Bobby.

Student Work Sample: Sheila

Name _____   Date _____

Tyler added 6 tenths and 3 hundredths to 26.78. What was the sum?

(A.) 27.41

B. 26.89

C. 27.68

D. 386.78

$$\begin{array}{r} \overset{1\ 1}{26.78} \\ +\ 6.3\downarrow \\ \hline 33.0\ 8 \end{array}$$

Explain your thinking.

I chose "A" because it was closest to the answer I got. I added 26.78 + 6.3 and I got 33.08.

A Conversation with Sheila	Teacher Insights
T: Sheila, I see that when you added, you got 33.08, but you circled 27.41 as your answer choice. Please tell me more about your thinking. **Sheila:** First I put six tens and three hundredths together, and I got six point three. Then I added them up. I started here [pointing at the 8 in 26.78]. Eight and zero is eight, so I wrote down an 8. Then I added seven and three and got ten. I put down the 0 and carried the 1. Six plus six plus one is thirteen. I put down the 3 and carried the 1. One plus two is three. I wrote down the 3 and—voila!—I was done. So I looked at the answer choices and my answer wasn't there, so I decided to estimate, and choice A, twenty-seven point forty-one, was closest to my answer. Is that right?	**T:** *There are several areas where Sheila might have misunderstandings. She may not realize that the correct way to read a decimal point is with the word* and. *There is evidence that she has fragile or no understanding of place value, judging by her verbal explanation and the way she set up the problem. She may also have misread the problem. In addition, she incorrectly estimated when trying to find the answer choice closest to the sum she had figured; choice C is actually closer to her sum than choice A.*
T: Let's talk about your thinking. Please read aloud for me the first sentence of the problem. [Sheila reads the sentence aloud.] Does the first sentence talk about tens or tenths? **Sheila:** Aren't they the same thing?	**T:** *Sheila's question provided important information about where to start. She has a foundational issue that must be addressed: she does not know the difference between tenths and tens.*

Informed Instructional Suggestions

Sheila marked the correct answer choice, but, when questioned, she revealed many possible areas of need. It is important for Sheila to have foundational place-value experiences that will help her understand ones, tens, hundreds, thousands, tenths, and hundredths and how they are related. This understanding is the underpinning of the base ten number system, and it is clear that Sheila needs conceptual development. Base ten blocks are excellent concrete models that Sheila can use to more clearly understand the base ten number system.

Student Work Sample: Boz

Name _____   Date _____

Tyler added 6 tenths and 3 hundredths to 26.78. What was the sum?

(A.)   27.41

B.   26.89

C.   27.68

D.   386.78

Explain your thinking.

$$2{,}678$$
$$+\quad 63$$
$$\overline{2741}$$

I changed the desimals to regular numbers and added 63 to get my sum.

A Conversation with Boz	Teacher Insights
T: Do any of these answer choices seem unreasonable to you?	**T:** *In this instance, what Boz did worked, although mathematically his thinking was misguided. It seemed important at this point to give him a counterexample to help him examine his thinking.*
Boz: I think that choice D is way too big.	
T: But when you solved the problem, you got 2,741. Choice D is the closest to the answer you got. Also, I am a bit confused because you circled choice A, 27.41. Please help me understand your thinking.	
Boz: It was quite easy actually. First I added six-tenths to three-hundredths and got sixty-three–hundredths. Then I changed the numbers to regular numbers and added.	
T: What if Tyler added 0.6 to 26.78? What would the sum be?	**T:** *Boz marked the correct answer, but he had some misguided thinking. Our conversation put him in a state of disequilibrium—he exhibited some confusion but also a need to find out why his strategy did not work as expected—the perfect environment for learning.*
Boz: [Pauses for a moment. Then, using his original thinking, he writes the following problem.]	
$$\begin{array}{r}2{,}678\\+\quad 6\\\hline 2{,}684\end{array}$$	
T: The correct answer is 27.38. What do you think happened?	
Boz: I checked my work, and I added correctly. Maybe I should write it as decimals. [Writes the following problem.]	
$$\begin{array}{r}26.78\\+\quad .6\\\hline 27.38\end{array}$$	
I guess I can't just change them into regular numbers because it just doesn't exactly work. I am not sure why.	

Informed Instructional Suggestions

Boz needs to explore why his thinking did not work. He could use base ten blocks to concretely test his idea. It would also be helpful to engage Boz in conversation about what he was thinking as he explored. In addition, he could create problems to test his ideas and theories to help him think like mathematicians do, making and verifying conjectures.

Student Work Sample: Melody

Name _____ Date _____

Tyler added 6 tenths and 3 hundredths to 26.78. What was the sum?

(A.) 27.41

B. 26.89

C. 27.68

D. 386.78

Explain your thinking.

6 0 to 3 = 09

I hade to right
6 tenths and 3 hundredths

A Conversation with Melody	Teacher Insights
T: Please tell me about your thinking, Melody. **Melody:** I added six-tenths and three-hundredths and got nine. I didn't really know what to do next, so I guessed. I knew that choice D was way too big, but I didn't really know about the other three.	**T:** Melody has some of the basic vocabulary of decimal numbers but was not accurate when she added six-tenths and three-hundredths. In her verbal explanation, she stated the sum was nine, and in her written explanation, she indicated the sum was nine-hundredths.

Informed Instructional Suggestions

Melody circled the correct answer choice, but her understanding is very limited. She even admitted to guessing. The multiple-choice answer alone would have masked her need for instructional support and would have left her with incomplete foundational knowledge. Because her needs are basic, she could benefit from some of the same experiences we recommended for Sheila.

Student Work Sample: Jacques

Name _____ Date _____

Tyler added 6 tenths and 3 hundredths to 26.78. What was the sum?

A. 27.41

B. 26.89

C. 27.68

D. 386.78

Explain your thinking.

I rounded it so I got 27.41. We have not learned this yet

$26.78 \rightarrow 27.41$

A Conversation with Jacques	Teacher Insights
T: Jacques, please tell me about your thinking. **Jacques:** Like I wrote, we haven't learned this yet. It was hard. I just decided maybe I should round twenty-six point seventy-eight to the closest answer choice. Seventy-eight is bigger than fifty, so I rounded up to twenty-seven. Twenty-seven point forty-one is closer to twenty-six point seventy-eight than twenty-seven point sixty-eight.	**T:** *There are several areas of concern here. First, Jacques had indeed been exposed to adding decimals but apparently didn't recognize what the problem was asking him to do. Second, he was not reading the decimal correctly. Third, he showed little understanding of tenths and hundredths or even rounding.*

Informed Instructional Suggestions

Jacques marked the correct answer, but his explanations indicated that his needs are similar to those of Melody and Sheila. He needs work at the foundational level of understanding decimals.

Student Work Sample: Damon

Name _____ Date _____

Tyler added 6 tenths and 3 hundredths to 26.78. What was the sum?

A. 27.41

B. 26.89

(C.) 27.68

D. 386.78

$$\begin{array}{r} 26.78 \\ +\ \ \ \ 6 \\ +\ \ 30 \\ \hline 27.68 \end{array}$$

Explain your thinking.

What I did was, I added 26.78 to 6 tenths and
3 hundredths and got 27.68.

$$\begin{array}{r} 26.78 \\ .6 \\ +\ \ .03 \\ \hline 27.41 \end{array}$$

A Conversation with Damon	Teacher Insights
T: Please tell me more about how you solved this problem, Damon. **Damon:** First, I rewrote all the numbers. Next, I added them up. Uh-oh! I see a mistake. I didn't put in the decimal point for six-tenths, and I wrote .30 instead of .03. But I still got the right answer, didn't I? How did that happen? **T:** Why do you think you got the correct answer? **Damon:** I got the right answer because my answer was one of the answer choices, so it has to be right. **T:** Rewrite the problem correctly and see what answer you get. **Damon:** [Damon writes the problem on his paper and performs the calculation.] Oh, I see now. I guess I should check my work more carefully. I got a different answer and it is also one of the answer choices. That is really tricky. It's like they know what mistakes we'll make and then make up wrong answers based on those mistakes!	**T:** *Damon made an error that he was able to catch and correct himself. Although he marked an incorrect answer, he does have the skills needed to solve this problem.*

Informed Instructional Suggestions

Damon's wrong answer alone would have indicated a need for additional instruction. Through the brief conversation, though, it became clear that additional instruction wouldn't be necessary. Damon does need to read problems more carefully and remember to check all aspects of his work for accuracy, but he is ready to explore thousandths. The instructional suggestions we made for Bobby would also be appropriate for Damon.

Student Work Sample: Gerti

Name _____ Date _____

Tyler added 6 tenths and 3 hundredths to 26.78. What was the sum?

A. 27.41

B. 26.89

C. 27.68

(D.) 386.78

Explain your thinking.

A Conversation with Gerti	Teacher Insights
T: Please tell me what you think this problem is about, Gerti. **Gerti:** I have to add some tens and hundreds. I drew a picture to show six tens and three hundreds. That would equal 360. Then I added that to the third number in the problem. That's how I got my answer. **T:** How do you read the number you got for your answer? **Gerti:** I don't know. **T:** The problem says that Tyler added six-tenths. You drew a picture of six tens. Are tens and tenths the same thing? **Gerti:** I don't really know. It sounds like it could be.	**T:** *Gerti solved the problem as if it involved whole numbers rather than decimal fractions. She indicated that she does not know the difference between tens and tenths.*

Informed Instructional Suggestions

Gerti is confused and needs more time and many more experiences to develop her conceptual understanding of the skills needed to solve this problem. Gerti would benefit from the types of activities we suggested for Sheila.

Reassessment

1. Use a similar problem at the same level of difficulty.

    Sydney added 7 tenths and 1 hundredth to 34.59. What was the sum?

    A. 35.30
    B. 34.67
    C. 204.59
    D. 35.39

    Explain your thinking.

2. Choose a problem that is similar but slightly more challenging.

    Bart added 73 hundredths and 5 tenths to 45.68. What was the sum?

    A. 46.91
    B. 53.48
    C. 46.46
    D. 46.81

    Explain your thinking.

ⓟⓡⓞⓑⓛⓔⓜ ⓕⓞⓤⓡ

Overview

This problem asks students to put together two clues to determine which pair of numbers is correct. It is helpful if students are familiar with the mathematics vocabulary words *product* and *sum*. Facility with basic addition and multiplication facts is also helpful in solving this problem.

Sample Problem

When the ages of two sisters are added, the sum is 16. When the ages are multiplied, the product is 63. What are their ages?

A. 11 and 5
B. 9 and 6
C. 10 and 6
D. 7 and 9

Explain your thinking.

Possible Student Solution Strategies

o Students use their knowledge of basic addition and multiplication facts to solve the problem, showing their thinking in a variety of ways: pictures, numbers, friendly facts, and repeated addition.
o Students attend to only one clue, for example, they choose an answer based only the sum and ignore the product.
o Students make errors in the usage of basic facts.

Conversation Starters

o What is this problem asking you to do?
o How can you solve this problem in another way?
o How could you explain your thinking to a younger student?
o How would you use pictures or numbers to help you solve this problem? How would you solve it another way?
o What is unusual about this problem?
o What skills do you already know that could help you solve this problem?

Student Work Sample: Mark

Name _____ Date _____

When the ages of two sisters are added, the sum is 16. When the
ages are multiplied, the product is 63. What are their ages?

A.   11 and 5

B.   9 and 6

C.   10 and 6

●   7 and 9

Explain your thinking.

sum = answer to an addition problem.
product = answer to a multiplication problem.

I first added and multiplied
each answer and found out
which one was right.

A = 11+5=16
11×5=55

B = 9+6=15
9×6=54

C = 10+6=16
10×6=60

D = 7+9=16
7×9=63

A Conversation with Mark	Teacher Insights
T: Your written explanation is very clear and complete. I appreciate that because it helps me more clearly know about your thinking. What was unusual to you about this problem? **Mark:** I thought it was just a little tricky or maybe unusual because I had to think about two things at once. I had to think about two numbers that, when added together, were sixteen, and when the same two numbers were multiplied, equaled sixty-three. That was a little tricky. **T:** How would you explain your thinking to a younger student? **Mark:** First, I would make sure that the person knew what *sum* and *product* were. I wrote that on my paper. Then I would go to each choice and first find the sum. Eleven plus five equals sixteen. Then I would find the product of those same two numbers. Eleven times five is fifty-five. For eleven and five, the sum is sixteen, which works, but the product is fifty-five, which doesn't work. It is supposed to be sixty-three. Choice A doesn't work. I'd do that for the other three choices.	**T:** *Mark had a clear understanding and approach to this problem, which he was easily able to articulate.*

Informed Instructional Suggestions

Mark is ready to explore other problems similar to this one yet more complex (e.g., using clues to find three numbers instead of two, or using clues with subtraction and division). He would also benefit from writing his own problems like this one for others to solve.

Student Work Sample: Leah

Name _____ Date _____

When the ages of two sisters are added, the sum is 16. When the ages are multiplied, the product is 63. What are their ages?

A. 11 and 5

B. 9 and 6

C. 10 and 6

(D.) 7 and 9

I knew the answer was D because 7+9=16 and 7×9=63.

Explain your thinking.

addition

7 ⅲⅲⅱ II
+ 9 ⅲⅲⅱ IIII
16 ⅲⅲⅱ ⅲⅲⅱ I

multiplication

A Conversation with Leah	Teacher Insights
T: You did a complete job of explaining your thinking. What is another way you could explain what you did?	*T: Leah had no trouble with this problem and was able to discuss clearly more than one way to verify her answer choice.*
Leah: Well, for the addition problem, truthfully, I knew what 7 plus 9 equaled. But unless I show you, you can't know. I drew tallies to prove my answer. But I could have taken 1 from the 7 and made it 6 and put the 1 with the 9 to make it 10. Then all I would have to do is add 10 plus 6, which is really easy. It's 16. Or I could have taken a 1 from the 9 and added it to the 7 to make 8. Eight plus 8 is 16, which is also easy because it is a double. For the multiplication part I could have multiplied 10 times 7, which is 70, and then subtracted one group of 7 to get 63.	
T: Why would you need to subtract a group of seven?	
Leah: Because I thought 10 groups of 7 and got 70, and it is only supposed to be 9 groups of 7, so I have to take away a group of 7 from 70 to get back to 9 groups of 7.	
T: Why did you multiply seven by ten?	
Leah: It's a really easy fact. Anything times ten is easy.	

Informed Instructional Suggestions:

Leah has strong understanding and command of this problem. Like Mark, she is ready to explore more complex problems and write and solve her own problems to share with others.

Student Work Sample: Otto

Name _____ Date _____

When the ages of two sisters are added, the sum is 16. When the ages are multiplied, the product is 63. What are their ages?

~~A.~~   11 and 5

~~B.~~   9 and 6

~~C.~~   10 and 6

(D.)   7 and 9

Explain your thinking.

First I tried addition. I knew that 8+8 =16, however 8×8 does not equal 63. Then I tried multiplication. I knew 7×9=63 *Second I tried multiplication* and 7+9=16. Sister #1's age was 7, and sister #2's age was 9.

A Conversation with Otto	Teacher Insights
T: Otto, I see that you started with eight plus eight. That is an interesting place to start. Please tell me more about your thinking. **Otto:** I knew I had to add. And I knew that eight plus eight is sixteen. That wasn't a choice, but it was a place where I could start to think about this question. As I said, eight plus eight is sixteen! Bingo! But then I thought to myself, "What is eight times eight?" Uh-oh! Not good because eight times eight is sixty-four. But then I remembered that seven times nine is sixty-three. I added seven and nine and it was sixteen. Victory is mine! I figured it out. The sisters are seven and nine.	**T:** *Like Mark and Leah, Otto had an effective strategy for solving this problem. He made use of his knowledge of basic facts.*

Informed Instructional Suggestions

Otto is ready for the same kinds of experiences and explorations as Leah and Mark.

Student Work Sample: Franny

Name _____ Date _____

When the ages of two sisters are added, the sum is 16. When the ages are multiplied, the product is 63. What are their ages?

A.   11 and 5

B.   9 and 6

C.   10 and 6

D.   7 and 9

Explain your thinking.

I think choice D. 7 and nine because, 7+9 = 16 $\frac{3}{3}$ 16÷2=8. So it maknes senee for it to be D. 7 and nine.

A Conversation with Franny	Teacher Insights
T: I noticed that you used division in this problem. Please tell me about what the problem is asking you to do and why you used division. **Franny:** There are two sisters. Their ages equal 16. So I added the numbers in the answer choices to see which ones were equal to 16. All of them did except for choice B; it was equal to 15. I did this in my head because it is just basic facts. Since there were two sisters, I divided 16 by 2. That equals 8. I noticed that 7 and 9 were choices, and if I take away 1 from one of the 8s, that leaves 7, and I can put that 1 with the other 8, and that will equal 9. Then to be sure, I multiplied 7 times 9, which is 63. Seven and 9 make sense.	**T:** *Initially, Franny's use of division seemed confused. But through her verbal explanation, it became clear that she had command of the problem and the skills needed to solve it.*

Informed Instructional Suggestions

Franny would benefit from the same instruction and activities as Mark, Leah, and Otto.

Student Work Sample: Albert

Name _____ Date _____

When the ages of two sisters are added, the sum is 16. When the ages are multiplied, the product is 63. What are their ages?

A. 11 and 5

B. 9 and 6

C. 10 and 6

(D.) 7 and 9

Explain your thinking.

$9 + 7 = 16$

$9 \times 10 = 90 - 27 = 63$

$9 \times 3 = 27$ (9 & 7)

A Conversation with Albert	Teacher Insights
T: Please tell me more about what you wrote on your paper, Albert. **Albert:** I know the basic addition facts, which is where I started in my head. I looked at all the pairs of numbers and they all equal sixteen when you add them, except for nine and six, and they equal fifteen. I can only eliminate choice B. That means I have to multiply. Ugh! I don't know the multiplication facts very well. I started to feel sort of sad. But I looked again and thought, "Hey, this won't be hard. I can use multiplying by ten and eleven. Easy!" I know eleven times five is fifty-five. Can't be choice A. I don't have to worry about choice B. Ten times six is sixty, easy! It can't be choice C. That leaves only choice D. But I have to show my thinking. I thought nine times ten is ninety. But that is three groups of nine too many. Three times nine is twenty-seven. So I have to subtract the twenty-seven from ninety, which is sixty-three. Choice D is right!	**T:** *Albert was able to find a solution strategy that worked for him. He admitted he doesn't know the multiplication facts well, but he does know how to multiply by ten and eleven, which helped him greatly in this circumstance.*

Informed Instructional Suggestions

Albert needs additional opportunities to become more fluent with the multiplication facts. He has a clear understanding of the concept of multiplication, as demonstrated by his verbal explanation. To boost his fluency and confidence, Albert could play games to practice the facts, such as multiplication tic-tac-toe or multiplication bingo. Playing the card game war using multiplication would be another engaging way for Albert to practice.

Student Work Sample: Chris

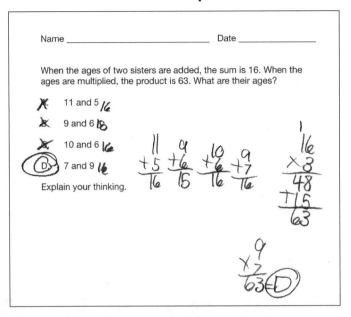

Name _____ Date _____

When the ages of two sisters are added, the sum is 16. When the ages are multiplied, the product is 63. What are their ages?

✗ 11 and 5 *16*

✗ 9 and 6 *15*

✗ 10 and 6 *16*

Ⓓ 7 and 9 *16*

Explain your thinking.

A Conversation with Chris	Teacher Insights
T: Please tell me about what you think this problem is asking you to do.	**T:** *Chris had some understanding of the situation and did mark the correct answer. However, his written and verbal explanations indicated some confusion about what he needed to do with respect to finding the product. It was a coincidence that his thinking generated a correct answer.*
Chris: I have to find the sums of each pair of numbers. That means I have to add them. I did that. Then I wasn't too sure.	
T: I can see that you were able to figure out a next step. Please tell me about what you did and why.	
Chris: The problem said I needed to find a product. I noticed there were three sixteens in the sums, so I multiplied sixteen times three. I got forty-eight. I still had one sum that was fifteen, so I added that to the forty-eight. Forty-eight and fifteen equals sixty-three. I also know that seven times nine equals sixty-three because I memorized it, so the right answer has to be choice D.	
T: Why did you multiply sixteen times three?	
Chris: Because there were three sums of sixteen. I knew I had to multiply.	

Informed Instructional Suggestions

Chris needs some guiding questions to help him use the knowledge he has to solve problems like this one. If we help him focus on what the question is asking about the sum and the product of each pair of numbers, it might help him see why multiplying sixteen by three was an error in his thinking.

Student Work Sample: Andre

Name _____ Date _____

When the ages of two sisters are added, the sum is 16. When the ages are multiplied, the product is 63. What are their ages?

A. 11 and 5

B. 9 and 6

C. 10 and 6

(D.) 7 and 9

Explain your thinking.

$16 - 10 = 6 \times 2 = 12$

$10 \times 2 = {}^{+}20$
_____
32

$11 \times 2 = 22$
$5 \times 2 = {}^{+}10$
_____
32

$7 \times 2 = 14$
$9 \times 2 = {}^{+}18$
_____
32

$7 \times 9 = 63$
$9 \times 7 = 63$

A Conversation with Andre	Teacher Insights
T: Andre, I see that you multiplied by two. Please explain your thinking. **Andre:** There were two sisters, so I had to multiply all of the numbers by two. After I multiplied the numbers by two, I added them up. **T:** Why did you subtract ten from sixteen? **Andre:** The problem said the sum was sixteen. I didn't know what sixteen times two was, so I subtracted six and got ten. I know what two times ten and two times six are. I wrote it here. [Andre points to his paper.] I added up the two numbers and got thirty-two. **T:** Andre, in your words, please tell me what you think this problem is asking you to do. **Andre:** It is asking me to multiply each number in the choices by two because there are two sisters. Then I have to add the numbers together because it says sum, and that means to add.	*T: Andre showed confusion about what the problem was asking him to do. He appeared to know what* sum *means and worked to incorporate this understanding into his problem solution. His written solution and verbal explanations thus far indicated little understanding of what the second sentence of the problem was asking for.*

Informed Instructional Suggestions

Andre marked the correct answer but did not understand the problem. He needs help with reading problems carefully and determining what they are asking him to do. Andre would benefit from receiving guidance in how to solve this type of problem and many opportunities to practice similar problems before moving on.

Student Work Sample: Zorba

Name _____ Date _____

When the ages of two sisters are added, the sum is 16. When the
ages are multiplied, the product is 63. What are their ages?

A.   11 and 5

B.   9 and 6

C.   10 and 6

Ⓓ   7 and 9

Explain your thinking.

because if the 2 girls were twins it would say 8 Years old. and it Isa good anser.

A Conversation with Zorba	Teacher Insights
T: Why do you think choice D is a good choice? **Zorba:** If the girls were twins, then they could be eight years old. But that's not a choice, so I know they aren't twins. I noticed that choices A, C, and D all add up to sixteen, so I knew it had to be one of them. I looked at Juan's paper and he had choice D. Seven and nine add up to sixteen, so it seemed like a good choice. **T:** Please read the second sentence of the problem aloud. [Zorba reads.] Is the product of seven and nine sixty-three? **Zorba:** I don't know that one yet. Maybe? I didn't know, so I skipped that part.	**T:** *Zorba marked the correct answer but had little understanding of the problem. He used good reasoning to figure out that the girls were not twins but didn't seem to know what to do next. He didn't know how to multiply nine times seven and simply skipped the part of the problem that was difficult for him.*

Informed Instructional Suggestions

Like Chris and Andre, Zorba needs help with figuring out how to solve problems such as this one. He also needs to work on fluency with the multiplication facts. The suggestions we made for Albert would also be appropriate for Zorba.

Student Work Sample: Patti

Name _____ Date _____

When the ages of two sisters are added, the sum is 16. When the ages are multiplied, the product is 63. What are their ages?

(A.)   11 and 5   *A is the only ansc left so thats why I chose A.*

B.   9 and 6

~~C.~~   ~~10 and 6~~

D.   7 and 9

Explain your thinking.

A Conversation with Patti	Teacher Insights
T: Patti, how would you explain your thinking and work to the class or another student? **Patti:** I know that when you add each pair of numbers, the sum should be 16, and when you multiply them, the answer should be 63. I know the addition facts and so I didn't have to figure out the addition, but I am not sure of all of the multiplication facts, so I had to figure them out or check to be sure what I thought was correct. I started with choice C. I actually know 10 times 6, but I wanted to show it, so I used circles and tallies. Ten times 6 equals 60 and 10 plus 6 equals 16. The 16 part works but not the 60. Not choice C! Then I went to choice D. Seven plus 9 equals 16 and that's good. I don't know 7 times 9, so I had to figure it out and I got 31. Can't be choice D. Then I did choice B, which I already know is wrong because 9 plus 6 equals 15. Nine times 6 equals 54, so I know it's wrong for two reasons. That leaves choice A, so it must be choice A. I chose it.	*T: Patti knows how to approach a problem such as this one. Her error was computational and showed a lack of number sense; the answer of thirty-one as the product of seven times nine is unreasonable, especially within the context of the figuring she did.*

Informed Instructional Suggestions

Patti understands this type of problem but needs to focus on fluency with multiplication facts. Also, Patti needs to remember to test all the answer choices. She did not check the numbers in choice A. Had she done so, she might have reconsidered her previous work and discovered the error she had made when figuring seven times nine.

Student Work Sample: Samantha

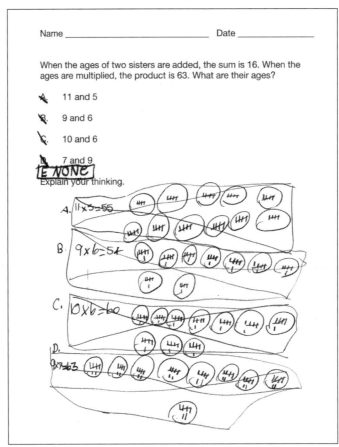

A Conversation with Samantha	Teacher Insights
T: I see you did a lot of work to figure out the multiplication. **Samantha:** I actually know these facts, but I wanted to show it. The problem is that none of these is equal to sixteen. So there is no correct answer given. **T:** What do you think the problem is asking you to do? **Samantha:** Find the numbers that have a product of sixteen. **T:** Please reread the problem aloud. **Samantha:** [Samantha reads.] Oh no! I'm not supposed to find the product of sixteen; I am supposed to find a product of sixty-three and a sum of sixteen. No wonder there wasn't a right answer! **T:** Do you still think that the answer of "none" is the correct answer? **Samantha:** No. Choice D has sixty-three and if I add seven plus nine it's sixteen, so the answer is choice D.	*T: Samantha is a second language learner. Although she is fluent in many aspects of English, sometimes reading comprehension can be a challenge for her. Rereading the problem aloud helped her better understand what was being asked of her, and she was able to solve the problem correctly.*

Informed Instructional Suggestions

Samantha's incorrect response was misleading. She was able to use her skills and reasoning to solve the problem once she understood the question. Samantha needs help in the areas of language and comprehension. It would also be useful to ask Samantha to explore similar problems. This will reinforce her mathematical understanding and language development.

Reassessment

1. Use a similar problem at the same level of difficulty.

   When the ages of two brothers are added, the sum is 18. When the ages are multiplied, the product is 72. What are the brothers' ages?

   A. 9 and 9
   B. 7 and 11
   C. 10 and 7
   D. 12 and 6

   Explain your thinking.

2. Choose a problem that is similar but slightly more challenging.

    When the ages of three cousins are added, the sum is 14. When the ages are multiplied, the product is 70. What are the cousins' ages?

    A. 8, 2, and 4
    B. 9, 1, and 4
    C. 9, 2, and 4
    D. 5, 7, and 2

    Explain your thinking.

PROBLEM FIVE

Overview

The objective of this question is to add whole and mixed numbers with uncommon denominators. Students must be able to pull the information from the problem and correctly add to find the sum in simplest terms.

Sample Problem

Juan ran $2\frac{1}{2}$ kilometers on Tuesday, $3\frac{1}{4}$ kilometers on Wednesday, and 3 kilometers on Thursday. How many kilometers did he run in those three days?

A. $5\frac{3}{4}$ kilometers
B. 7 kilometers
C. $8\frac{3}{4}$ kilometers
D. 8 kilometers

Explain your thinking.

Possible Student Solution Strategies

o   Students correctly add the whole numbers and then the fractions or do the reverse.
o   Students convert the fractions to decimals and then add the decimals and convert the decimal answer to a fraction.
o   Students use pictures to help them add.
o   Students add the whole numbers and then, when adding the fractions, they first add the numerators and then add the denominators.
o   Students incorrectly convert the fractions.
o   Students add only the mixed numbers, failing to add the whole numbers.

Conversation Starters

o   What do you know about this problem? What do you need to find out?
o   Is there more than one way to solve this problem? Tell about it.
o   How do you know that your answer is reasonable?
o   Convince me that your idea makes sense.

Student Work Sample: Sheila

Name _____ Date _____

Juan ran $2\frac{1}{2}$ kilometers on Tuesday, $3\frac{1}{4}$ kilometers on Wednesday, and 3 kilometers on Thursday. How many kilometers did he run in those three days?

A. $5\frac{3}{4}$ kilometers

B. 7 kilometers

C. $8\frac{3}{4}$ kilometers

D. 8 kilometers

① $\begin{array}{r} 3 \\ 3 \\ +2 \\ \hline 8 \end{array}$ ② $\begin{array}{r} 1/2 \\ +1/4 \\ \hline 3/4 \end{array}$

③ $8 + 3/4 = 8\frac{3}{4}$

Explain your thinking.

Well first I added the whole numbers $(3, 3+2)$ and I got 8. Then I added $\frac{1}{2} + \frac{1}{4}$ and I knew that $\frac{1}{2}$ is equal to $\frac{2}{4}$ so all I had to do was add one more forth and I got $\frac{3}{4}$. Then all I had to do was put $8 + \frac{3}{4}$ together and get $8\frac{3}{4}$!

A Conversation with Sheila	Teacher Insights
T: What do you know about this problem? **Sheila:** I know that Juan ran for three days. The problem wants me to find out how many kilometers he ran. That means I have to add up all the kilometers. **T:** That makes sense to me. Please convince me that your answer is reasonable. **Sheila:** It's pretty easy, actually. First I added up the whole numbers. That's three plus three plus two. That makes eight. Then I had to add one-half and one-fourth. I know that one-half is equal to two-fourths. Two-fourths plus one-fourth is three-fourths. Eight plus three-fourths is eight and three-fourths, and that's answer C.	**T:** *Sheila was easily able to think about this problem and solve it. Both her written and verbal explanations were clear and sound.*

Informed Instructional Suggestions

Sheila is ready to continue to explore similar problems with fractions that are less friendly than fourths and halves. It would be beneficial to have her work with fractions materials to reinforce her conceptual understanding of fractions.

Student Work Sample: Moises

Name _____ Date _____

Juan ran $2\frac{1}{2}$ kilometers on Tuesday, $3\frac{1}{4}$ kilometers on Wednesday, and 3 kilometers on Thursday. How many kilometers did he run in those three days?

A. $5\frac{3}{4}$ kilometers

B.   7 kilometers

C. $8\frac{3}{4}$ kilometers

D.   8 kilometers

Explain your thinking.

$$
\begin{array}{ll}
2\ ^1/_2 & 2.50 \\
3\ ^1/_4 & 3.25 \\
3 & +\ 3 \\
\hline
 & 8.75
\end{array}
$$

I made it a little easier for me. I knew $2\frac{1}{2}$ is 2.50 and I knew $3\frac{1}{4}$ is 3.25 an 3 is just 3 so I added everything together and got 8.75 and I knew that is $8\frac{3}{4}$

A Conversation with Moises	Teacher Insights
T: Do you think there is more than one way to solve this problem? **Moises:** I know there are at least two ways. One way is with fractions and the other is with decimals. I did decimals because it is easier for me. **T:** Please tell me more. **Moises:** I know that $2\frac{1}{2}$ in decimals is 2.50. Three and one-fourth is 3.25. It's like adding money, so it's easy. And 3 is just 3. So then I just added it all up and I got 8.75, and 0.75 is like $\frac{3}{4}$, so the answer is $8\frac{3}{4}$. **T:** How could you solve this problem without using decimals? **Moises:** Well, I know that $\frac{1}{2}$ is equal to $\frac{2}{4}$. It's like money, $\frac{1}{2}$ of a dollar is two quarters. Two-fourths plus $\frac{1}{4}$ is $\frac{3}{4}$. Add up the whole numbers and that's still 8. The answer is $8\frac{3}{4}$.	**T:** *Moises was able to solve this problem using both decimal and common fractions. He indicated that he is more comfortable using decimals than fractions, which he did when originally solving the problem.*

Informed Instructional Suggestions

Like Sheila, Moises is ready for work involving fractions that are less friendly than halves and fourths. He should work on fraction activities that continue to build on his comfort with decimals when appropriate. Moises and Sheila could work together and Moises could help Sheila expand her understanding by explaining his thinking about the connections between common and decimal fractions.

Student Work Sample: Jackie

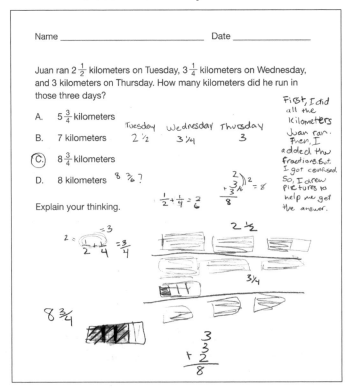

Name _____ Date _____

Juan ran $2\frac{1}{2}$ kilometers on Tuesday, $3\frac{1}{4}$ kilometers on Wednesday, and 3 kilometers on Thursday. How many kilometers did he run in those three days?

A. $5\frac{3}{4}$ kilometers

B. 7 kilometers

C. $8\frac{3}{4}$ kilometers

D. 8 kilometers

Explain your thinking.

A Conversation with Jackie	Teacher Insights
T: Please tell me more about how you approached this problem, Jackie. **Jackie:** Well I got confused, so I drew pictures. I drew a picture of $2\frac{1}{2}$, $3\frac{1}{4}$, and 3. Once I had the pictures, it was pretty easy. I could see that $\frac{1}{2}$ and $\frac{1}{4}$ equal $\frac{3}{4}$. **T:** What confused you? **Jackie:** Well, at first I added the numerators of the fractions and got two. Then I added the denominators and got six. So the fraction was two-sixths. That was wrong. So I drew pictures and I could see the answer.	**T:** *Jackie initially made a common error by adding the numerators and then the denominators. When she drew a picture, she was able to solve the problem accurately. Jackie is a student who often benefits from seeing models of mathematical situations.*

Informed Instructional Suggestions

Jackie should be encouraged to continue to use pictures to help her solve problems. She needs opportunities to explore fractions using concrete materials to support her emerging understanding and bolster her confidence. It would also be a good idea to offer Jackie experiences that would help her see why adding the denominators doesn't work to develop her understanding.

Student Work Sample: Vicki

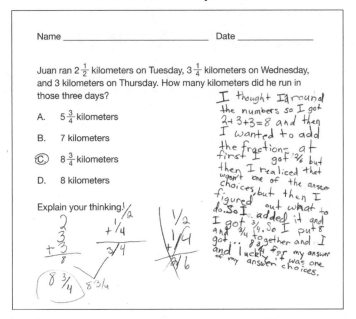

Name _____ Date _____

Juan ran $2\frac{1}{2}$ kilometers on Tuesday, $3\frac{1}{4}$ kilometers on Wednesday, and 3 kilometers on Thursday. How many kilometers did he run in those three days?

A. $5\frac{3}{4}$ kilometers

B.   7 kilometers

C. $8\frac{3}{4}$ kilometers

D.   8 kilometers

Explain your thinking!

I thought I'd round the numbers so I got 2+3+3=8 and then I wanted to add the fractions at first I got 13/6 but then I realiced that wasn't one of the answer choices, but then I figured out what to do. So I added it and I got 3/4. So I put 8 and 3/4 together and I got... 8 3/4 and luckly for me my answer was one of my answer choices.

A Conversation with Vicki	Teacher Insights
T: What did you discover when you solved this problem? **Vicki:** I did the problem and the answer I got wasn't there. I added and got $8\frac{2}{6}$. Eight was a choice and so was $8\frac{3}{4}$, but not $8\frac{2}{6}$. I was confused so I thought for a while. When I thought, I thought that $\frac{2}{6}$ was less than $\frac{1}{2}$, and it didn't make sense that I should add something to $\frac{1}{2}$ and get a smaller answer. Then I remembered that $\frac{1}{2}$ is like $\frac{2}{4}$, and $\frac{2}{4}$ and $\frac{1}{4}$ is $\frac{3}{4}$. I knew $8\frac{3}{4}$ was the right answer. **T:** How would you explain your mistake to another student? **Vicki:** I would tell another student that you are not supposed to add the bottom number of the fractions. When I got the wrong answer, I added the top numbers together, then I added the bottom numbers together and I got a smaller fraction than I started with. That's weird, I think.	**T:** *Vicki was able to use her number sense to realize that her initial answer was incorrect. Because the fractions were familiar, she was able to reason her way to a correct solution.*

Informed Instructional Suggestions

Although Vicki marked the correct response, questions remain about how strong her understanding really is. If her incorrect response had been a choice, she would have selected it. The next step should be to provide more experiences with fractions to further assess Vicki's level of understanding and to reinforce the number sense that she does have. Vicki would benefit from using fraction kits and other fraction manipulatives. Vicki also needs to develop and use the correct vocabulary associated with fractions, such as *numerator* and *denominator*.

Student Work Sample: Sharisa

Name _____ Date _____

Juan ran $2\frac{1}{2}$ kilometers on Tuesday, $3\frac{1}{4}$ kilometers on Wednesday, and 3 kilometers on Thursday. How many kilometers did he run in those three days?

A. $5\frac{3}{4}$ kilometers

B.   7 kilometers

Ⓒ $8\frac{3}{4}$ kilometers

D.   8 kilometers

Explain your thinking.

What I did was that I added 3+2+3=8 that's how I got the 8. Then I + ½ + ¼ = $\frac{1}{75}$, then I did $\frac{1}{75} = \frac{3}{4}$. That's how I got my answer.

$$\begin{array}{r} 2 \\ 3 \\ +\,3 \\ \hline 8 \end{array}$$

$$\frac{1}{2} + \frac{1}{4} = \frac{1}{75}$$

$$\frac{1}{75} = \frac{3}{4}$$

$$= 8\frac{3}{4}$$

A Conversation with Sharisa	Teacher Insights
T: When you added one-half and one-fourth, you got the sum of one–seventy-fifth. Please tell me more about this. **Sharisa:** Well, if you add a quarter and fifty cents, you get seventy-five cents. That's three-quarters of a dollar. I think that one–seventy-fifth and three-fourths are the same amount.	**T:** *Sharisa showed confusion in both her written and verbal explanations that needs to be corrected.*

Informed Instructional Suggestions

Although Sharisa marked the correct answer, there is a serious flaw in her thinking. One–seventy-fifth is not equivalent to three-fourths. Sharisa needs concrete experiences with money and experiences using various fractions materials to help her see and learn about equivalent fractions. If we had not learned about her confusion through her explanations, we would have let her move forward with a gap in her knowledge and misunderstandings that might have spilled into other areas.

Student Work Sample: Bobby

Name _____ Date _____

Juan ran $2\frac{1}{2}$ kilometers on Tuesday, $3\frac{1}{4}$ kilometers on Wednesday, and 3 kilometers on Thursday. How many kilometers did he run in those three days?

A. $5\frac{3}{4}$ kilometers

B. 7 kilometers

C. $8\frac{3}{4}$ kilometers

D. 8 kilometers

Explain your thinking.

Whell I kind of of guess because I took the two that were totally wrongh and thought about the problem. Then I added 2+3+3 and got eight so I choose C.

$$\begin{array}{r} 2 \\ +3 \\ +3 \\ \hline 8 \end{array}$$

Tuesday
+ 2½

Wednesday
+ 3¼

Thursday
+ 3

A Conversation with Bobby	Teacher Insights
T: Which two answer choices do you think are totally wrong?	**T:** *Bobby reasoned his way to a correct answer without using the skills being assessed.*
Bobby: I think choice B and choice D. If you add up the whole numbers, you know the answer has to be at least eight, so choice B won't work. And there are fractions, so I don't think choice D would work because it is a whole number, eight, but I know there is more than eight. It is eight and some more because of the fractions.	
T: Does choice A seem reasonable to you?	
Bobby: Not really, because the whole number part is five, and that is less than eight. I didn't think of it before, but now when I think of it, it is totally wrong too. So, that leaves choice C.	
T: Do you know what one-half plus one-fourth is?	
Bobby: I thought it was two-sixths, but that's not a choice, so I don't know.	

Informed Instructional Suggestions

Bobby marked the correct answer by using his reasoning, but his explanations showed that he is unable to add fractions with uncommon denominators. Bobby needs concrete experiences with adding fractions and mixed numbers. He also needs activities that will help him see why it doesn't work to add the denominators.

Student Work Sample: Zolli

Name _____ Date _____

Juan ran $2\frac{1}{2}$ kilometers on Tuesday, $3\frac{1}{4}$ kilometers on Wednesday, and 3 kilometers on Thursday. How many kilometers did he run in those three days?

A. $5\frac{3}{4}$ kilometers

B. 7 kilometers

C. $8\frac{3}{4}$ kilometers

(D.) 8 kilometers

Explain your thinking.

$$\begin{array}{r} 2\frac{1}{2} \\ +3\frac{1}{4} \\ \underline{3\phantom{\frac{1}{4}}} \\ 8\frac{3}{6} \end{array}$$

I added 2 ½, 3 ¼, and 3 which equalled 8 ⅜ but that wasn't the anseuer so I gussed the closets to 8 ⅜ which is 8 and that was anseuer so I chose it

A Conversation with Zolli	Teacher Insights
T: I see that the answer you figured was $8\frac{2}{6}$, but you circled 8 on your paper. Please tell me more about that. **Zolli:** I added up all the whole numbers. Then I did the fractions. I added the top numbers first and got 2 and then I added the bottom numbers and got 6. I noticed $8\frac{2}{6}$ wasn't there, so I chose 8 because I think it is closer than $8\frac{3}{4}$, but I am not really sure.	**T:** *Zolli made the same error as Jackie and Vicki did, and it's a common mistake for students of this age. While Jackie and Vicki reasoned that their initial answers were incorrect, Zolli did not. She handled the problem by selecting an answer choice that seemed the closest to the answer she got.*

Informed Instructional Suggestions

Like several of the previous students, Zolli needs to develop conceptual understanding of what it means to add fractions and why adding the denominators does not work. Concrete materials would be useful in helping Zolli acquire this understanding.

Reassessment

1. Use a similar problem at the same level of difficulty.

   Cami swam $5\frac{1}{4}$ laps on Monday, $7\frac{1}{2}$ laps on Tuesday, and 6 laps on Wednesday. How many laps did she swim in those three days?

   A. $18\frac{3}{4}$

   B. $12\frac{3}{4}$

   C. $18\frac{2}{6}$

   D. $19\frac{2}{6}$

   Explain your thinking.

2. Choose a problem that is similar but slightly more challenging.

   Charlie wrote $7\frac{1}{4}$ pages of his report on Wednesday, $6\frac{1}{8}$ pages on Thursday, and $1\frac{1}{2}$ pages on Friday. How many pages did Charlie write in the three days?

   A. $14\frac{3}{8}$

   B. $14\frac{7}{8}$

   C. $14\frac{3}{14}$

   D. $14\frac{3}{4}$

   Explain your thinking.

⒫⒭⒪⒝⒧⒠⒨ ⒮⒤⒳

Overview

This question asks students to apply their knowledge of money and fractions to solve the problem.

Sample Problem

Which of the following has the same value as 10 nickels?

A. $\frac{1}{10}$ of a dollar

B. $\frac{1}{5}$ of a dollar

C. $\frac{1}{2}$ of a dollar

D. $\frac{1}{4}$ of a dollar

Explain your thinking.

Possible Student Solution Strategies

o   Students prove their answer by applying their knowledge of money. They understand the value of a nickel relative to a dollar and what amount is represented by each of the fractions presented in the answer choices.

o   Students figure the value of 10 nickels with multiplication, skip-counting, or pictures.

o   Students misread or misunderstand 10 nickels and figure the problem as if a nickel were equivalent to one-tenth of a dollar rather than one-twentieth of a dollar.

Conversation Starters

o   Why does your solution make sense?

o   How did pictures help you solve this problem?

o   Is there more than one possible answer? Explain.

o   How could you solve this problem in another way?

Student Work Sample: Johnson

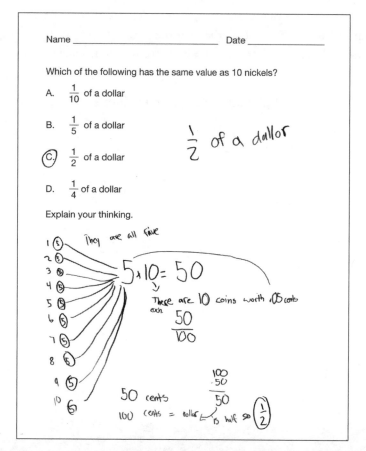

Name _____ Date _____

Which of the following has the same value as 10 nickels?

A. $\frac{1}{10}$ of a dollar

B. $\frac{1}{5}$ of a dollar

C. $\frac{1}{2}$ of a dollar   *(circled)*

D. $\frac{1}{4}$ of a dollar

$\frac{1}{2}$ of a dallor

Explain your thinking.

(handwritten) They are all five

1 (5) 2 (5) 3 (5) 4 (5) 5 (5) 6 (5) 7 (5) 8 (5) 9 (5) 10 (5)

$5 \times 10 = 50$

These are 10 coins worth .05 cents each

$\frac{50}{100}$

$\begin{array}{r} 100 \\ -50 \\ \hline 50 \end{array}$

50 cents

100 cents = dollar is half so $\left(\frac{1}{2}\right)$

A Conversation with Johnson	Teacher Insights
T: Please tell me about how you used pictures to help you solve this problem. **Johnson:** It was easy, really. I drew ten coins because there were ten nickels. Then I put a five in each to show they are worth five cents. My picture is a picture of ten groups of five cents. I already knew that ten times five is fifty. I know that half of a dollar is fifty cents, and I proved it by subtracting fifty from one hundred and it was fifty. **T:** If we read the times sign as "groups of," does your picture match your multiplication sentence? **Johnson:** Hmm, the number sentence says five groups of ten, huh? I did it backwards. But I also know that the number sentence could be read as five ten times. It works if you read it that way.	**T:** *As part of classroom instruction, we had talked about the importance of making sure number sentences matched pictures. It was good to note that Johnson had internalized this information and was able to apply it in this discussion. Johnson's written work was clear and indicated that he understands the ideas needed to solve this problem.*

Informed Instructional Suggestions

Johnson understands this type of problem and is ready to move to similar problems involving amounts over one dollar, for example, determining that 25 dimes is the same amount as $2\frac{1}{2}$ dollars. Fluency with these ideas will also reinforce and support place-value understanding and decimals.

Student Work Sample: Jamie

Name _____ Date _____

Which of the following has the same value as 10 nickels?

A. $\frac{1}{10}$ of a dollar

B. $\frac{1}{5}$ of a dollar

C. $\frac{1}{2}$ of a dollar $10 \times 5 = 50¢ = \frac{1}{2}$ of a dollar

D. $\frac{1}{4}$ of a dollar   (A) $\frac{1}{10} = 10¢$ of a dollar

Explain your thinking.   (B) $\frac{1}{5} = 20¢$ of a dollar

(D) $\frac{1}{4} = 25¢$ of a dollar

A Conversation with Jamie	Teacher Insights
T: I see you selected choice C. Do you think that there is more than one possible answer? Why or why not? **Jamie:** For this problem and these answers, there is only one correct choice and that is choice C. None of the other choices is the same as ten nickels. But if there weren't answer choices, I think there could be more right answers. Like maybe fifty pennies is the same as ten nickels or five dimes is the same as ten nickels. Or maybe if there were two dollars, then ten nickels could equal one-fourth of two dollars? Maybe . . . I am not too sure. **T:** I agree with your thinking, Jamie. Thanks for stretching your brain a bit on this.	**T:** *Jamie has mastered the content needed to answer this question accurately.*

Informed Instructional Suggestions

Jamie's needs are very similar to those of Johnson and she would benefit from the same explorations and activities we suggested for him.

Student Work Sample: Andy

Name _____ Date _____

Which of the following has the same value as 10 nickels?

A. $\frac{1}{10}$ of a dollar

B. $\frac{1}{5}$ of a dollar

C. $\frac{1}{2}$ of a dollar

D. $\frac{1}{4}$ of a dollar

Explain your thinking.

$$\frac{1}{2} \times \frac{1}{5} = \frac{1}{10}$$

$$\frac{1}{5} \times \frac{1}{50} =$$

$$\frac{1}{5} \times \frac{1}{50} = \frac{1}{250}$$

A Conversation with Andy	Teacher Insights
T: Why does your answer of one-half of a dollar make sense? **Andy:** I multiplied $\frac{1}{2}$ times $\frac{1}{5}$ because I wanted to get to $\frac{1}{10}$ because there are ten nickels. Also, I knew that nickels are worth five cents, so I used $\frac{1}{5}$, and $\frac{1}{2}$ is $\frac{1}{2}$ dollar. Then I multiplied $\frac{1}{5}$, because a nickel is five cents, times $\frac{1}{50}$, because $\frac{1}{2}$ of a dollar is fifty cents, and that equaled $\frac{1}{250}$. **T:** Wow, that is quite an explanation! Based on your explanation, how did you decide to choose one-half of a dollar as your answer? **Andy:** I don't really know. It was a guess mostly. Did I guess right? **T:** You did guess correctly, but we need to talk some more about your thinking and see if I can better understand it.	**T:** *Andy is clearly confused and needs help with money. He also needs to develop a better understanding of when it is appropriate to multiply fractions and how to multiply fractions.*

Informed Instructional Suggestions

Andy's correct answer masked his confusion. He needs additional opportunities to solve problems similar to this one using manipulatives such as coins or pictures. He also needs to develop a conceptual understanding of multiplication of fractions so that he can apply the related skills when appropriate.

Student Work Sample: Nellie

Name _____ Date _____

Which of the following has the same value as 10 nickels?

A. $\frac{1}{10}$ of a dollar .10

B. $\frac{1}{5}$ of a dollar .5

C. $\frac{1}{2}$ of a dollar .10

D. $\frac{1}{4}$ of a dollar .20

Explain your thinking.

Chnnged fraction to money

A Conversation with Nellie	Teacher Insights
T: I see that you wrote a decimal beside each answer choice. What you wrote is interesting. Please tell me how you figured each. **Nellie:** One-tenth of a dollar is ten cents, and that's what I wrote. One-fifth of a dollar is five cents, and I wrote that. One-half of a dollar is ten cents, so I wrote ten cents, and one-fourth of a dollar is twenty cents. **T:** It's interesting to me that you wrote that one-tenth of a dollar and one-half of a dollar are both ten cents. **Nellie:** Uh-oh, that's wrong. I think maybe one-tenth of a dollar is maybe ten cents and one-half is more than that. But I am not exactly sure how much more it is. But one-tenth would be like a dime; a dime is ten cents, you see, and I know there are ten dimes in a dollar.	**T:** *Nellie's grasp of money is weak at best. There were many examples of her confusion in both her written work and her verbal explanation. Also, in all cases but choice A, Nellie wrote incorrect money amounts using decimal notation. Nellie was not certain how much half of a dollar is.*

Informed Instructional Suggestions

It is important to find out first what knowledge Nellie has and does not have with respect to money. She correctly answered the question, but she has little understanding of the skills being tested by this problem. Once we establish Nellie's base-level knowledge, we need to give her concrete manipulatives to develop her understanding. Along the way, it will be important to introduce the symbols to notate money. It would also be helpful to establish what knowledge Nellie has of place value. For example, does she understand that ten ones make a ten or that ten tenths equal one? Working with money can be a helpful way to develop beginning understanding of tenths and hundredths.

Student Work Sample: Darren

Name _____ Date _____

Which of the following has the same value as 10 nickels?

A. $\frac{1}{10}$ of a dollar

B. $\frac{1}{5}$ of a dollar

C. $\frac{1}{2}$ of a dollar

D. $\frac{1}{4}$ of a dollar

Explain your thinking.

$\frac{1}{2}$ is the answer because 5 is half
of ten. 5+5=10 $\frac{1}{2}+\frac{1}{2}=$ whole

A Conversation with Darren	Teacher Insights
T: Why does your solution make sense, Darren? **Darren:** Well, I drew a picture to show that one-half plus one-half equals a whole. I also showed that five plus five equals ten. I did the five because nickels are five cents and I did the ten because there are ten nickels. Hmm . . . I am getting confused. Well, I was confused before and chose one-half. The other fractions seem too tricky. Mostly, I guessed.	**T:** *Darren has some correct ideas about one-half but went astray in his thinking when solving this problem.*

Informed Instructional Suggestions

Darren marked the correct answer, but his understanding is muddled. Like Nellie, Darren needs to develop foundational money skills and he needs to work with money. He would benefit from the same activities as Nellie, and the two might benefit from working together.

Student Work Sample: Steve

Name _____ Date _____

Which of the following has the same value as 10 nickels?

A. $\frac{1}{10}$ of a dollar

B. $\frac{1}{5}$ of a dollar

C. $\frac{1}{2}$ of a dollar

D. $\frac{1}{4}$ of a dollar

Explain your thinking.

a half of a dollar is 2 quarters

A Conversation with Steve	Teacher Insights
T: I see you wrote about quarters. How does that relate to this problem? **Steve:** It takes two quarters to make one-half of a dollar. **T:** Please reread the question aloud. [Steve reads.] Could you think of a way to use quarters that might help you solve this problem? **Steve:** I don't think so. The problem is about nickels. I didn't read the problem. I just decided to use quarters to make one-half of a dollar. **T:** Now that you have read the problem, do you want to keep your answer or change it? **Steve:** Maybe change it. Nickels are worth five cents, so maybe one nickel is worth one-fifth of a dollar.	*T: Like Andy, Nellie, and Darren, Steve has some significant deficits in his understanding of both money and fractional representations. Even after rereading the problem and with some guiding questions, Steve was still confused.*

Informed Instructional Suggestions

Steve has significant gaps and misunderstandings about both money and fractions. His needs are very similar to those of the previous three students.

Student Work Sample: Kelly

Name _____ Date _____

Which of the following has the same value as 10 nickels?

A. $\frac{1}{10}$ of a dollar

B. $\frac{1}{5}$ of a dollar

C. $\frac{1}{2}$ of a dollar

D. $\frac{1}{4}$ of a dollar

Explain your thinking.

I chose A becaus when you flip it,
it is $\frac{10}{1}$ whien equals 10

A Conversation with Kelly	Teacher Insights
T: Please share with me what you did to solve this problem. **Kelly:** I saw that there are supposed to be 10 of something, so I just flipped $\frac{1}{10}$ over and it became 10 over 1, which is the same thing as 10. **T:** Please read the problem to yourself and then tell me in your own words what you think it is asking. **Kelly:** Oh, I see, I'm not supposed to find a fraction that is equal to ten at all. I'm supposed to find out what part of a dollar is ten nickels. Oopsie! I should read the problem, huh? I just looked at the numbers and not the words. **T:** Now that you understand the problem, what could you do to solve it? **Kelly:** It's easy, actually. I can do it in my head. I know that ten nickels is fifty cents, which is one-half of a dollar. I also know that there are twenty nickels in a dollar, so ten nickels has to be one-half of a dollar. **T:** What did you learn from this? **Kelly:** I have to read everything on the page or I might make a mistake like I just did.	**T:** *Kelly's multiple-choice answer and her written explanation showed confusion. But after rereading the question, she was able to solve the problem easily and efficiently in two ways.*

Informed Instructional Suggestions

Kelly does not need remediation or further opportunities to explore similar problems on this level. Although she marked the incorrect answer, her needs are similar to those of Johnson and Jamie. She also needs work with fractions to help her understand that fractions such as $\frac{1}{10}$ and $\frac{10}{1}$ are not the same.

Student Work Sample: Nina

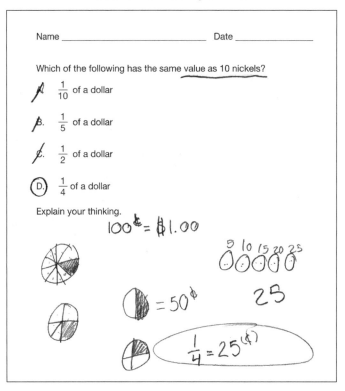

Name _____ Date _____

Which of the following has the same value as 10 nickels?

A. $\frac{1}{10}$ of a dollar

B. $\frac{1}{5}$ of a dollar

C. $\frac{1}{2}$ of a dollar

D. $\frac{1}{4}$ of a dollar

Explain your thinking.

$100¢ = \$1.00$

$\bigcirc = 50¢$

$5\ 10\ 15\ 20\ 25$

25

$\frac{1}{4} = 25(¢)$

A Conversation with Nina	Teacher Insights
T: Nina, please read the problem aloud. [Nina reads.] What is it asking you to do? **Nina:** I have to figure out how much ten nickels are worth. I did that. Right here on my paper. I counted five five times because each nickel is five cents and . . . oh no! I only figured out what five nickels is. It was supposed to be ten nickels. The right answer is really one-half of a dollar.	**T:** *Like Kelly, Nina does possess the understanding to correctly solve this problem, although she chose an incorrect answer. Nina's verbal realization and explanation provided important insights to her true level of understanding.*

Informed Instructional Suggestions

Nina is ready for the same activities and learning opportunities as Johnson and Jamie.

Reassessment

1. Use a similar problem at the same level of difficulty.

   Which of the following has the same value as 15 nickels?

   A. $\frac{15}{100}$ of a dollar
   B. $\frac{1}{4}$ of a dollar
   C. $\frac{1}{2}$ of a dollar
   D. $\frac{3}{4}$ of a dollar

   Explain your thinking.

2. Choose a problem that is similar but slightly more challenging.

   Which of the following has the same value as 15 dimes?

   A. $1\frac{1}{2}$ dollars
   B. $\frac{1}{2}$ of a dollar
   C. $\frac{15}{100}$ of a dollar
   D. $1\frac{1}{4}$ of a dollar

   Explain your thinking.

Name _____

Measurement

+5min +20
10:40   11:00   +10 min

11:10   +5min

11:1

30min + 10 min = 40 min

PROBLEM ONE

Overview

To solve this problem, students need to know the value of coins and be able to count or add money. It is also important that they are able to compare money amounts to determine the greatest amount.

Sample Problem

Four friends counted their change. Study their coins. Then answer the question below.

Marci had 7 dimes.
Sam had 3 quarters and 2 nickels.
Kyle had 1 quarter and 5 dimes.
Monte had 16 nickels.

Which friend had the most money?

A. Marci
B. Sam
C. Kyle
D. Monte

Explain your thinking.

Possible Student Solution Strategies

o Students use pictures to show monetary amounts.
o Students use addition to determine the value of the coins.
o Students use multiplication to determine the value of the coins.
o Students use skip-counting to determine the value of the coins.
o Students determine the number of coins rather than the value of the coins.
o Students miscalculate or misrepresent the value of the coins.

Conversation Starters

o What is alike and what is different about your solution and those of others?
o Is there more than way to solve this problem? How do you know?
o How did you think about this problem?
o How would you use manipulatives or pictures to help you solve this problem?
o How could you explain your thinking to another student?

Student Work Samples: Mary and Suri

Name _____ Date _____

Four friends counted their change. Study their coins. Then answer the question below.

Marci had 7 dimes.
Sam had 3 quarters and 2 nickels.
Kyle had 1 quarter and 5 dimes.
Monte had 16 nickels.

Which friend had the most money?

A.   Marci

B.   Sam

C.   Kyle

D.   Monte

Explain your thinking.

I already showed you right here!

Name _____ Date _____

Four friends counted their change. Study their coins. Then answer the question below.

Marci had 7 dimes.
Sam had 3 quarters and 2 nickels.
Kyle had 1 quarter and 5 dimes.
Monte had 16 nickels.

Which friend had the most money?

A.   Marci

B.   Sam

C.   Kyle

D.   Monte

Explain your thinking.

Marci has 7 dimes =70¢
Sam has 3 quarters and 2 nickles=85¢
Kyle has 1 quarter and 5 dimes= 50¢
Monte has 16 nickles= 80¢
So it is B.

A Conversation with Mary and Suri	Teacher Insights
T: Mary and Suri, please share your work with each other. As you share your work, think about how your work is similar and how it is different. **Suri:** I used words and numbers to show my thinking and you used pictures and numbers. **Mary:** I like to draw pictures when I use money. It helps me see the coins and count them. Let's compare our answers. **Suri:** We both got seventy cents for seven dimes. **Mary:** I got ninety cents and you got eighty-five cents for three quarters and two nickels. **Suri:** Hmm. Let's count using your picture. Twenty-five, fifty, seventy-five, eighty, and one more nickel is eighty-five. **Mary:** Oops! I put five cents too much. **Suri:** For Kyle, I put twenty-five cents, but when I look at your picture, I see I forgot to add the quarter! You were right. **Mary:** We both got eighty cents for Monte. We both made mistakes, but we got the right answer! **Suri:** I think we both need to check our work. Your picture helped me to see my mistake.	**T:** *Both Mary and Suri know the value of coins and can figure out the value of a group of coins. However, they both made computational errors and should be encouraged to carefully check their work.*

Informed Instructional Suggestions

Mary and Suri are ready for similar problems using more coins and groups of coins totaling more than one dollar. Writing and solving their own problems similar to this one would also provide useful practice and reinforcement.

Student Work Sample: Colleen

Name _____ Date _____

Four friends counted their change. Study their coins. Then answer the question below.

Marci had 7 dimes.
Sam had 3 quarters and 2 nickels.
Kyle had 1 quarter and 5 dimes.
Monte had 16 nickels.

$$\begin{array}{r} 75 \\ +20 \\ \hline 95¢ \end{array} \qquad \begin{array}{r} 25 \\ +50 \\ \hline 75 \end{array}$$

Which friend had the most money?

$10+10+10+10+10+10+10=7$

A. Marci

$5+5+5+5+5+5+5+5+5+5$

(B.) Sam

$+5+5+5+5+5=80$

C. Kyle

D. Monte

Explain your thinking.

I know it is Sam because Sam has 95¢ Marci has 70¢ Kyle has 75¢ Monte has 80¢ and the highest number is 95 and that how I know it's Sam.

A Conversation with Colleen	Teacher Insights
T: I like how you showed all of your work. That helps me more clearly understand your thinking. Please tell me about how you got seventy-five cents and twenty cents in your first problem.	**T:** *Colleen has the skills necessary to solve this problem. She made an error and should be encouraged to check her work for accuracy.*
Colleen: The problem says that Sam has three quarters and two nickels. The seventy-five is because three quarters make seventy-five cents and the twenty cents is because two nickels make twenty cents.	
T: That's interesting. Is there anywhere else you had to add nickels?	
Colleen: Yes, Monte.	
T: How much did two nickels equal when you figured out Monte's coins?	
Colleen: Five and five is ten, so two nickels is ten cents.	
T: How many nickels did Sam have?	
Colleen: Two . . . oh no, I put two nickels make twenty cents, but really two nickels make ten cents! Sam really has eighty-five cents, not ninety-five cents. Sam still has the most.	

Informed Instructional Suggestions

Colleen's needs are similar to those of Mary and Suri. She should practice a few similar problems to improve her accuracy. The activities and lessons we suggested for Mary and Suri would also be appropriate for Colleen.

Student Work Sample: Charlie

Name _____ Date _____

Four friends counted their change. Study their coins. Then answer
the question below.

Marci had 7 dimes.
Sam had 3 quarters and 2 nickels.
Kyle had 1 quarter and 5 dimes.
Monte had 16 nickels.

Which friend had the most money?

A.   Marci

B.   Sam

C.   Kyle

D.   Monte

$$\begin{array}{c} 5 \\ \times \\ 16 \\ \hline 80 \end{array} \qquad \begin{array}{c} 5 \\ \times 5 \\ \hline 25 \end{array} \qquad \begin{array}{c} 25 \\ 25 \\ +25 \\ \hline 75 \end{array} \qquad \begin{array}{c} 10 \\ \times 7 \\ \hline 70 \end{array}$$

$$\begin{array}{c} 25 \\ +25 \\ \hline 50 \end{array} \qquad \begin{array}{c} 25 \\ +10 \\ \hline 85 \end{array}$$

Explain your thinking.

I think it is Sam becau
I added their change and
85 is the biggest and thats what
Sam got.

A Conversation with Charlie	Teacher Insights
T: How could you explain your thinking to another student about how you got the answer to five times sixteen?	**T:** *Charlie, like Colleen, made a computational error. However, he has the skills necessary to correctly solve the problem.*
Charlie: I know that 10 times 16 is 160, so 5 is half of 10, and half of 160 is 80. I could also count by 5s.	
T: I like the way you used your number sense to figure out five times sixteen. Your next arrow shows how you figured the amount of money that Kyle had. Please tell me more.	
Charlie: Kyle has five dimes, so I wrote . . . oops! I wrote 5 × 5, and it should be 5 × 10. Kyle should have fifty cents in dimes plus a quarter. He has seventy-five cents, not fifty.	

Informed Instructional Suggestions

Like Colleen, Charlie needs to check to be sure that his solution matches the problem. Charlie should have additional practice with solving and checking problems similar to this one. Then he can move on to solving similar problems with larger numbers.

Student Work Sample: Suzie

Name _____ Date _____

Four friends counted their change. Study their coins. Then answer the question below.

Marci had 7 dimes.
Sam had 3 quarters and 2 nickels.
Kyle had 1 quarter and 5 dimes.
Monte had 16 nickels.

Which friend had the most money?

Tip
quarter = 25¢
dime = 10¢
penny = 1¢
nickle = 5¢

A. Marci

B. Sam

C. Kyle

● Monte

Marci 7 dimes = 70¢

Explain your thinking. *Sam 3 quarters = 75¢ 75¢+10¢=85¢*

Kyle 1 quarter=25¢ 25¢+5 dimes=75¢

Monte 16 nickels = (80¢)

A Conversation with Suzie	Teacher Insights
T: I like how you gave a tip about how to solve this question! I can see you know some important things about money. It looks like you figured out the amount of money each person had. You circled eighty cents. Why did you do that?	**T:** *Suzie marked an incorrect answer; however, she understands the skills needed to solve this problem.*
Suzie: It's the most.	
T: Let's look back at the amounts of money each person had. Please read them aloud.	
Suzie: Marci had seventy cents, Sam had eighty-five cents, Kyle had seventy-five cents, and Monte had eighty cents. Wait a minute, eighty-five is more than eighty! Sam had the most. He had eighty-five cents. I made a mistake!	

Informed Instructional Suggestions

Suzie's incorrect response implied she had not mastered these skills when in fact she has. When asked to explain her thinking, she showed clearly all that she does know. She made an error that she caught during her verbal explanation. Suzie needs experiences and activities similar to those we recommended for Mary and Suri. She also needs encouragement to check her answers.

Student Work Sample: Lucy

Name _____ Date _____

Four friends counted their change. Study their coins. Then answer the question below.

Marci had 7 dimes.
Sam had 3 quarters and 2 nickels.
Kyle had 1 quarter and 5 dimes.
Monte had 16 nickels.

Which friend had the most money?

A.   Marci

B.   Sam

C.   Kyle

D.   Monte

Explain your thinking.

Handwritten work:

Marci—7+0=7
✗ Sam— 3+2=5
✗ Kyle—5+1=6
✓ Monte— 16+0=16

A Conversation with Lucy	Teacher Insights
T: How did you think about this problem? What is it asking you to do? **Lucy:** I have to find who has the most money. I see numbers, so I just add them up to find out. I didn't even have to add them all because Monte has sixteen and that's the most. Marci has seven coins, Sam has five coins, and Kyle has six. I showed it on my paper. **T:** Is the problem asking you to count the number of coins or the amount of money? **Lucy:** It's the same thing. The more coins you have, the more money you have. **T:** Which is more, five pennies or one nickel? **Lucy:** Five pennies is more. Five coins is more than one coin.	*T: Lucy clearly demonstrated her ability to count coins but showed virtually no understanding of what the problem was asking her to do. She seemed to confuse the word* money *with the word* coins, *a common problem among children who are learning a second language or who have other issues with language. She also indicated no awareness of the value of coins, stating that five pennies were worth more than one nickel.*

Informed Instructional Suggestions

Lucy needs foundational experiences to help her develop understanding of the value of coins and then how to count money. Using concrete materials such as play money would support Lucy in acquiring these basic understandings.

Reassessment

1. Use a similar problem at the same level of difficulty.

    Four friends counted their change. Study their coins. Then answer the question below.

    Jessica had 19 nickels.
    Juan had 2 quarters and 3 dimes.
    Max had 9 dimes.
    Rachel had 1 quarter and 7 nickels.

    Which friend had the most money?

    A. Jessica
    B. Juan
    C. Max
    D. Rachel

    Explain your thinking.

2. Choose a problem that is similar but slightly more challenging.

    Five friends counted their change. Study their coins. Then answer the question below.

    Jack had 5 quarters and 3 dimes.
    Monica had 15 dimes.
    Chin had 6 quarters and 6 nickels.
    Charlie had 7 quarters.
    Brooke had 10 nickels, 6 dimes, and 6 pennies.

    Which friend had the most money?

    A. Jack
    B. Charlie
    C. Chin
    D. Brooke

    Explain your thinking.

PROBLEM TWO

Overview

This problem asks students to find the area of an irregular shape. Each square represents 6 square feet. This twist in the problem requires that students read carefully all information and multiply the number of shaded squares by six.

Sample Problem

If one square unit equals 6 square feet, what is the area of the shaded figure?

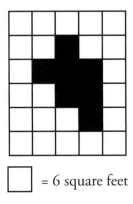

= 6 square feet

A. 7 square feet
B. 48 square feet
C. 36 square feet
D. 42 square feet

Explain your thinking.

Possible Student Solution Strategies

o   Students correctly figure the area by first counting the shaded squares and then multiplying by six.
o   Students correctly figure the area by skip-counting by sixes.
o   Students correctly figure the area using repeated addition.
o   Students correctly figure the area using pictures.
o   Students figure the area of the unshaded squares.
o   Students only count the shaded squares and do not account for the value of each square.

Conversation Starters

o   Is there more than one way to solve this problem?
o   What did you do to check your answer?
o   How did you think about this problem?

Student Work Sample: Suri

Name _____ Date _____

If one square unit equals 6 square feet, what is the area of the shaded figure?

☐ = 6 square feet

A.   7 square feet

B.   48 square feet

C.   36 square feet

D.   42 square feet

Explain your thinking.

This is the shaded part...

one box = 6 square feet.....

×6
──
42 = anwser!

A Conversation with Suri	Teacher Insights
T: Please tell me how you thought about this problem. **Suri:** Well, when I read the problem I noticed that it was more than just counting the squares. I had to make sure that each square counted as six rather than one. So I drew a picture and put a 6 in each square. There were seven squares, so I multiplied seven times six and got forty-two. It's a basic fact.	**T:** *Both Suri's written and oral explanations of her thinking were clear.*

Informed Instructional Suggestions

Suri is ready to explore similar problems with larger numbers. Another activity that would benefit Suri and other students would be for her to create similar problems at varying degrees of difficulty, find the solution to each problem in one or more ways, and then share the problems with other students.

Student Work Sample: Jill

Name _____ Date _____

If one square unit equals 6 square feet, what is the area of the shaded figure?

☐ = 6 square feet

A. 7 square feet

B. 48 square feet

C. 36 square feet

D. 42 square feet

Explain your thinking.

$$6+6+6+6+6+6+6=42$$

$$7 \times 6 = 42$$

A Conversation with Jill	Teacher Insights
T: I see that you used more than one way to solve this problem. Can you think of another way still? **Jill:** I'm not sure. I used pictures. I drew seven squares because there are seven shaded squares. Then, under each square, I showed skip-counting. Then I did repeated addition. I wrote seven 6s because there are seven groups of six. Then I wrote the multiplication sentence. I suppose I could combine two sixes to make twelve and count by twelve three times and then add the last six, but I didn't think of that. **T:** You have a lot of ways of thinking about this. Another important thing is that in all the ways you showed on your paper, you got the same answer. That's important. What does it mean when you do different ways and get different answers? **Jill:** It means I made a mistake somewhere and I need to go back and redo my work. **T:** I also like the way that your multiplication sentence matches your thinking of this as seven groups of six.	**T:** *Jill had multiple solution strategies for this problem. She was even able to stretch her thinking to come up with an additional verbal explanation, an indicator of her ability to think flexibly.*

Informed Instructional Strategies

Jill's needs are similar to those of Suri, and she would benefit from the same instructional strategies and activities. It would also be helpful to both girls if they worked together to explore their ideas.

Student Work Sample: Franny

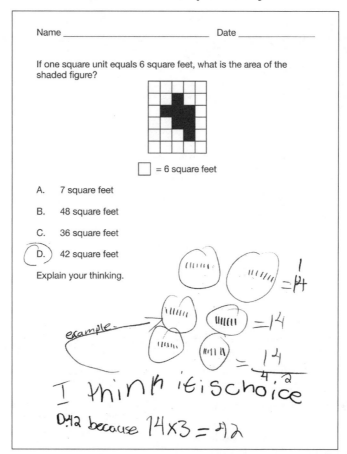

Name _____   Date _____

If one square unit equals 6 square feet, what is the area of the shaded figure?

☐ = 6 square feet

A.   7 square feet

B.   48 square feet

C.   36 square feet

D.   42 square feet

Explain your thinking.

example

I think it is choice D.42 because 14×3 = 42

A Conversation with Franny	Teacher Insights
T: I am a bit confused by your paper. Please tell me more about how you thought about this problem. **Franny:** I knew that I had to multiply seven times six because there are seven shaded squares and each one is worth 6. So I drew six circles and put seven lines in each one. Then I put two sevens together to make fourteen. I got three fourteens and added those up to get forty-two. Then I wrote *14 × 3 = 42*.	**T:** *There are two ways to think of multiplication. The number sentence 7 × 6 can be thought of as seven groups of six, as Jill thought of it, or seven six times, as Franny thought of it. Jill's way of thinking is more common than Franny's, but both are correct.*

Informed Instructional Suggestions

Franny would benefit from the same experiences as Suri and Jill. Also, asking Franny to share her thinking with Suri and Jill would provide them with an opportunity to hear a different idea.

Student Work Sample: Samantha

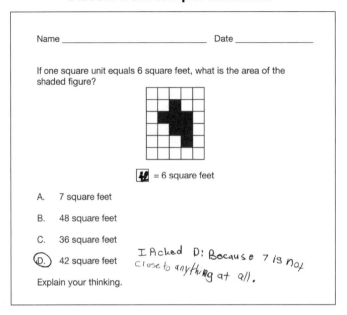

Name _____ Date _____

If one square unit equals 6 square feet, what is the area of the shaded figure?

= 6 square feet

A.   7 square feet

B.   48 square feet

C.   36 square feet

(D.)   42 square feet   I Picked D: Because 7 is not
                          close to anything at all.

Explain your thinking.

A Conversation with Samantha	Teacher Insights
T: Please tell me about your thinking. I notice that you first circled choice A and then erased that and circled choice D. **Samantha:** I counted up seven shaded squares. That's why I circled choice A. But then I saw the number 6 and got confused. I don't know why there is a 6 there when there are seven squares. So I looked at Harvey's paper and he put choice D. So I did. **T:** Please read the problem aloud and tell me in your own words what it says. **Samantha:** I didn't read it before. I just saw shaded squares and counted because that's what you usually do for problems like this. The directions say that each square equals 6 square feet. I guess that's where the 6 comes from. **T:** Now that you have read the problem and know about the 6, what would you do to correctly solve this problem? **Samantha:** I am not sure. I'd probably still check my neighbor's paper to see what he did.	**T:** Samantha marked the correct answer but was very confused about what this problem was asking her to do. She attempted to use prior experience with counting shaded squares to find the area of a polygon, but in this case it didn't work because of the value represented by each square.

Informed Instructional Suggestions

Samantha's confusion would have been hidden by her copied correct answer had she not also explained her thinking. Her written and verbal explanations revealed her difficulties and provided insight into her specific needs. Because Samantha does understand how to count area when each square represents 1, she would benefit from similar experiences with each square unit having a value other than 1. She could also use tiles or other similar manipulatives as a way to keep track of what she has and has not counted.

Student Work Sample: Reggie

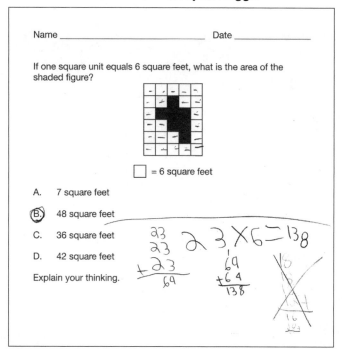

Name _____ Date _____

If one square unit equals 6 square feet, what is the area of the shaded figure?

☐ = 6 square feet

A.   7 square feet

Ⓑ   48 square feet

C.   36 square feet

D.   42 square feet

Explain your thinking.

A Conversation with Reggie	Teacher Insights
T: Reggie, I notice that you got 138 but you circled 48. Please tell me about that.	*T: At first glance, Reggie's paper showed confusion. But by taking a few moments to explore his thinking, I learned that in fact he has the skills and understands the concepts necessary to solve this problem.*
Reggie: I counted up all of the unshaded squares and there were 23. Because each square equals 6, I multiplied 23 times 6. I didn't know how to do that, so I added 23 three times and got 69. Three is only half of 6, so I had to do another three 23s, so that's the same as 69 twice. I added 69 plus 69 and that was 138. But that was trouble! That answer wasn't there. I checked my work and got the same answer, so I knew I was right. I decided to choose the highest answer, and that was 48.	
T: Reggie, please reread the problem.	
Reggie: Uh-oh! I worked way too hard. I only had to count the shaded squares, and I counted the unshaded squares. There are seven shaded squares, so I have to multiply seven times six, and that's forty-two.	

Informed Instructional Suggestions

Reggie is ready to move forward. He should work on the same activities we suggested for Suri. In addition, Reggie needs to remember to read carefully.

Student Work Sample: Tony

Name _____ Date _____

If one square unit equals 6 square feet, what is the area of the shaded figure?

$\boxed{7}$ = 6 square feet

A. 7 square feet

B.   48 square feet

C.   36 square feet

D.   42 square feet

Explain your thinking.

A Conversation with Tony	Teacher Insights
T: Please reread this problem and then tell me what you think it is asking you to do. **Tony:** It says to count the shaded squares. **T:** What else does it tell you? **Tony:** I don't know. **T:** What does each square equal? **Tony:** Um, 6 square feet? **T:** Why is that important? **Tony:** I don't get it; there are seven shaded squares, not six. And in the past, I always just had to count up the squares and that was the answer.	**T:** *Tony was unable to break away from past experiences to accurately apply his strategy of counting squares as a method to find the area when the value of each square was something other than 1.*

Informed Instructional Suggestions

Tony has a beginning understanding of the skills needed to solve this problem, since he can count area when the unit is equal to one. However, he needs more practice. Tony would benefit from experiences similar to those we suggested for Samantha, in which a square unit represents something other than 1.

Reassessment

1. Use a similar problem at the same level of difficulty.

    If one square unit equals 4 square feet, what is the area of the shaded figure?

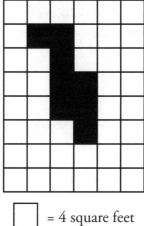

    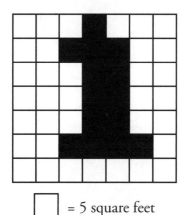 = 4 square feet

    A. 32 square feet
    B. 8 square feet
    C. 40 square feet
    D. 36 square feet

    Explain your thinking.

2. Choose a problem that is similar but slightly more challenging.

    If one square unit equals 5 square feet, what is the area of the unshaded space?

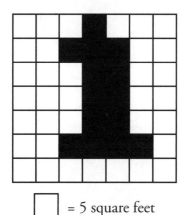

    = 5 square feet

    A. 70 square feet
    B. 175 square feet
    C. 35 square feet
    D. 150 square feet

    Explain your thinking.

ⓅⓇⓄⒷⓁⒺⓂ ⓉⒽⓇⒺⒺ

Overview

The objective of this question is to test students' skills in finding elapsed time. To successfully solve the problem, students need foundational knowledge about time, for example, how to read an analog clock, how to count time, and how to add or subtract time.

Sample Problem

Sam arrived at the bus station at 11:15 p.m. but found out that his bus had left at 10:35 p.m. By how many minutes did he miss his bus?

A. 50 minutes
B. 20 minutes
C. 30 minutes
D. 40 minutes

Explain your thinking.

Possible Student Solution Strategies

o Students estimate to get an approximate answer and then figure the exact answer.
o Students use 11:00 as a landmark, then use addition, subtraction, or a number line to figure the number of minutes.
o Students draw a clock and count the elapsed time in five- or ten-minute increments.
o Students incorrectly add or subtract.

Conversation Starters

o What do you know about this problem? What do you need to find out?
o How could a picture help you solve this problem?
o How could you prove your answer?
o Can you solve this problem in another way?

Student Work Sample: Sheila

Name _____ Date _____

Sam arrived at the bus station at 11:15 p.m. but found out that his bus
had left at 10:35 p.m. By how many minutes did he miss his bus?

A.   50 minutes

B.   20 minutes

C.   30 minutes

D.   40 minutes *(circled)*

Explain your thinking.

> To get my answer I fist took 10:35 p.m.
> and saw that 11:15 was rufly about 45 minuts
> apart. so than I dicided to take 10:35 p.m.
> and round up all the way till I got to
> 11:00. and that turned out to be 25
> minuts But, than I looked a 11:15.p.m.
> and saw that I had to add 15
> more minuts to get my answer.
> so I did the math and got
> 40, because 15 plus 25 is 40.
> minuts. So sam was 40 minuts
> late,

A Conversation with Sheila	Teacher Insights
T: What do you know about this problem? **Sheila:** I know that Sam missed the bus. I also know that he missed it by about forty-five minutes. Then I figured out the exact number of minutes. I knew that it was twenty-five minutes from 10:35 to 11:00. Then I just had to add fifteen more minutes to get to 11:15. Twenty-five and fifteen is forty. **T:** Can you solve the problem in another way to verify your answer? **Sheila:** Yes. I could start at 10:35 and count by fives until I get to 11:15. There are five fives, or twenty-five, to get to 11:00 and the three fives more, or fifteen, to get to 11:15. That's forty minutes.	*T: Sheila had a clear understanding of how to solve this problem and was able to state a second problem solution.*

Informed Instructional Suggestions

Sheila is ready to investigate and solve more complex problems involving elapsed time, such as figuring elapsed time to the minute when not in increments of five minutes, or figuring elapsed time beyond 60 minutes.

Student Work Sample: Don

Name _____ Date _____

Sam arrived at the bus station at 11:15 p.m. but found out that his bus had left at 10:35 p.m. By how many minutes did he miss his bus?

A.   50 minutes

B.   20 minutes

C.   30 minutes

D.   40 minutes

Explain your thinking.

$$30 \text{ min} + 10 \text{ min} = 40 \text{ min}$$

A Conversation with Don	Teacher Insights
T: Please tell me about the strategy you used to solve this problem.	**T:** *Like Sheila, Don had strong understanding and at least two strategies to solve this problem.*
Don: I just used a number line. I put 10:35 on the left side. Then I added five minutes to get to 10:40. Then I added twenty minutes more to get to 11:00. Next I added ten more minutes to get to 11:10 and then I added five minutes and I was on 11:15. I figured out how many minutes I added altogether, and that was my answer.	
T: What's another way you could solve this problem?	
Don: I could draw a picture of a clock and count how many minutes between 10:35 and 11:15 using the clock.	

Informed Instructional Suggestions

Don's needs are similar to Sheila's, and perhaps they could work together to explore more challenging, complex problems involving elapsed time.

Student Work Sample: Belinda

Name _____ Date _____

Sam arrived at the bus station at 11:15 p.m. but found out that his bus had left at 10:35 p.m. By how many minutes did he miss his bus?

A.   50 minutes

B.   20 minutes

C.   30 minutes

D.   40 minutes

Explain your thinking.

A Conversation with Belinda	Teacher Insights
T: Please tell me about what you did. **Belinda:** I drew a clock and showed 10:35. Then I counted by fives from 10:35 to 11:15. I got forty minutes. I circled choice D.	**T:** *Like Sheila and Don, Belinda has good understanding of the skills needed to solve this problem.*

Informed Instructional Suggestions

Belinda should work on the same activities we recommended for Sheila and Don.

Student Work Sample: Bart

Name _____ Date _____

Sam arrived at the bus station at 11:15 p.m. but found out that his bus had left at 10:35 p.m. By how many minutes did he miss his bus?

A.   50 minutes

B.   20 minutes

C.   30 minutes

D.   40 minutes

Explain your thinking.

Because 10:35 + 40 = 10:75 but sence the mins colum is over 60 by 15 so it has to be 11:15

A Conversation with Bart	Teacher Insights
T: Your thinking is very interesting. Please tell me more about it. **Bart:** I started with 10:35 and counted up by fives by looking at the clock on the back wall. I got forty. So to check my answer I added forty to 10:35 and got 10:75. But I know you can't do that because there are only sixty minutes in an hour, so you have to start over again when you get to sixty. Seventy-five is fifteen more than sixty, so that's 11:15. So I was right.	**T:** *While Bart's thinking was unusual, he showed strong understanding that when adding and subtracting time, he was not working in the base ten system. Rather, he had to remember that hours have sixty minutes, so when he went over sixty minutes, he had to add another hour. Therefore, seventy-five minutes would need to be communicated as one hour and fifteen minutes.*

Informed Instructional Suggestions

Bart's needs are the same as those of the previous students. Asking the students to share their thinking with one another or with the rest of the class would provide various strategies for all to consider.

Student Work Sample: Betsy

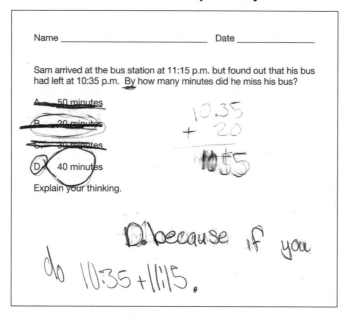

Name _____ Date _____

Sam arrived at the bus station at 11:15 p.m. but found out that his bus had left at 10:35 p.m. By how many minutes did he miss his bus?

A. ~~50 minutes~~

B. ~~20 minutes~~

C. ~~30 minutes~~

D. 40 minutes

Explain your thinking.

$$10.35$$
$$+ \ 20$$
$$\overline{10.55}$$

D. because if you do 10:35 + 11:15.

A Conversation with Betsy	Teacher Insights
T: Please tell me more about how you solved this problem. **Betsy:** I tried to add 10:35 plus twenty because it was one of the answer choices. I got 10:55 and erased it. Then I tried to add 10:35 plus 11:15. That didn't make too much sense because when I thought about it, the answer would be 21-something. I knew from my first attempt that twenty was too low, so I just doubled twenty to get forty. **T:** How could you prove that forty works? **Betsy:** I am not sure. I think I might be able to use the clock on the back wall somehow, but I'm not really sure what to count.	**T:** *Betsy used a good strategy for taking multiple-choice tests. She tried one of the answers to see if produced the desired result. In this case it did not, but it did give her a bit of direction. Continuing with this strategy might have led her to an answer that made sense to her. Instead of continuing, however, she tried to add the two times given. She did realize that the answer she produced made no sense. Then she essentially guessed. At the end of our discussion, she surmised that she could use the clock on the classroom wall as a tool to solve this question.*

Informed Instructional Suggestions

Betsy's correct answer alone would have indicated she understood the content and skills involved, but she arrived at that answer through confusion. Betsy needs opportunities to help her develop understanding and meaningful strategies for working with time. Using an analog clock would be a good way for Betsy to practice figuring elapsed time. She could also work with a drawing of a clock face or a cardboard clock face with attached minute and hour hands that she could manipulate. She did use a good test-taking strategy when she tried an answer choice, and we plan to acknowledge and reinforce this strategy.

Student Work Sample: Zorba

Name _____ Date _____

Sam arrived at the bus station at 11:15 p.m. but found out that his bus had left at 10:35 p.m. By how many minutes did he miss his bus?

A.   50 minutes

B.   20 minutes

C.   30 minutes

D.   40 minutes

Explain your thinking. 25

50

becaus it is right in the middle and it could be the right anser.

A Conversation with Zorba	Teacher Insights
T: Zorba, please tell me more about what you mean by "right in the middle." **Zorba:** It's not the smallest and it's not the largest, so it could be the right answer. **T:** Are you saying that the smallest answer choice or the largest answer choice will never be the right answer? **Zorba:** Yep. Usually when I figure out all the choices, it's not the largest or the smallest, and it's usually choice C or D because they want you to figure out all the choices. I suppose it could have been thirty minutes, but I chose forty.	*T: Zorba was lucky enough to guess the correct answer. Interestingly, what Zorba has noticed about multiple-choice tests tends to be true in many cases.*

Informed Instructional Suggestions

Zorba's lucky guess that led to a correct answer did not represent understanding, and his explanations told us nothing about his knowledge of time. A reasonable next step would be to ask Zorba to use an analog clock as a tool to work through the problem to find a logical solution.

Student Work Sample: Bobby

Name _____ Date _____

Sam arrived at the bus station at 11:15 p.m. but found out that his bus
had left at 10:35 p.m. By how many minutes did he miss his bus?

A.   50 minutes

B.   20 minutes

C.   30 minutes

D.   40 minutes

Explain your thinking.

well, I really just guessed on s this one.

$$10\overset{3}{3}5$$
$$\underline{20}$$
$$1055$$

$$10{:}35$$
$$\underline{50}$$
$$1085$$

$$10{:}35$$
$$\underline{\times40}$$
$$1075$$

A Conversation with Bobby	Teacher Insights
T: I see that you guessed, but I also see that you did a lot of work. What made you guess the way you did? **Bobby:** I knew I could try to get the correct answer by trying all of the answer choices, so I did. But I started to get answers that weren't in normal time. They weren't making sense to me. I did notice that when I added twenty to 10:35, I got something that was sensible but not sensible enough. I even tried to subtract, but I crossed that out. I just guessed.	**T:** *Bobby tried to make sense of this problem, and like Betsy, he tried the answer choices. He realized that his answers didn't make sense, but he didn't know what to do with that information. Unlike Bart, Bobby does not understand that when working in hours, a time over sixty minutes needs to be converted into an hour and the remaining minutes.*

Informed Instructional Suggestions

Bobby needs experiences with working with hours, minutes, and cardboard clocks to help him learn how to correctly figure and convert time.

Student Work Sample: Suri

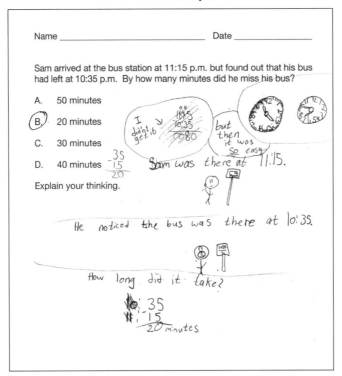

Name _____ Date _____

Sam arrived at the bus station at 11:15 p.m. but found out that his bus had left at 10:35 p.m. By how many minutes did he miss his bus?

A.   50 minutes

(B.)   20 minutes

C.   30 minutes

D.   40 minutes

Explain your thinking.

A Conversation with Suri	Teacher Insights
T: Suri, I like the way you restated the problem using your own words. Please tell me about why at the bottom of the page you crossed off the hours in your figuring.	*T: Suri needs to practice finding elapsed time, including how to set up the problem correctly. She had some understanding about the minutes but failed to incorporate the hours into her figuring.*
Suri: I didn't need them because I was figuring out minutes.	
T: I see you also drew two clocks. Please use one of the clocks and start counting at 10:35 and see where you are after adding twenty minutes.	
Suri: Ohh, adding twenty minutes only gets to 10:55! That's not right. I have to get to 11:15. [Suri continues to count using the clock she had drawn on her paper.] Oh, I see now: it's forty minutes.	

Informed Instructional Suggestions

Suri needs to practice using strategies to figure elapsed time. Analog clocks are useful for this. Another approach that could be helpful would be mentally counting by fives from the first time to the second time to find the elapsed time. Suri would also benefit from hearing Sheila's and Don's strategies.

Student Work Sample: Kitty

Name _____ Date _____

Sam arrived at the bus station at 11:15 p.m. but found out that his bus had left at 10:35 p.m. By how many minutes did he miss his bus?

A.   50 minutes

Ⓑ.   20 minutes

C.   30 minutes

D.   40 minutes

Explain your thinking.

What I did was thought the way of math that I would do the problem. I thought subtraction I got 1 hour and 20 minutes so I picked The closest answer to it because for me the question was confusing.

11:15 pm
10:35 pm

$$11:15 \\ -\ 10:35 \\ \hline 1:20$$

A Conversation with Kitty	Teacher Insights
T: I see you used subtraction. Why did it make sense to you to do this? **Kitty:** I had to find the difference between the two times, so that means I have to subtract. **T:** Your answer says that when you subtracted, you got one hour and twenty minutes, but you chose fifty minutes. **Kitty:** I did that because I really didn't get the problem. I know that the answer should be there, but I didn't know what else to do, so I picked the closest one.	*T: When Kitty subtracted, she revealed two areas of difficulty. First, she tried to use the standard algorithm for subtraction and made a typical mistake by not regrouping when she should have. Second, she failed to recognize that she was working with groups of sixty minutes.*

Informed Instructional Suggestions

Kitty's needs are similar to those of Bobby. She would benefit from the same kinds of instructional experiences we recommended for him.

Reassessment

1. Use a similar problem at the same level of difficulty.

   Jasmine arrived at the train station at 2:20 p.m. but found out that her train had left at 1:45 p.m. By how many minutes did she miss her train?

   A. 45 minutes
   B. 35 minutes
   C. 40 minutes
   D. 30 minutes

   Explain your thinking.

2. Choose a problem that is similar but slightly more challenging.

   Maxwell arrived at the airport at 9:25 a.m. for his 11:00 a.m. flight. He noticed that his flight was delayed for 40 minutes. How long did Maxwell have to wait before his flight left?

   A. 1 hour, 15 minutes
   B. 2 hours
   C. 1 hour, 45 minutes
   D. 2 hours, 15 minutes

   Explain your thinking.

PROBLEM FOUR

Overview

Students are given the measurements of two angles of a triangle and must figure out the measurement of the third angle. Using the knowledge that the interior angles of a triangle add up to 180 degrees, they must first find the sum of the known angles and then subtract the sum from 180 degrees to find the measurement of the missing angle.

Sample Problem

What is the measure of ∠C?

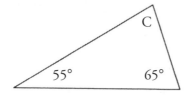

A. 120°
B. 60°
C. 70°
D. 100°

Explain your thinking.

Possible Student Solution Strategies

o   Students add to find the sum of the known angles and then subtract that sum from 180 degrees.
o   Students make an estimation of the third angle based on the size of the known angles.
o   Students add the known angles only without subtracting the sum from 180 degrees.

Conversation Starters

o   What do you know about this problem? What do you need to find out?
o   How did you reach your answer?
o   Is there more than one possible correct answer? Explain.

Student Work Sample: Yolanda

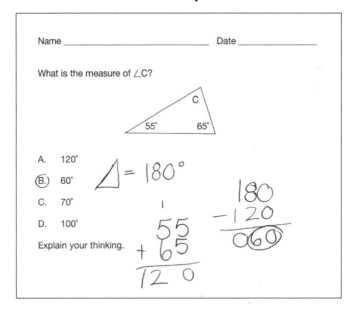

Name _____ Date _____

What is the measure of ∠C?

A.   120°

B.   60°

C.   70°

D.   100°

Explain your thinking.

A Conversation with Yolanda	Teacher Insights
T: What do you know about this problem?	**T:** *Yolanda was able to apply the necessary information to solve this problem confidently and accurately. She also made a good case for why there is only one correct answer for this particular question. After a bit of thought, Yolanda was able to share a second solution strategy.*
Yolanda: I know how big two of the angles are and I know that the degrees of the angles of a triangle add to 180 degrees.	
T: What do you need to find out?	
Yolanda: I have to figure out the size of the third angle. I can do that by adding the two angles and then subtracting the sum from 180 degrees. That will be the size of the angle without the measurement.	
T: Is there more than one possible correct answer?	
Yolanda: I don't think so. There is always 180 degrees in a triangle and that can never change. The first two angles are labeled and can't change either. There really is only one correct answer.	
T: Is there more than one way to get the correct answer?	
Yolanda: I think so. I think that by looking at the two labeled angles and the one without a measurement you can estimate about what the correct answer will be. When I look at the answers, I know that 60 and 70 are the only reasonable answers. Then if I add just the tens—seven tens, six tens, and five tens—I get eighteen tens, which is 180. When I add the ones in, the sum is too big because it is over 180. The answer has to be 60 degrees.	

Informed Instructional Suggestions

Yolanda has a strong understanding of these skills and concepts. She is ready to explore similar problems with other polygons, such as quadrilaterals, whose interior angles will always have a sum of 360 degrees.

Student Work Sample: Eddie

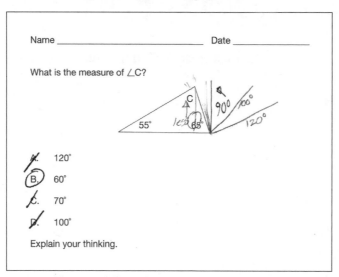

Name _____   Date _____

What is the measure of ∠C?

A. 120°

(B.) 60°

C. 70°

D. 100°

Explain your thinking.

A Conversation with Eddie	Teacher Insights
T: Your drawing is very interesting to me. Please tell me more about your thinking and how your drawing helped you think about this problem.	**T:** *Eddie's pictures and labels indicated some knowledge of angles. He used a right angle as a landmark to help him think about angles in general. He was unaware that the interior angles of triangles add to 180 degrees.*
Eddie: I know what a 90-degree angle is and I drew it to help me with the other angles. Then I drew a picture of a hundred-degree angle and a 120-degree angle. That way I could show that choices A and D were not correct. I know the missing angle is less than 90 degrees, which leaves choices B and C. So just by looking at the angle that's 65 degrees, I guessed that the missing angle was less because it looks smaller. That means choice B must be the right answer.	
T: What is the sum of the interior angles in a triangle?	
Eddie: I don't know.	

Informed Instructional Suggestions

Eddie chose the correct answer based on his partial understanding. Without written or verbal explanations, Eddie's true needs would not have been revealed. It would be helpful to provide Eddie with experiences that would allow him to discover for himself that the sum of the three interior angles of all triangles is 180 degrees. For example, he could use a protractor to measure the angles of a variety of accurately drawn triangles. Or Eddie could find examples of triangles in his world that he could measure using a protractor to further strengthen this understanding.

Student Work Sample: Lilli

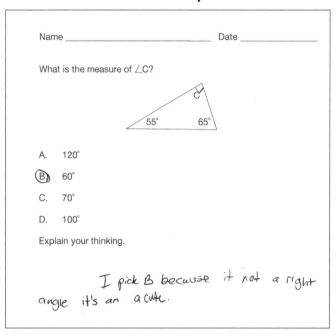

Name _____ Date _____

What is the measure of ∠C?

A.   120°

Ⓑ   60°

C.   70°

D.   100°

Explain your thinking.

I pick B because it not a right angle it's an a cute.

A Conversation with Lilli	Teacher Insights
T: What is a right angle? **Lilli:** It's like a corner on this paper. [Lilli uses her finger to indicate a corner of the paper.] **T:** What is an acute angle? **Lilli:** It's less than a right angle. **T:** What does that mean? **Lilli:** It's like this angle that says 55 degrees. **T:** What made you circle choice B, 60 degrees? **Lilli:** Sixty degrees must look something like the two in the triangle because the numbers are about the same.	*T: Lilli has partial understanding. She knows what is a right angle. She has some understanding of acute angles. She does not seem to know that there are 180 degrees in a triangle. She gauged her answer on the two angles that were labeled.*

Informed Instructional Suggestions

Lilli's correct answer did not expose her needs. Her next steps should be similar to those of Eddie. She needs experiences that will further develop her conceptual understanding of angles, as well as experiences that will help her discover that the three interior angles of all triangles always add to 180 degrees.

Student Work Sample: Ian

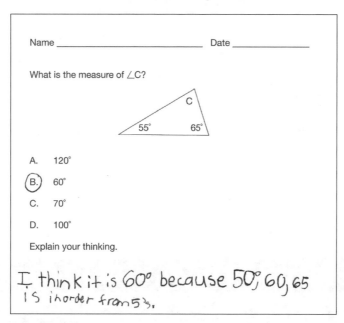

A Conversation with Ian	Teacher Insights
T: Please tell me about your thinking. **Ian:** I noticed a pattern. I found out that all I had to do was count by fives. Fifty-five, sixty, sixty-five. It's done! **T:** Do you know how many degrees the three interior angles of a triangle should add to? **Ian:** I know there are three sides in a triangle. Why would I need to measure how hot the triangle is?	*T: Ian did mark the correct answer but for reasons that are not relevant to this problem. He indicated an understanding of simple patterns but little understanding of angles, triangles, or how degrees relate to angles and triangles.*

Informed Instructional Suggestions

Ian needs foundational experiences to develop understanding of angles and how to measure them. He also needs to discover that the three interior angles of all triangles add to 180 degrees and that when two of those angles are known, he can find the measurement of the third one by subtracting the sum of the other two angles from 180 degrees.

Student Work Sample: Ellen

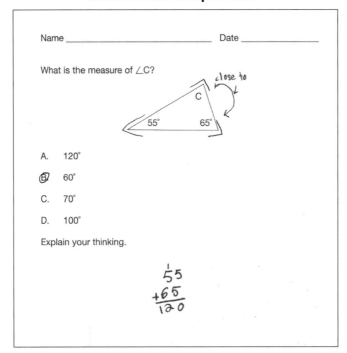

Name _____ Date _____

What is the measure of ∠C?

A.   120°

B.   60°

C.   70°

D.   100°

Explain your thinking.

A Conversation with Ellen	Teacher Insights
T: How did you think about this problem? **Ellen:** I know I have to find out the degrees in the third angle. So I added the degrees in the two that are labeled and I got 120 degrees. I know that if I subtract the sum from 360, I will know the missing measurement. But when I did that, I got 240 degrees and that makes no sense and isn't an answer choice. So I crossed it out. Then I looked at the triangles and the third angle looks sort of like the other two. It especially looks close to the angle that is 65 degrees. So I chose 60.	**T:** *Ellen has some good strategies for solving problems such as this one. However, she doesn't know that the three interior angles of a triangle add to 180 degrees. Like some other students, she ended up using visual clues to help her choose an answer.*

Informed Instructional Suggestions

Although Ellen marked the correct answer, she needs to spend more time working with triangles. She would benefit from the same activities and instructional suggestions as Eddie.

Student Work Sample: Dusty

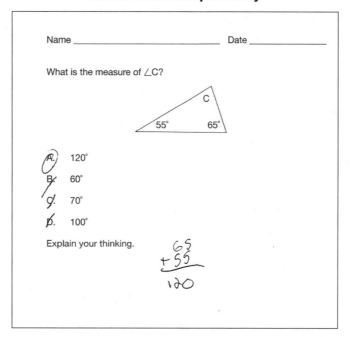

Name _____ Date _____

What is the measure of ∠C?

A.) 120°

B. 60°

C. 70°

D. 100°

Explain your thinking.

$$\begin{array}{r} 65 \\ + 55 \\ \hline 120 \end{array}$$

A Conversation with Dusty	Teacher Insights
T: How did you think about this problem? **Dusty:** I had to find the size of the third angle. So I just added the two that were there. I got 120 degrees, and that was choice A, so I chose that! Easy, huh? **T:** Do you know how many degrees the three interior angles of a triangle should add to? **Dusty:** Sure, 180 degrees. **T:** How could you use that information to help you with this problem? **Dusty:** I don't see how that could help me.	*T: Dusty has partial understanding. He has yet to learn that he can find a missing angle by subtracting the sum of the degrees of two known angles from the total number of degrees in a triangle.*

Informed Instructional Suggestions

Dusty needs instructional activities and problems to help him discover how to find the measurement of an unknown angle in a triangle when the other two angles are known. Once he understands this and can apply it to accurately solve similar problems, he will be ready for similar experiences with quadrilaterals.

Reassessment

1. Use a similar problem at the same level of difficulty.

    What is the measure of ∠A?

    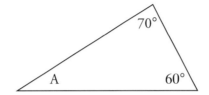

    A. 55°
    B. 130°
    C. 80°
    D. 50°

    Explain your thinking.

2. Choose a problem that is similar but slightly more challenging.

    What is the measure of ∠B?

    A. 64°
    B. 100°
    C. 116°
    D. 124°

    Explain your thinking.

PROBLEM FIVE

Overview

To correctly solve this problem, students need to know that there are 36 inches in 1 yard. Students must also be able to subtract correctly. In this problem, the word *a* indicates one. This may be problematic for students who are learning English.

Sample Problem

Tony has a piece of rope that is 27 inches long. How much less than a yard is the rope?

A. 12 inches
B. 72 inches
C. 9 inches
D. 36 inches

Explain your thinking.

Possible Student Solution Strategies

o Students use their knowledge of inches and yards to correctly answer the question using addition or subtraction.
o Students misuse their knowledge of measurement to find an answer.

Conversation Starters

o What do you need to know to solve this problem?
o How can you prove your answer?
o How could you explain your thinking to another student?

Student Work Sample: Carrie

Name _____ Date _____

Tony has a piece of rope that is 27 inches long. How much less than a yard is the rope?

A. 12 inches

B. 72 inches

C. 9 inches

D. 36 inches

Explain your thinking.

1 yard = 3 feet

27 in. = 2 feet 9 in.

1 foot = 12 in.

3 feet = 36 in

$$\begin{array}{r} 36 \\ -27 \\ \hline 09 \text{ in.} \end{array}$$

A Conversation with Carrie	Teacher Insights
T: What did you need to know to solve this problem? **Carrie:** I needed to know how many inches in a yard. Otherwise I would be stuck. **T:** How could you explain your thinking to another student? **Carrie:** I knew that there are 36 inches in a yard. Tony's rope was 27 inches. So all I had to do was to subtract twenty-seven from thirty-six to figure out how much less than a yard was his rope. **T:** How can you prove your answer? **Carrie:** To prove I got the right answer, all I have to do is add nine and twenty-seven and if I am right, the answer will be thirty-six. And it is! **T:** Why did you write 27 inches equals 2 feet, 9 inches? **Carrie:** Oh, 9 inches is the difference between 27 inches and 1 yard, but really 27 inches is the same as 2 feet, 3 inches.	**T:** *Carrie was able to accurately and efficiently solve this problem. She applied all necessary skills and was able to prove that her answer was correct.*

Informed Instructional Suggestions

Carrie is ready to move to more difficult problems in linear measurement as well as in other areas of measurement.

Student Work Sample: Beth

Name _____ Date _____

Tony has a piece of rope that is 27 inches long. How much less than a yard is the rope?

~~A.~~ 12 inches

~~B.~~ 72 inches

Ⓒ 9 inches

~~D.~~ 36 inches

Explain your thinking.

yard = 3ft. = 36in. I used My fingers and counted how Many numbers I have to count to get to 36, and it was 9 numbers so it's 9 inches.

A Conversation with Beth	Teacher Insights
T: What information did you need to know that this problem didn't tell you?	*T: Beth's written and verbal explanations showed she had a solid solution strategy for this problem.*
Beth: I needed to know that there were 36 inches in a yard because I had to find out how many inches less than a yard was Tony's rope. The rope was 27 inches, and the problem told me this.	
T: How could you explain your solution to someone else?	
Beth: I knew that Tony's rope was 27 inches long, so I used my fingers to count up from twenty-seven to thirty-six. I got nine. I know the answer must be nine.	

Informed Instructional Suggestions

Beth and Carrie have very similar instructional needs. It may be helpful for both girls to share their solution strategies with each other, as this would provide a different correct strategy for each to consider.

Student Work Sample: Lilli

Name _____ Date _____

Tony has a piece of rope that is 27 inches long. How much less than a yard is the rope?

A.   12 inches

B.   72 inches

C.   9 inches

D.   36 inches

Explain your thinking.

A Conversation with Lilli	Teacher Insights
T: I can see you did a lot of figuring on your paper. Please tell me what you were trying to do. **Lilli:** I know that there are 36 inches in a yard. If Tony's rope is 27 inches, then all I have to do is to add each of the answer choices to 27 until I get the sum of 36 inches.	**T:** *Lilli has the skills necessary to solve this problem and she was able to apply them effectively.*

Informed Instructional Suggestions

Lilli would benefit from the same experiences and instructional activities we mentioned for Carrie and Beth.

Student Work Sample: Darren

Name _____ Date _____

Tony has a piece of rope that is 27 inches long. How much less than a yard is the rope?

A.   12 inches

B.   72 inches

C.   9 inches

D.   36 inches

Explain your thinking.

there is 27 inches in the rope. if you divied 27 by 3 you get nine.

A Conversation with Darren	Teacher Insights
T: Please tell me about your thinking. **Darren:** I know that there are 3 feet in a yard and 36 inches in a yard too. Tony's rope is 27 inches and it needs 9 more inches to make a yard, so 27 inches divided by 3 feet is 9 inches.	**T:** *Darren was moving back and forth between linear measurements without regard to what they represented. His explanations made this confusion evident.*

Informed Instructional Suggestions

Darren marked the correct answer but he used an incorrect strategy to select that answer and does not understand what inches, feet, and yards represent. Darren needs to participate in multiple hands-on experiences involving linear measurement with inches, feet, and yards, so that he can fully understand their relationships and what each of the measures represents. He should also work on problems that would help him practice converting between these measures.

Student Work Sample: Kelly

Name _____ Date _____

Tony has a piece of rope that is 27 inches long. How much less than a yard is the rope?

A.   12 inches

B.   72 inches

C.   9 inches

D.   36 inches

Explain your thinking.

well a x3 =27

A Conversation with Kelly	Teacher Insights
T: I see you used multiplication to help you to solve this problem. Please tell me why this makes sense to you. **Kelly:** I knew that there were 3 feet in a yard. So I had to figure out which number times three is equal to twenty-seven. I knew my multiplication facts and I knew that three times nine is twenty-seven. So I picked choice C. **T:** How many inches do you think there are in a yard? **Kelly:** Twenty-seven. That's what the problem says.	**T:** *Kelly does not know how many inches are in a yard but thinks that there are 27 because this number was used in the problem. She does know that there are 3 feet in a yard. Also, Kelly did not understand that she needed to find the difference between the length of Tony's rope and 1 yard.*

Informed Instructional Suggestions

Kelly's correct answer hid her misconceptions. Her written and verbal explanations showed that she needs many more experiences with linear measurement and solving problems similar to this before she will be proficient. Kelly's needs are similar to those of Darren.

Student Work Sample: Rachel

Name _____ Date _____

Tony has a piece of rope that is 27 inches long. How much less than a yard is the rope?

A.   12 inches

B.   72 inches

C.   9 inches

(D.) 36 inches

$$
\begin{array}{r}
\overset{5}{6}3 \\
-\ 27 \\
\hline
36
\end{array}
$$

Explain your thinking.

I know it is (D) because a yard is 63 inches, so you subtract 27 fr 63 and you get 36.

A Conversation with Rachel	Teacher Insights
T: Rachel, please read aloud the problem and the answer choices. [Rachel reads.] I see you used the number 63 in your figuring. Where did you get that number? **Rachel:** I got it right here. [Points to choice D, 36.] Oh, wait a minute, it doesn't say 63, it says 36!	**T:** *Rachel sometimes struggles with reversals, as was the case in this situation. Rachel's written work, with the exception of her error of sixty-three, showed an understanding of the subtraction process involved in the problem.*

Informed Instructional Suggestions

Rachel's error is not mathematical and does not need remediation. However, she does need additional experiences with linear measurement involving inches, feet, and yards to strengthen her knowledge about these measurements. .

Reassessment

1. Use a similar problem at the same level of difficulty.

    Desmen has a piece of string that is 18 inches long. How much less than a yard is the string?

    A. 6 inches
    B. 18 inches
    C. 24 inches
    D. 12 inches

    Explain your thinking.

2. Choose a problem that is similar but slightly more challenging.

    Tess has a piece of yarn that is 42 inches long. How much longer than a yard is the yarn?

    A. 78 inches
    B. 14 inches
    C. 36 inches
    D. 6 inches

    Explain your thinking.

PROBLEM SIX

Overview

The purpose of problems such as this one is to test students' knowledge of and ability to work with volume. Students must also be able to multiply three factors accurately.

Sample Problem

How many 1-inch cubes could be stored in this box?

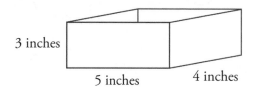

3 inches

5 inches

4 inches

A. 30
B. 60
C. 12
D. 24

Explain your thinking.

Possible Student Solution Strategies

o   Students correctly use the formula to find the volume of the box and, therefore, the number of cubes that would fill it.
o   Students multiply to find the area of a single layer of cubes and multiply that number by three layers.
o   Students misuse the formula to find the volume of the box, or the number of cubes that would fill it.
o   Students add the lengths of some of the edges.

Conversation Starters

o   Is there more than one possible answer to this problem?
o   How did your reach your answer?
o   Convince me that your thinking makes sense.

Student Work Sample: Alvin

Name _____ Date _____

How many 1-inch cubes could be stored in this box?

3 inches

5 inches   4 inches

A.   30

B.   60

C.   12

D.   24

$$5 \times 4 = 20$$
$$\underline{\times\ 3\ \ }$$
$$60$$

Explain your thinking.

When You find the Volume
You X a # then X the answer
with the other #

example

$$3 \times 5 = 15$$
$$\underline{\times\ 4\ }$$
$$60$$

A Conversation with Alvin	Teacher Insights
T: Alvin, how did you reach your answer? **Alvin:** I multiplied all of the numbers. **T:** What do the numbers represent? **Alvin:** The 3 inches is the height, so three cubes could be stacked. The 5 inches is how many cubes could go across the front. Then the 4 inches tells how many cubes go from the front to the back. Then when I multiply three times five, I know how many cubes it would take to cover the front. That's fifteen. Then I know I need four fifteens to fill the box. So four times fifteen is sixty.	**T:** *Alvin has strong conceptual understanding of the formula for finding volume, what it represents, and why it works.*

Informed Instructional Suggestions

Alvin is ready to explore the volume of other 3-D shapes. Since his understanding of this problem is so strong, it would make sense to have him work initially with other 3-D shapes that could be filled with cubes, such as a larger cube. Not all 3-D shapes, or polyhedra, can be filled with whole cubes, just like not all polygons can be filled with whole squares.

Student Work Sample: Steve

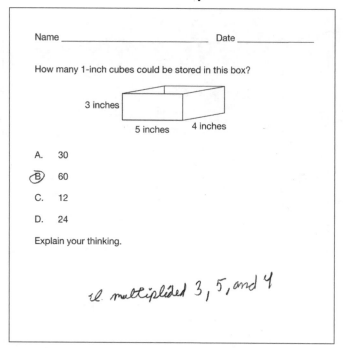

Name _____ Date _____

How many 1-inch cubes could be stored in this box?

3 inches

5 inches   4 inches

A.   30

Ⓑ   60

C.   12

D.   24

Explain your thinking.

I. multiplied 3, 5, and 4

A Conversation with Steve	Teacher Insights
T: Steve, you wrote that you multiplied. Why did you choose to do that? **Steve:** That's how I learned it. You find all of the numbers and then multiply them all together to figure out how much a box holds. **T:** What do the numbers represent? **Steve:** I don't know. I just did problems out of the book that way.	*T: Steve has memorized a formula for volume with no conceptual understanding. He does know how to multiply three factors.*

Informed Instructional Suggestions

Steve did get the correct answer because he had memorized a formula and was able to compute accurately. His correct answer by itself would have hidden his lack of understanding. Steve needs concrete experiences with filling rectangular prisms with smaller cubes and then recording the numbers to represent how many cubes tall a polyhedron is, how wide it is, and how deep it is. By doing this, Steve will develop number sense about what is reasonable. He will see what the numbers represent and why the formula for volume works.

Student Work Sample: Lilli

Name _____ Date _____

How many 1-inch cubes could be stored in this box?

3 inches

5 inches   4 inches

A. 30

B. 60

C. 12

D. 24

Explain your thinking.

$$\begin{array}{r} 4 \\ 5 \\ +3 \\ \hline 12 \text{ cubes} \end{array}$$

$$\begin{array}{r} 4 \\ \times 3 \\ \hline 12 \\ \times 5 \\ \hline 60 \text{ cubes} \end{array}$$

A Conversation with Lilli	Teacher Insights
T: You have solved this problem in two ways and you got two different answers. That's very interesting. Please tell me more. **Lilli:** I knew that I either had to add or multiply all of the numbers. So I did both. I really don't know which way to do it. So I just guessed and chose choice B. Twelve didn't seem big enough for a box that size. **T:** What do you think the numbers mean? **Lilli:** I know it's a measurement, but I don't know much else. I think if I knew more then I could probably know if I should add or multiply.	**T:** *Lilli possessed partial understanding of this problem. Because she was unclear about what the measurements represented, she was unable to reason her way to a solution confidently.*

Informed Instructional Suggestions

In order to more fully develop her understanding, Lilli needs concrete experiences like those we suggested for Steve.

Student Work Sample: Ian

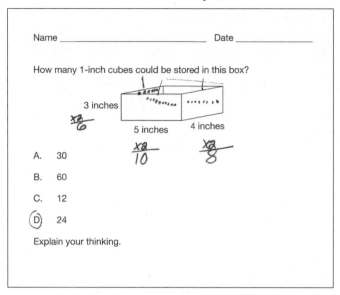

Name _____ Date _____

How many 1-inch cubes could be stored in this box?

3 inches

5 inches   4 inches

A.   30

B.   60

C.   12

(D)   24

Explain your thinking.

A Conversation with Ian	Teacher Insights
T: Please convince me that your thinking makes sense. **Ian:** I know that the front is 5 inches on the bottom. I can see that the front top edge is the same. That's 5 two times, so I multiplied and got 10. Then I saw the 4, and the opposite edge is also 4, so I multiplied it by 2 and that was 8. I can see one edge that is 3 inches but the opposite edge is partly covered, but I know it is there, so 3 two times is 6. Then I added up 6, 10, and 8, and that is 24 inches. I looked at the answer choices and twenty-four is choice D.	**T:** *Ian was able to clearly articulate his thinking, although it was incorrect. It appears that he does not conceptually understand volume.*

Informed Instructional Suggestions

Ian needs to develop foundational understanding of volume. He needs the same instruction as Steve.

Reassessment

1. Use a similar problem at the same level of difficulty.

   How many 1-inch cubes could be stored in this box?

   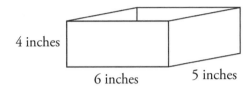

   A. 30
   B. 15
   C. 60
   D. 120

   Explain your thinking.

2. Choose a problem that is similar but slightly more challenging.

   How many 1-inch cubes could be stored in this box?

   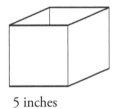

   A. 125
   B. 25
   C. 100
   D. 5

   Explain your thinking.

Date _____

Algebra

y + 20

14

plain your thinking.

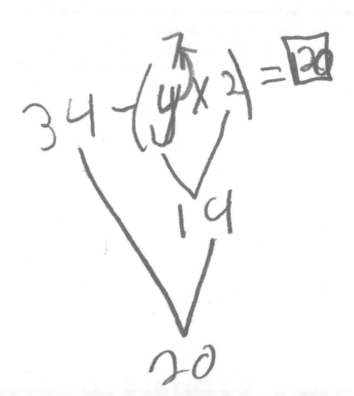

$$34 - (y \times 2) = \boxed{20}$$

14

20

ⓅⓇⓄⒷⓁⒺⓂ ⓄⓃⒺ

Overview

This problem requires students to demonstrate knowledge of relational symbols such as < and >. Students must also apply the knowledge that when the same variable is used within a problem, that variable represents the same number. In this problem, students add two variables to find a sum larger than the given number.

Sample Problem

Choose the number that goes into each box to make this number sentence true.

$$\square + \square > 334$$

A. 132
B. 157
C. 169
D. 92

Explain your thinking. Then choose an answer that doesn't work and explain why.

Possible Student Solution Strategies

o   Students double each answer choice to find the sum and then correctly compare the sum with 334.
o   Students divide 334 by 2 to get an estimate of what the variable might be.
o   Students attempt to find a number that would result in an equivalent expression.
o   Students misunderstand the meaning of the relational symbol and solve the problem incorrectly.

Conversation Starters

o   What do you know about this problem?
o   What did you need to do to find your answer?
o   How could you prove your answer?

Student Work Sample: Suri

Name _____ Date _____

Choose the number that goes into each box to make this number sentence true.

$\boxed{} + \boxed{} > 334$

A.   132

B.   157

Ⓒ   169

D.   92

Explain your thinking. Then choose an answer that doesn't work and explain why.

C. is the correct answer.
A., B, and D do not work because that number plus its number again is smaller than 334.

Like

too small   too small   too Small   good

A Conversation with Suri	Teacher Insights
T: What do you know about this problem?	*T: Suri was able to apply her knowledge and skills to solve this problem accurately.*
Suri: I know that the same number goes in both boxes and that when they are added together, they have to be larger than 334.	
T: What did you do to find your answer?	
Suri: I could tell from looking that 92 was too small. But I added it twice to be sure. Then I added each of the other answer choices two times to find out which was the right answer. Only 169 worked.	

Informed Instructional Suggestions

Suri is ready to explore other similar areas of algebra. For example, she could explore problems that use three addends, have different variables, or use other operations. Also, Suri would benefit from solving similar problems that don't provide multiple-choice answers.

Student Work Sample: Jackie

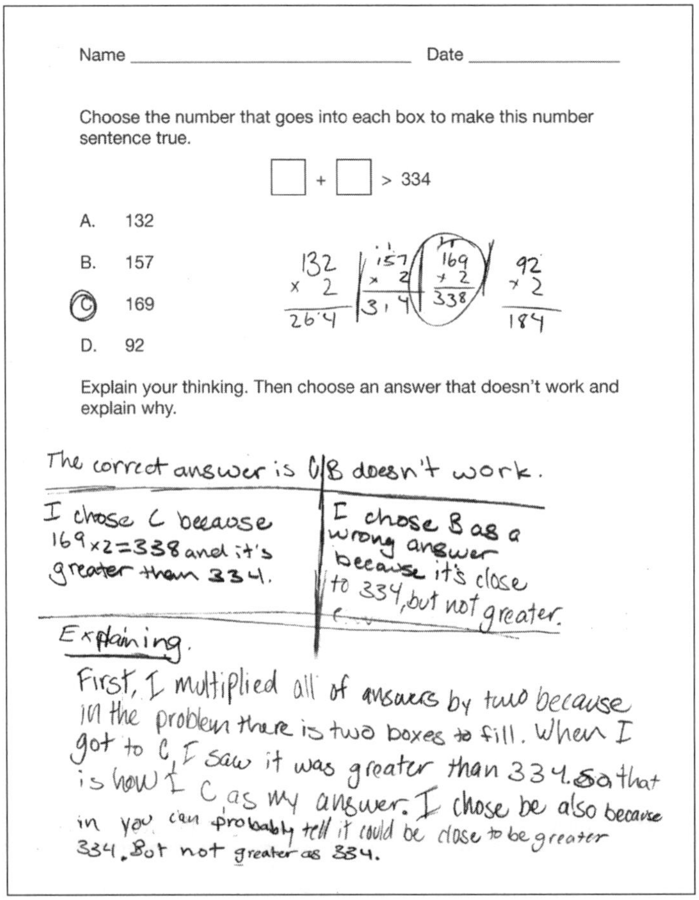

Name _____ Date _____

Choose the number that goes into each box to make this number sentence true.

$$\boxed{} + \boxed{} > 334$$

A.   132

B.   157

Ⓒ   169

D.   92

(handwritten work:)

$\begin{array}{r} 132 \\ \times\ 2 \\ \hline 26\ 4 \end{array}$ $\begin{array}{r} 157 \\ \times\ 2 \\ \hline 31\ 4 \end{array}$ $\begin{array}{r} 169 \\ +\ 2 \\ \hline 338 \end{array}$ $\begin{array}{r} 92 \\ \times\ 2 \\ \hline 184 \end{array}$

Explain your thinking. Then choose an answer that doesn't work and explain why.

(handwritten responses:)

The correct answer is C/B doesn't work.

I chose C because 169×2=338 and it's greater than 334.

I chose B as a wrong answer because it's close to 334, but not greater.

Explaining.

First, I multiplied all of answers by two because in the problem there is two boxes to fill. When I got to C, I saw it was greater than 334. So that is how I C as my answer. I chose be also because in you can probably tell it could be close to be greater 334. Bot not greater as 334.

A Conversation with Jackie	Teacher Insights
T: Jackie, I noticed that on your paper you used multiplication, but the problem is addition. Please explain your thinking. **Jackie:** Multiplying by two is the same as adding the same number twice. Because there are two boxes that are the same, I know that the missing numbers have to be the same. **T:** How did you know what to do? **Jackie:** I decided to multiply each answer choice by two. Then all I had to do was to find the one that was larger than 334. That number was 169. I also know that none of the other choices work because they all are too small.	**T:** *Like Suri, Jackie has a strong command of the skills required to solve this problem. She also used her knowledge about the relationship between doubling and multiplying by two.*

Informed Instructional Suggestions

Jackie's next steps should be the same as those for Suri.

Student Work Sample: Yolanda

Name _____ Date _____

Choose the number that goes into each box to make this number sentence true.

$$\boxed{169} + \boxed{169} > 334$$

A. 132

B. 157

C. 169

D. 92

$$\begin{array}{r} 92 \\ + 92 \\ \hline 184 \end{array}$$

$$\begin{array}{r} 1 \\ 169 \\ + 169 \\ \hline 338 \end{array}$$

Explain your thinking. Then choose an answer that doesn't work and explain why.

Answer: C: 169 I think the answer is C because 338 > 334 and 338 is C + C = 336 or 169+169= 338.

wrong answer: D AKA 92 the reason it's not 92 is D + D = 184 or 92+92= and 184 is < then 334.

A Conversation with Yolanda	Teacher Insights
T: Please tell me about your thinking. **Yolanda:** I know that I have to find two numbers that when added are greater than 334. So I started with choice D because I was pretty sure it would be less than 334. And it was. It was only 184. The problem also says I have to explain an answer that doesn't work and now I have done that. I went to choice C next. When I added 169 twice, I got 338. Jackpot! I found an answer that worked because 338 is greater than 334. **T:** Based on what you just explained, how do you know that choice A or B won't work? **Yolanda:** Choices A and B are smaller than 169, so when doubled, they will be smaller than 334.	*T: Yolanda, like Suri and Jackie, solved this problem correctly and indicated strong understanding in both her written and verbal explanations.*

Informed Instructional Suggestions

The suggestions we made for Suri would also be appropriate for Yolanda.

Student Work Sample: Ferguson

Name _____ Date _____

Choose the number that goes into each box to make this number sentence true.

☐ + ☐ > 334

A.   132

B.   157

Ⓒ   169

D.   92

Explain your thinking. Then choose an answer that doesn't work and explain why.

I know that its not A,B,or D because the number have to be biger I know that it's C because its a biger number

A Conversation with Ferguson	Teacher Insights
T: What do you know about this problem? **Ferguson:** I know the numbers in the box have to be big to be more than 334. I picked the biggest number and that was 169. All the others are smaller so I don't think they would work. **T:** Tell me how you could prove your idea. **Ferguson:** I could add 169 two times. I know that 100 plus 100 is 200. Sixty plus 60 is 120. Two hundred plus 120 is 320. Nine plus 9 is 18. Three hundred twenty plus 18 is 338, and that is bigger than 334.	**T:** *Ferguson is correct in the notion that only the greatest number will work for a multiple-choice question such as this one. When asked, he was able to support his idea and he was able to prove it worked by adding the greatest number twice.*

Informed Instructional Suggestions

Because Ferguson made a correct generalization about multiple-choice questions such as this one, it would benefit Ferguson and other students for him to share his strategy and prove why it works. However, Ferguson also needs to solve problems similar to this one that don't include multiple-choice answers so he can practice problem solving and computing.

Student Work Sample: Josie

Name _____ Date _____

Choose the number that goes into each box to make this number sentence true.

□ + □ > 334

A.   132

B.   157

C.   169

D.   92

Explain your thinking. Then choose an answer that doesn't work and explain why.

92 is the wrong one because it dosen't go into 334,

A Conversation with Josie	Teacher Insights
T: What do you know about this problem? **Josie:** I know that the boxes are the same number and that when they are added together they are greater than 334. I tried to divide because I knew that the boxes had to be the same number. But 92 does not go into 334. **T:** Why did you think you should divide? **Josie:** I divided because I knew the boxes had to have the same number. Hmm, maybe I should have divided by two since there are two boxes. I didn't think of that. **T:** Why did you choose choice C? **Josie:** I know that 92 plus 92 is less than 200 because 92 is less than a hundred, so two of them must be less than 200. I can estimate that 132 is about 260. I also can estimate that 157 added twice is about 300. So my best guess was 169.	*T: Josie realized that both boxes represented the same number. She also demonstrated good estimation skills. Her intuition about dividing to find the value of the boxes made sense, but she got confused about what she should be dividing. After explaining her thinking to me, she realized that division was a correct strategy, but, since there were two boxes, she should have divided 334 by 2. During future instruction with Josie, we need to talk about the idea that in this situation, when dividing by 2, the quotient will make the number sentence equivalent rather than nonequivalent.*

Informed Instructional Suggestions

Because Josie understood what she needed to do but got a bit confused, she would benefit from further opportunities to explore and practice similar problems before moving on.

Student Work Sample: Sharisa

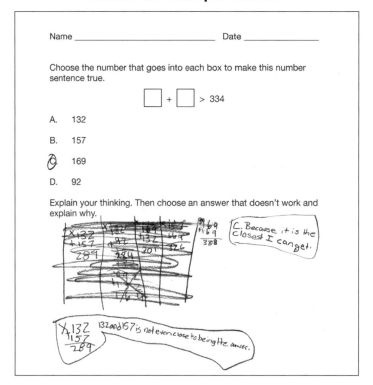

Name _____ Date _____

Choose the number that goes into each box to make this number sentence true.

☐ + ☐ > 334

A. 132

B. 157

Ⓒ 169

D. 92

Explain your thinking. Then choose an answer that doesn't work and explain why.

A Conversation with Sharisa	Teacher Insights
T: What do you know about this problem? **Sharisa:** I know that the box side of the problem is bigger than 334. **T:** What do you know about the boxes? **Sharisa:** Those are the missing numbers. **T:** Do they need to be the same numbers or can they be different? **Sharisa:** I am not sure. I tried a lot of ways and crossed them off because nothing seemed to work. All of the ways I did were less than 334 and I know that it has to be greater than 334. Finally I took the biggest number and added it twice and got a number that was bigger than 334.	**T:** *Sharisa understands relational symbols but lacks understanding that the same variable in the same problem represents the same number. She demonstrated accuracy in most of her calculating.*

Informed Instructional Suggestions

Sharisa found the correct answer, but her written and verbal explanations revealed areas of need. She needs experiences to help her better understand variables and what they represent. Once this is clear to her, she will be ready for learning experiences similar to those we recommended for Suri.

Student Work Sample: Jason

Name _____ Date _____

Choose the number that goes into each box to make this number sentence true.

☐ + ☐ > 334

A. 132

B. 157

C. 169

D. 92

92 won't work because it will be less than 334 and it is suppose to be bigger than 334.

Explain your thinking. Then choose an answer that doesn't work and explain why.

A Conversation with Jason	Teacher Insights
T: Please tell me what you know about this problem.	**T:** *Jason has the necessary skills to solve this problem. However, he is often resistant to showing his work, and in this case, he made an error in computation when trying to mentally add 132 two times.*
Jason: I know that the boxes have to have numbers and the numbers have to add up to something more than 334. I also know that 92 won't work because it is too small.	
T: How did you know that 132 when added twice would be more than 334?	
Jason: I know that 2 plus 2 is 4, 30 plus 30 equals 60, 100 plus 100 plus the 1 I have to carry is 364. That's bigger than 334. I did it in my head so I know.	
T: Please turn your paper over and add 132 twice, showing your work.	
Jason: [Jason performs the calculation.] Oopsie! I didn't have to carry that 1, and the answer is really 264. My brain failed me.	
T: Which of the answers do you think will work?	
Jason: I think 169. [Jason does the computation on the back of his paper and finds that 169 is the correct answer.]	

Informed Instructional Suggestions

Jason had the wrong answer because of an error in mental computation. Based on his multiple-choice answer alone, it would have appeared that Jason had not mastered the needed skills for this problem when in fact he has, as he demonstrated in his verbal explanation. We need to encourage him to show his thinking to help avoid errors such as he made. Jason is ready for the same instructional experiences we suggested for Suri.

Student Work Sample: Madison

Name _____ Date _____

Choose the number that goes into each box to make this number sentence true.

wrong
↓

$\boxed{92}$ + $\boxed{92}$ > 334

(A) 132

B. 157

C. 169 right

(D) 92

Explain your thinking. Then choose an answer that doesn't work and explain why.

132 is wrong because 132 is
to big and so are all
the others (And because
it can't fit in the box.)

132 → □?

A Conversation with Madison	Teacher Insights
T: What do you know about this problem? **Madison:** I know that I have to find a small number to put in the square because it is small. I know that 92 is the smallest and I had to squeeze it in. The others have three digits, and they'll never fit. A number with one digit would work even better.	**T:** *Madison did not understand what this problem was asking her to do. Her meaning of smaller and larger numbers is based on the length of the numbers and doesn't seem to relate to the quantity represented by the numbers. She indicated no awareness or understanding of the relational symbol.*

Informed Instructional Suggestions

Madison needs basic experiences to help her develop understanding of numbers before she is ready to engage in problems of this nature. While she is correct that a two-digit number is less than a three-digit number, she seems not to have a way to compare numbers of the same length. It would be helpful to spend time with Madison one-on-one to probe what she does and does not understand about the base ten number system. Base ten blocks would be a useful tool to help her develop understanding.

Reassessment

1. Use a similar problem at the same level of difficulty.

   Choose the number that goes into each box to make this number sentence true.

   $$\square + \square > 486$$

   A. 146
   B. 243
   C. 184
   D. 248

   Explain your thinking. Then choose an answer that doesn't work and explain why.

2. Choose a problem that is similar but slightly more challenging.

   Choose the number that goes into each box to make this number sentence true.

   $$821 > \square + \square$$

   A. 422
   B. 408
   C. 412
   D. 416

   Explain your thinking. Then choose an answer that doesn't work and explain why.

P R O B L E M   T W O

Overview

This question tests students' knowledge and application of substitution, variables, order of operations, and computational skills. Students must use these skills to find the value of an algebraic expression.

Sample Problem

What is the value of the expression below if $y = 7$?

$$34 - (y \times 2) = \square$$

A. 32
B. 20
C. $y + 20$
D. 14

Explain your thinking.

Possible Student Solution Strategies

o   Students apply their knowledge of substitution and the order of operations as well as computational skills to successfully find the value of the expression.

o   Students partially or incorrectly solve the problem, indicating confusion with one or more of these skills.

Conversation Starters

o   In your own words, please tell me what this problem is asking you to do.

o   Is there more than one correct answer? How do you know?

o   What knowledge do you need to know to solve this problem?

Student Work Sample: Max

Name _____ Date _____

What is the value of the expression below if $y = 7$?

$$34 - (y \times 2) = \boxed{20}$$

A.   32

B.   20

C. $y + 20$

D.   14

Explain your thinking.

$$34 - (y \times 2) = \boxed{20}$$
$$14$$
$$20$$

A Conversation with Max	Teacher Insights
T: What knowledge did you have to have to solve this problem? **Max:** I had to know that I should start with the parentheses first. Also, that's where the y is. So I replaced the y with a 7. I finished the part inside the parentheses by multiplying seven times two, and that's fourteen. The last thing I had to do was subtract fourteen from thirty-four. That equals twenty. **T:** Is twenty the only correct answer or is there more than one right answer? **Max:** There is only one right answer. If you do it again and get a different answer, then you made a mistake. It's kind of like asking if there is another correct answer to one plus one. The answer is two, and that is the only correct answer. The box number would change if y were equal to something else, but then you have changed the problem to a new problem.	**T:** *Max's understanding is strong and he is confident. He was able to explain his thinking both using written numbers and verbally.*

Informed Instructional Suggestions

Max is ready to explore similar problems that have larger numbers, more variables, or both. He would also benefit from writing and solving his own problems. Max could also try writing a story problem that could be represented by this expression or other similar expressions. For example: *Pierre had thirty-four baseball cards that he wanted to put in an album. He put them on seven pages in groups of two. How many cards remain?*

Student Work Sample: Nedmon

Name _____ Date _____

What is the value of the expression below if $y = 7$?

$$34 - (y \times 2) = \boxed{20}$$
$$7 \times 2 = 14$$

A. 32

(B.) 20

C. $y + 20$

D. 14

$+6 \quad +10 \quad +4 = 20$

$14 \quad 20 \quad 30 \quad 34$

Explain your thinking.

Well since $y = 7$ and $7 \times 2 = 14$, all I did was subtract 14 from 34 and I got 20.

A Conversation with Nedmon	Teacher Insights
T: What did you need to know to help you solve this problem? **Nedmon:** I needed to know that I have to substitute the *y* in the problem with 7. Then the parentheses tell me that that is the place to start. Next I have to figure out what goes in the box. **T:** You know a lot about this problem. How did you find the value of the expression? **Nedmon:** I first multiplied seven times two because that is what is in the parentheses. That equals fourteen. Then I had to subtract fourteen from thirty-four, and that equals twenty. Twenty is what goes in the box, and it is also the value of the expression. It's sort of like a code or logic game really; once you get it, it's really pretty easy.	**T:** *Like Max, Nedmon was able to easily solve this problem with confidence and understanding.*

Informed Instructional Suggestions

Nedmon has essentially the same needs as Max. They could work together on the same instructional activities. After writing their own problems, they could exchange and solve each other's problems.

Student Work Sample: Cassidy

Name _____ Date _____

What is the value of the expression below if $y = 7$?

$$34 - (y \times 2) = \boxed{}$$

A. 32

B. 20

C. $y + 20$

D. 14

Explain your thinking.

[handwritten student work:]

34
$-\ 7$
_____
27

I Sobtracted $34 - 7$ and I got 27 so I rounded I got 30 but 30 wasn't a answer so I went lower and I got 20.

A Conversation with Cassidy	Teacher Insights
T: In your own words, please tell me what this problem is asking you to do.	**T:** *Cassidy has partial understanding of the skills needed for this problem, but she also has some areas of weakness that need to be addressed, such as doing everything stated in an expression.*
Cassidy: The problem says that *y* is seven, and I have to figure out what goes in the box.	
T: Please tell me more about your thinking.	
Cassidy: Well, I knew that *y* is equal to seven, so I subtracted. I did thirty-four minus seven and got twenty-seven. Twenty-seven wasn't an answer choice. I thought, "Uh-oh!" Since my answer wasn't there, I decided to choose twenty because it was sort of close to twenty-seven. I knew thirty-two wasn't right because I was already down to twenty-seven when I subtracted.	
T: Cassidy, please read the expression aloud. [Cassidy reads.] When you explained your thinking, I heard you use the number thirty-four and you did talk about seven because *y* is equal to seven, but what about this part of the expression that says times two?	
Cassidy: Oh, I didn't think about that. I just did thirty-four minus seven. No wonder my answer wasn't there. I didn't know I had to do anything else. Do you mean that whatever else is in parentheses I have to do?	
T: If it is in the expression, you have to do it. You can't ignore it.	

Informed Instructional Suggestions

Cassidy's correct answer by itself would have indicated a mastery of the skills needed to solve this problem. Both her written and verbal explanations proved otherwise. Cassidy needs experiences that will strengthen her foundational algebraic skills and understanding, such as working with problems involving parentheses.

Student Work Sample: Alma

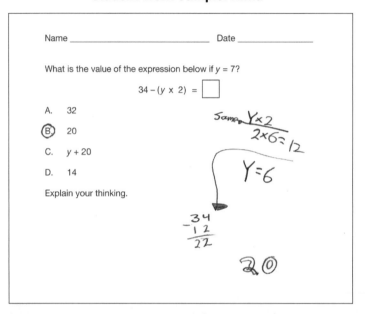

A Conversation with Alma	Teacher Insights
T: In your own words, please tell me what this problem is asking you to do. **Alma:** I know that I have to make y into a number. I decided to make y into six. Then I multiplied two times six because now there is a 6 in place of y. That makes twelve. Thirty-four minus twelve is twenty-two. **T:** Why did you choose six? **Alma:** I knew the number that went in the box had to be one of the answer choices, but I got twenty-two and it's not a choice. I knew that choice C didn't really make sense for this problem. I really didn't know what to do and so I chose twenty because it is close to twenty-two. **T:** What does the problem say that y represents? **Alma:** It says y is equal to seven. Does that mean I have to make y into seven? [I nod.]	**T:** *Alma essentially made up her own problem. She was unaware of how to solve problems involving substitution. Also, Alma seemed unconcerned that her answer did not match any of the answer choices. She simply picked the answer choice closest to her answer instead of reconsidering the problem.*

Informed Instructional Suggestions

The correct answer choice Alma selected provided a misleading picture of Alma's skill and understanding. She needs experiences involving substitution and how to use substitution to solve problems similar to this one. It would be helpful to give her simple problems to support her growing understanding. For example, *What is* y + 4? y = 5 followed by *What is* y + 4? y = 6, and so on. A series of problems like that would help Alma understand how changes in the value of *y* affect the expression. Alma could also use tiles or other counters to see what happens when the value of *y* changes.

Student Work Sample: Kanisha

Name _____ Date _____

What is the value of the expression below if $y = 7$?

$$34 - (y \times 2) = \boxed{}$$

A. 32

● 20

C. y + 20

D. 14

$Y = 10$

$10 \times 2 = 20$

Explain your thinking.

A Conversation with Kanisha	Teacher Insights
T: Please tell me more about your thinking.	**T:** *It is apparent that Kanisha does not understand problems such as this one. She asked about substitution during our conversation. To find an answer for this problem, she essentially made up her own problem to fit one of the answer choices. She seemed unaware of the 34 and the subtraction sign.*
Kanisha: I really wasn't too sure about this problem. I looked at the words and I looked at the math sentence and I looked at the answer choices. I saw 20 was an answer choice and I noticed that one part of the problem was some number times 2, so I thought I could make the *y* into a 10 and then multiply 10 times 2 to equal 20.	
T: Please reread the problem to find out what number is represented by *y*.	
Kanisha: [Kanisha reads.] Oh, I see the problem says that *y* equals seven. Do I just take out the *y* and put in the 7?	

Informed Instructional Suggestions

Kanisha marked the correct answer as a result of making up her own problem to fit that answer. Kanisha needs experiences that will help her develop basic ideas of algebra. She needs to build an understanding of substitution. Instructional activities similar to those we suggested for Alma would also help Kanisha.

Student Work Sample: Lainie

Name _____ Date _____

What is the value of the expression below if $y = 7$?

$$34 - (y \times 2) = \boxed{}$$

A. 32

B. 20

C. $y + 20$

D. 14

Explain your thinking.

It says in the directions that the y in the problem stands for 7 so the problem really is 34-(7×2)=___

7×2=14 right? so it is 34-14=___ right?

$$\begin{array}{r} 34 \\ -14 \\ \hline 14 \end{array}$$

14   4+20   10+30

	A Conversation with Lainie	Teacher Insights

T: I see that you did a lot of explaining and showed a lot of work on your paper. I am a bit confused by two things. First, is thirty-four minus fourteen really fourteen?

Lainie: Um, yes, I think so. I showed it on a number line. Wait a minute, I only went to thirty on the number line and I should have gone to thirty-four! Oh lizard breath! I see another mistake. To go from fourteen to twenty is really six, not four! Where is my brain?

T: I agree that there are two errors in your figuring. Now that you have found them, can you figure the correct answer?

Lainie: Yes, actually that's not too hard. I have to add two more for the part of the number line that goes from fourteen to twenty, and I have to add four more to go from thirty to thirty-four. That's a total of six. Fourteen plus six equals twenty. The answer should really be twenty, and that's choice B.

Teacher Insights

T: *Lainie made two errors in computation, but her written explanation showed clear understanding of the algebra involved in the problem. She was able to find her own errors and correct her mistakes to find the right answer.*

Informed Instructional Suggestions

Lainie's incorrect answer choice did not accurately represent her skill level and understanding. In fact, she has good understanding of the algebraic skills involved in the problem and does not need remediation. She does need to work more carefully and to check her work for accuracy, but her instructional needs are really like those of Max and Nedmon.

Student Work Sample: Jona

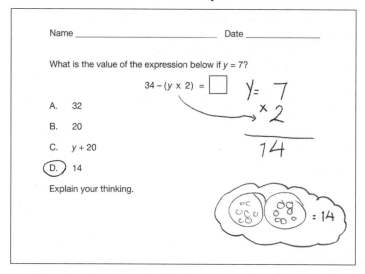

Name _____ Date _____

What is the value of the expression below if $y = 7$?

$$34 - (y \times 2) = \boxed{}$$

A. 32

B. 20

C. $y + 20$

(D.) 14

Explain your thinking.

A Conversation with Jona	Teacher Insights
T: In your own words, please tell me what this problem is asking you to do.	**T:** *Jona's verbal explanation helped me better understand what she knows. Her incorrect answer choice along with her written explanation indicated misunderstanding, when in reality they were the result of her having to leave class briefly. Her verbal explanation revealed that she did understand how to solve the problem.*
Jona: The problem says that y is equal to seven. Then it says in the parentheses seven times two, so that's fourteen. I drew seven two times to prove it.	
T: What about the part of the problem that says thirty-four minus? Why do you think that is there?	
Jona: It's there because I am supposed to subtract fourteen from thirty-four. I did finish the problem and I circled twenty, but then I had to go to speech class and when I came back, I looked at my paper and saw the picture of fourteen. I erased my answer of twenty and circled fourteen. I got distracted and forgot what I was supposed to be doing! The right answer should be thirty-four minus fourteen equals twenty. I really do know how to do this!	
T: Your verbal explanation helped me know that you understand.	

Informed Instructional Suggestions

Jona's needs are similar to those of Max and Nedmon. She is ready for more challenging problems and would also benefit from creating her own problems.

Reassessment

1. Use a similar problem at the same level of difficulty.

    What is the value of the expression below if $y = 9$?

    $$42 - (y \times 3) = \Box$$

    A. 45
    B. 39
    C. 15
    D. 27

    Explain your thinking.

2. Choose a problem that is similar but slightly more challenging.

    What is the value of the expression below if $y = 12$?

    $$y + (y - 2) = \Box$$

    A. $2y$
    B. 22
    C. 10
    D. 2

    Explain your thinking.

PROBLEM THREE

Overview

To solve this problem, students must first study a T-chart, find the rule for that T-chart, and then represent the rule and the T-chart with an equation. The rule for this T-chart involves multiplication, so in this situation, students must also recognize patterns involving multiplication by two, or doubling.

Sample Problem

What is the equation for the rule in this chart?

x	y
1	2
4	8
8	16
12	24

A. $x = 2y$
B. $x + 1 = y$
C. $x + 4 = y$
D. $2x = y$

Explain your thinking.

Possible Student Solution Strategies

o   Students recognize the pattern in the T-chart and correctly select the equation that represents it.
o   Students misinterpret the T-chart or equations and select an incorrect answer.

Conversation Starters

o   Why does your solution make sense?
o   Is there more than one possible correct answer? Why do you think that?
o   How could you solve this problem in another way?
o   Put this problem into your own words.

Student Work Sample: Damon

Name _____ Date _____

What is the equation for the rule in this chart?

x	y
1	2
4	8
8	16
12	24

X	Y
1 x2= 2
4 x2= 8
8 x2= 16
12 x2=24

A. $x = 2y$

B. $x + 1 = y$

C. $x + 4 = y$

(D.) $2x = y$

Explain your thinking.

I know this because one x two = two, four x two = eight, eight x two = sixteen and twelve x two = twentyfour

A Conversation with Damon	Teacher Insights
T: In your own words, please tell me what this problem is about. **Damon:** There is a chart. What goes in on the *x* side follows a rule and then comes out on the *y* side. To make the *y* numbers, the same rule happens to all the numbers on the *x* side. **T:** Why does your answer make sense? **Damon:** In the chart I drew I wrote *times two* next to each number on the *x* side. That's because all the *x* numbers are multiplied by two to make the *y* numbers. One times two is two, four times two is eight, and so on. **T:** Is there another way you could solve this problem? **Damon:** Yep, times two is the same thing as doubling. But doubling is really an adding problem so I think that multiplying by two is more correct when you look at the answer choices. I think doubling would be written as $x + x = y$ or something like that instead of $2x = y$.	**T:** *Damon understood this problem and even had some ideas about the different ways doubling and multiplying by two would be represented by equations. He was thinking, conjecturing, and exploring new ideas.*

Informed Instructional Suggestions

Damon is ready for additional exploration of similar but more complex problems. He could expand his thinking about doubling versus multiplying by two through discussion with others. Another avenue for Damon to explore would be situations in real life that could be represented by this T-chart, for example, the number of wheels on bicycles or the number of legs on chickens. He could also investigate how this T-chart would look when made into a coordinate graph. And he could extend all of these ideas by working with charts with other patterns.

Student Work Sample: Cherisse

Name _____ Date _____

What is the equation for the rule in this chart?

x	y
double 1	2
double 4	8
double 8	16
double 12	24

A. $x = 2y$

B. $x + 1 = y$

C. $x + 4 = y$

D. $2x = y$

Explain your thinking:

I know the answer is D because 2 of any numbers in the x column like for example if you double 12 it will equal 24. When ever you double a number on the x columns, it will equal the number next to it in the Y column.

A Conversation with Cherisse	Teacher Insights
T: I see that you have found a doubling pattern in the T-chart. Tell me more about your thinking and how you discovered that pattern. **Cherisse:** Doubling is like multiplying by two. I noticed when I looked at the chart that all the *y* numbers are double the *x* numbers. I looked at the answer choices and I knew I could eliminate choices B and C because they are adding. Besides, when I add one to *x*, like choice B says, it doesn't come out to *y* except for the first one, and when I add four to *x*, like choice C says, it only works for the second one. The rule has to work for all of the *x* numbers. That leaves choices A and D. Choice A means that two *y*'s are equal to *x*. That doesn't work; for example, two twos doesn't equal one. It's really the other way around. Two ones equal two. So choice A doesn't work. That leaves choice D. Then I checked to see if two of all the *x* numbers are equal to the *y* number next to it. Choice D means two *x*'s equal one *y*, and it was true for all of them. **T:** That was a very complete and clear explanation. It helped me know about your thinking. Thank you.	**T:** *Like Damon, Cherisse has a solid understanding.*

Informed Instructional Suggestions

Cherisse is ready to take the same next steps we suggested for Damon.

Student Work Sample: Roberto

Name _____ Date _____

What is the equation for the rule in this chart?

x	y
1	2
4	8
8	16
12	24

A. $x = 2y$

B. $x + 1 = y$

C. $x + 4 = y$

D. $2x = y$

Explain your thinking.

Because 8 + 8 = 16   1 + 1 = 2   4 + 4 = 8   12 + 12 = 24.

A Conversation with Roberto	Teacher Insights
T: Roberto, please tell me why your solution makes sense. **Roberto:** If I add each of the numbers in the *x* column to itself, it equals the one next to it in the *y* column. **T:** I agree that you found a pattern that involves adding, but you chose an answer choice that is multiplication. Why does that make sense to you? **Roberto:** Hmm, that does seem a little weird, but really it's not. Adding a number to itself like I did is just another way of multiplying by two. It's the same thing just written another way. **T:** Is there another possible answer choice? **Roberto:** Not here, but I think another way to write a correct equation is $x + x = y$. Then it would more closely match what I wrote, but $2x = y$ works because *y* is the *x* number two times.	**T:** *Roberto was able to do a nice job of explaining his understanding and thinking verbally. He had a firm understanding of this problem.*

Informed Instructional Suggestions

Roberto's mastery and needs are similar to those of Damon and Cherisse, so he could work on the same activities we recommended for them.

Student Work Sample: Cambria

Name _____ Date _____

What is the equation for the rule in this chart?

x	y
1	2
4	8
8	16
12	24

A.　$x = 2y$

B.　$x + 1 = y$

C.　$x + 4 = y$

D.　$2x = y$ *(circled)*

Explain your thinking.

$2 \div 1 = 2$　　$8 \div 4 = 2$　　$16 \div 8 = 2$　$24 \div 2 = 2$

$2x = y$

A Conversation with Cambria	Teacher Insights
T: I noticed that you used division to solve this problem but you chose an equation that involves multiplication. Please share you thinking about that. **Cambria:** I saw a pattern. I noticed that all of the y numbers divided by two equal the x numbers. That's what I wrote on my paper. But I know that the inverse of multiplication is division, so the inverse of division must be multiplication. I looked and—bingo!—there it was: $2x = y$. I can prove it works. Take any number on the x side and multiply it by two and it equals the y number. I get this!	**T:** *Like the students before her, Cambria understood this problem. Her written work could be misleading at first glance, but in reality it represented strong thinking and understanding, as shown in her verbal explanation.*

Informed Instructional Suggestions

The suggestions we made for Damon would be helpful for Cambria as well.

Student Work Sample: Zolli

Name _____ Date _____

What is the equation for the rule in this chart?

x	y
1	2
4	8
8	16
12	24

A. $x = 2y$

B. $x + 1 = y$

C. $x + 4 = y$

D. $2x = y$

Explain your thinking.

I just knew that on the chart that it was 2x=y.

A Conversation with Zolli	Teacher Insights
T: Zolli, please tell me more about your thinking. **Zolli:** I really don't know much about this. I don't really see any patterns in the chart. I was really confused. I picked D because the x on the chart was on the left and the x in the equation was on the left too. The y on the chart was on the right and it was on the right in the equation. It could have been choice A too, but choice D seemed better. I am pretty sure it's not choices B or C because they are adding and look too easy.	**T:** *Zolli made a guess. She tried to use valid reasoning to make her guess, and her guess was correct, but her explanation revealed that she has minimal understanding.*

Informed Instructional Suggestions

Zolli's verbal explanation indicated that she needs experiences that will support her conceptual development. One concrete way to help her would be to show her a real-life representation of the numbers in the T-chart. For example, we could create a T-chart on the board and label the left column *Number of People* and the right column *Number of Ears*. Then we could ask one person to stand up. Zolli could count the ears on that student and record the information on the T-chart. Next we could have four students stand and Zolli could count the ears on them and fill in the chart. We could continue this until Zolli began to see a pattern and she connected how the T-chart represented a real situation.

Student Work Sample: Jason

Name _____ Date _____

What is the equation for the rule in this chart?

x	y
1	2
4	8
8	16
12	24

(A.) $x = 2y$

B. $x + 1 = y$

C. $x + 4 = y$

D. $2x = y$

Explain your thinking.

$1 \times 2 = 2$
$4 \times 2 = 8$
$8 \times 2 = 16$
$12 \times 2 = 24$

A Conversation with Jason	Teacher Insights
T: Please tell me in your own words what this problem is asking you to do. **Jason:** I have to figure out the pattern in the T-chart and then figure out an equation that matches the pattern. I chose choice A because I notice that one side of the chart is two times the other side. Choice A says *x* equals two times *y*. **T:** What do you think the *x* and *y* mean? Where can you find them on the chart? **Jason:** Hmm, let me look. Oh I see, the *x* and *y* are at the top of the columns. **T:** Let's look at the first pair of numbers on the chart, 1 and 2. Which one is the *x* number and which one is the *y* number? **Jason:** One is *x* and 2 is *y*. **T:** Choice A says *x* equals two times *y*. Is the *x* number, 1, equal to two *y*'s, or, in this case, two 2s? **Jason:** No way. That's not right. But two is equal to two ones. I am confused. **T:** Look at the other choices and see if there is an equation that more closely matches your thinking about *x* and *y*. **Jason:** Oh, choice D works. Yeah, that's right. Choice D says two *x*'s equal *y*. Two 1s equal 2, two 4s equal 8, two 8s equal 16, and two 12s equal 24. That's tricky!	*T: Jason's observations of the patterns on this T-chart were correct. However, he showed only partial understanding of the relationship between a T-chart and an equation that represents it. With a few guiding questions, he was able to move forward and select an equation that represented his thinking about x and y.*

Informed Instructional Suggestions

Jason made an incorrect response, but he did have partial understanding and was able to find the correct response during the conversation. Jason needs more practice with problems similar to this one. Then he will be ready for the same instructional activities as Damon.

Reassessment

1. Use a similar problem at the same level of difficulty.

    What is the equation for the rule in this chart?

x	y
5	15
7	21
10	30
11	33
0	0

    A. $x + 10 = y$
    B. $3x = y$
    C. $x + x = y$
    D. $x = 3y$

    Explain your thinking.

2. Choose a problem that is similar but slightly more challenging.

    What is the equation for the rule in this chart?

x	y
6	3
10	5
2	1
32	16
42	21

    A. $x \div 2 = y$
    B. $x - 3 = y$
    C. $2x = y$
    D. $x \div 3 = y$

    Explain your thinking.

PROBLEM FOUR

Overview

To solve this problem, students have to apply their knowledge of the order of operations. They must also compute accurately using whole number operations.

Sample Problem

Solve the following problem using the correct order of operations.

$$3 \times 12 - 10 \div 2 \times 4 =$$

A. 24
B. 16
C. 0
D. 52

Explain your thinking.

Possible Student Solution Strategies

o   Students solve the equation correctly using the order of operations.
o   Students disregard the order of operations and solve the equation from left to right.

Conversation Starters

o   What do you need to know to correctly solve this equation?
o   What is one error that could be made with this problem?
o   Is there more than one correct answer? Explain.
o   How could you explain your thinking to another student?
o   Why does your solution make sense?

Student Work Sample: Kylie

Name _____ Date _____

Solve the following problem using the correct order of operations.

$$3 \times 12 - 10 \div 2 \times 4 =$$

A.   24

B.   16   (circled)

C.   0

D.   52

Student handwritten work:

$36 - 5 \times 4 =$
$3 \times 12 - 10 \div 2 \times 4 =$
$36 - 5 \times 4 =$
$36 - 20 = \boxed{16}$

Explain your thinking. I first followed the order of operations starting with multiplication, $3 \times 12 = 36$. I then did $10 \div 2 = 5$. After that, I did $36 - 5 \times 4$ and solved $5 \times 4 = 20$. Lastly, I did $36 - 20 = 16$.

A Conversation with Kylie	Teacher Insights
T: What did you need to know to correctly solve this equation? **Kylie:** I had to know that there is a correct order that I had to use to solve this equation. For this problem, I had to go from left to right and do the multiplication and division. Then I had to go back and do the subtraction. **T:** What is one error that could be made with this problem? **Kylie:** If you just do the problem from left to right or in any old order, you'll get the wrong answer. You have to do the multiplication and division in order from left to right and then do the subtraction. **T:** How could you explain your solution to another student? **Kylie:** Like I said, I have to go from left to right and do all of the multiplication and division. So first I multiplied three times twelve, and that's thirty-six. For now I skip the subtraction part and go to ten divided by two. That's equal to five. I multiply five times four, which is twenty. Then I go back to the subtraction part. Thirty-six minus twenty equals sixteen. Sixteen is the correct answer to the equation. **T:** What if there are parentheses or exponents in the problem? **Kylie:** You would have to do those parts before the multiplication, division, addition, or subtraction. **T:** Your written and verbal explanations have been very helpful. Thank you for sharing.	**T:** *Kylie's understanding of the order of operations is strong and she was able to apply her knowledge to accurately solve this equation. She also understands that if the order of operations is not followed, a different, incorrect answer will likely result.*

Informed Instructional Suggestions

Kylie would benefit from doing additional work with problems similar to this, to reinforce her learning, as well as those that are more difficult. She might also benefit from writing and solving her own problems.

Student Work Sample: Gayle

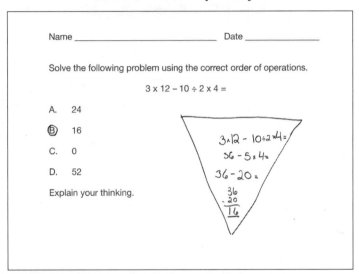

Name _____ Date _____

Solve the following problem using the correct order of operations.

$$3 \times 12 - 10 \div 2 \times 4 =$$

A. 24

Ⓑ 16

C. 0

D. 52

Explain your thinking.

(handwritten work:)
$3 \times 12 - 10 \div 2 \times 4 =$
$36 - 5 \times 4 =$
$36 - 20 =$
$\begin{array}{r} 36 \\ -20 \\ \hline 16 \end{array}$

A Conversation with Gayle	Teacher Insights
T: Your numerical solution is very useful in helping me see your thinking. Please tell me more about it. **Gayle:** I know that I have to do certain things first. In this problem, I have to go from left to right and do all of the multiplication and division. I showed that with my numbers. Three times twelve is thirty-six. Then I divided ten by two, and that's five. So in the second line of my figuring I wrote $36 - 5 \times 4$ to show what I did in the first line. Then I multiplied five times four, and that equals twenty. In the third line of my figuring, I wrote $36 - 20$. Thirty-six minus twenty is sixteen. **T:** What would happen if you did the computation as it is written from left to right? **Gayle:** I might get a different answer. Let's see . . . 3 times 12 is 36, minus 10 is 26, divided by 2 is 13, times 4 is . . . hmm. I can do this. Thirteen is the same as 10 plus 3. Ten times 4 is 40. Three times 4 is 12. Forty plus 12 is 52. So if you just did the problem in the order it is written, the answer would be 52. **T:** Thank you for talking with me and exploring a little bit. Your sharing has helped me better understand your knowledge and thinking.	**T:** *Gayle, like Kylie, indicated a strong understanding of the order of operations. She also used a good strategy to solve multiplication problems mentally and with paper and pencil.*

Informed Instructional Suggestions

Gayle and Kylie have a similar understanding of the order of operations. They would benefit from working together as well as independently to practice similar problems and then move on to more complex problems requiring these skills.

Student Work Sample: Chrystal

Name _____   Date _____

Solve the following problem using the correct order of operations.

$$3 \times 12 - 10 \div 2 \times 4 = $$ PEMDAS
( ) I^2 x ÷ + –

A.   24

B.   16

C.   0

D.   52

Explain your thinking.

$3 \times 12 - 10 \div 2 \times 4 =$
36   8

$\frac{12}{3}$ → 36   2×4=8

36

A Conversation with Chrystal	Teacher Insights
T: Please tell me more about this word you wrote at the top of your paper. What is PEMDAS?	**T:** *Chrystal learned PEMDAS from her brother, and this mnemonic seemed a useful way to help her remember the order of operations. What Chrystal did not understand was that when multiplying and dividing, she must compute from left to right. The same is true for addition and subtraction. Had Chrystal known this, she would have been able to successfully complete this problem.*
Chrystal: My brother taught me that. It helps me to remember the order of operations to solve equations. The *P* means parentheses, and that's what you do first. The *E* is exponents, and that's what you do second. The *M* is multiply. The *D* is divide. *A* is addition and *S* is subtraction. You do the problem in that order.	
T: How did you use *PEMDAS* to help you?	
Chrystal: I looked at the equation. There were no parentheses or exponents. So I began with doing all of the multiplication. I did three times twelve and got thirty-six. Then I did two times four and got eight. Then I got a little stuck. Ten divided by eight has a remainder. So then I had to sort of guess. I know the answer isn't zero or fifty-two. Fifty-two doesn't work because the problem is thirty-six minus something. Zero is ridiculous. That leaves sixteen or twenty-four. So I picked sixteen.	
T: Thank you, Chrystal. Your explanations have been very helpful.	

Informed Instructional Suggestions

Chrystal's correct answer choice does not reveal that she has only partial understanding. Her written and verbal explanations were helpful in establishing that she still has needs in this area. Chrystal needs instruction and practice with problems involving the order of operations, in particular, when it is necessary to compute from left to right across the equation. It would also be helpful for Chrystal to explore what happens when this convention is not followed. Once Chrystal has developed understanding and proficiency, she will be ready for experiences like those we suggested for Kylie and Gayle.

Student Work Sample: Veronica

Name _____ Date _____

Solve the following problem using the correct order of operations.

$$3 \times 12 - 10 \div 2 \times 4 =$$

A. 24

B. 16 *(circled)*

C. 0

D. 52

PEMDAS
( ) 4^2 x ÷ + −

Explain your thinking.

I used Pemdas to answer my question in the order Pemdas told me to.

A Conversation with Veronica	Teacher Insights
T: Please tell me more about why your answer makes sense to you. I don't see from looking at your paper what you did. **Veronica:** I used *PEMDAS*. See, I wrote it on my paper. I also showed what each of the letters in PEMDAS mean. I just did it in the order that PEMDAS said. **T:** What order was that? **Veronica:** There weren't any parentheses or exponents. That's what the *P* and *E* mean. So I did multiplication and division. That's the *M* and *D* in *PEMDAS*. Three times 12 is 36. Then I did 2 times 4, which is 8. But I realized that 10 divided by 8 would have a remainder. I thought, "What now?" But wait a minute, I remembered something: you have to multiply and divide in order from left to right. "Ah!" I said to myself as I started again, and this time I did 3 times 12, which is 36. Then I divided 10 by 2, which is 5, and then I multiplied 5 times 4 to get 20. The last thing I did was subtract 20 from 36, which is 16.	**T:** *Veronica got the correct answer and circled it on her paper. Her written explanation was not useful for discerning what she knew or what instruction she needed next. In this case, taking a few minutes to speak with Veronica allowed me to uncover a need for reinforcement. She understood that there is an order of operations and she used PEMDAS as a mnemonic to help her remember that order, but initially she forgot that she needed to work from left to right when multiplying and dividing.*

Informed Instructional Suggestions

Veronica's needs are similar enough to those of Chrystal that they could benefit from the same instructional activities and experiences.

Student Work Sample: Inga

Name _____ Date _____

Solve the following problem using the correct order of operations.

$$3 \times 12 - 10 \div 2 \times 4 =$$

A.   24

B.   16

C.   0

D.   52

Explain your thinking.

$3 \times 12 = 36$
-10
$26 \div 8 = 16$

P
E
M
D
A
S

A Conversation with Inga	Teacher Insights
T: What did you need to know to solve this problem? **Inga:** I had to know PEMDAS and how to multiply, divide, and subtract. **T:** Please tell me more about how you solved this problem. **Inga:** I started with three and multiplied three times twelve to get thirty-six. Then I subtracted ten from thirty-six to get twenty-six. I divided twenty-six by eight, and that was sixteen. **T:** You divided twenty-six by eight. Where did you get the eight? **Inga:** I got the eight from multiplying two times four. **T:** I see you have *PEMDAS* written on your paper. Please tell me more about that. **Inga:** I don't really know too much, but it does say rules about what to do first and second.	**T:** *There is more than one area of concern with Inga. She did mark the correct answer, but she has little understanding of the order of operations. She knows that PEMDAS exists, but she hasn't connected it as a mnemonic tool for problems such as this one. Inga also incorrectly solved 26 ÷ 8.*

Informed Instructional Suggestions

Inga's correct answer choice was misleading. She was not able to apply skills meaningfully to correctly solve this problem. Inga needs foundational activities that will help her develop understanding of the order of operations. If she is going to use PEMDAS as a mnemonic, then she needs to clearly see how to use it as a problem-solving tool. Also, it is important that Inga understand when to work from left to right across the problem.

Student Work Sample: Nina

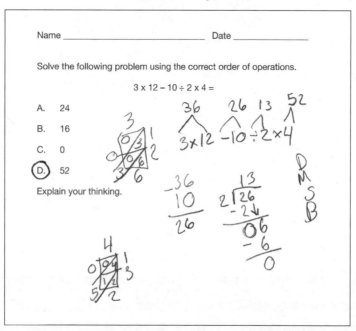

Name _____ Date _____

Solve the following problem using the correct order of operations.

3 x 12 – 10 ÷ 2 x 4 =

A. 24

B. 16

C. 0

D. 52

Explain your thinking.

A Conversation with Nina	Teacher Insights
T: Please tell me more about why your solution and answer make sense to you. **Nina:** I started with the three and did all the things the problem told me to do and I got fifty-two. I multiplied three times twelve, and that's thirty-six. Then I subtracted ten from thirty-six, and that's twenty-six. Then I divided twenty-six by two, and that's thirteen. Then I multiplied thirteen by four, and that's fifty-two. And there you have it!	**T:** *Nina's incorrect answer was the result of a failure to use the order of operations. She is able to subtract, multiply, and divide accurately. She used lattice multiplication to solve the multiplications involved and the traditional division algorithm to do the needed division.*

Informed Instructional Suggestions

Nina's needs are very much like those of Inga. She needs experiences to help her develop foundational understandings about the order of operations.

Student Work Sample: Gerti

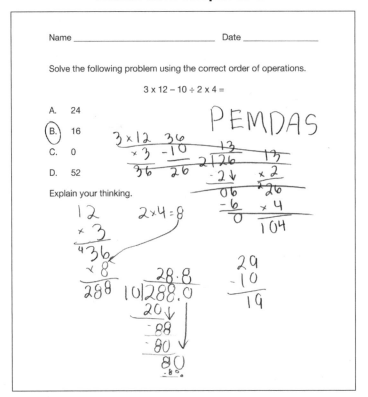

Name _____ Date _____

Solve the following problem using the correct order of operations.

3 x 12 – 10 ÷ 2 x 4 =

A.   24
B.   16
C.   0
D.   52

Explain your thinking.

A Conversation with Gerti	Teacher Insights
T: Gerti, I see *PEMDAS* on your paper and some figuring. Please tell me more about what you did. **Gerti:** We have been studying about PEMDAS so that's why I wrote it on my paper. It tells you the order to do things. The *P* is for parentheses and the *E* is for exponents and there aren't any of those things in this problem, so I went to *M*, which is multiplication. I did all of the multiplication. I did 3 times 12, and that's 36. I did 2 times 4, and that's 8. Then I multiplied 36 times 8, and that's 288. Then I divided 288 by 10, and that's 28.8. That rounds up to 29. Then I subtracted 10 from 29 to get 19. Nineteen was not a choice, so I chose the closest one, and that's 16. **T:** Thank you for sharing your thinking. I have a better idea of what we need to do next.	**T:** *Gerti has partial understanding of order of operations. She is confused and has not learned that when both multiplication and division are in the same problem, it is necessary to work from left to right across the problem. The same is true for addition and subtraction. Also, she got lost in her calculating and sometimes used a number more than once. For example, she divided by ten and subtracted ten. Her written explanation showed another attempt to solve this problem. In the other attempt, like Nina, Gerti worked across the problem from left to right without regard to the order of operations. However, Gerti used the number 2 twice. She divided by two and she multiplied by two. Gerti is able to accurately multiply and divide.*

Informed Instructional Suggestions

Gerti's needs are foundational, and she would benefit from the same instructional experiences we suggested for Inga.

Reassessment

1. Use a similar problem at the same level of difficulty.

   Solve the following problem using the correct order of operations.

   $$5 \times 8 + 32 \div 4 \times 2 =$$

   A. 36
   B. 56
   C. 18
   D. 9

   Explain your thinking.

2. Choose a problem that is similar but slightly more challenging.

   Solve using the correct order of operations.

   $$16 - 3 \times (6 + 2) \div 8 + 1 =$$

   A. 15
   B. 12
   C. 7
   D. 14

   Explain your thinking.

PROBLEM FIVE

Overview

For this problem, students need to apply their knowledge of algebra skills to solve for the variable, x. Understanding of the use of inverse operations would be helpful in solving this equation.

Sample Problem

Solve the following problem.

$$x + 239 = 372$$
$$x = \boxed{}$$

A. 147
B. 611
C. $x - 239$
D. 133

Explain your thinking.

Possible Student Solution Strategies

o Students use subtraction, the inverse operation of addition, to solve for x.
o Students count up to find the missing addend.
o Students solve for x by using substitution, replacing x with each answer choice.

Conversation Starters

o What did you do to solve this question?
o Is there more than one correct answer? How do you know?
o How could you use a picture or manipulatives to help you solve the problem or prove this answer?
o Convince me that your thinking makes sense.
o How could you use estimation to help you with this problem?

Student Work Sample: Penny

Name _____ Date _____

Solve the following problem.

$$x + 239 = 372$$

$$x = \boxed{}$$

~~A.~~   147

~~B.~~   611

~~C.~~ $x - 239$

(D.)   133

$$
\begin{array}{r}
3\overset{6}{\cancel{7}}\overset{12}{\cancel{2}} \\
-\ 2\ 3\ 9 \\
\hline
1\ 3\ 3
\end{array}
$$

The 1st thing I did was I looked at all of my answers A, B, C, & D. Then I eliminated the ones that didn't make sense. Then once I got rid of the 2 that didn't make sense I subtracted 372 & 239 to find what "x" equals. I found that the answer was 133, D.

Explain your thinking.

~~A. 147~~

~~B. 611~~ - no because if you are adding this # cant be bigger than the sum.

~~C. x = 239~~ - no because you want to find "x" so you would subtract 372 & 239.

(D. 133)

A Conversation with Penny	Teacher Insights
T: What did you do to solve this problem?	**T:** *Penny showed clear understanding of the skills needed to solve this problem. Both her written explanation and the discussion indicated her strength and flexible thinking.*
Penny: I knew that the amount on the left side of equation is equal to amount on the right side. The equal sign tells me this. That means I have to figure out what number added to 239 is equal to 372. I can find out by subtracting 239 from 372. Next I looked at the answer choices to see which ones made no sense. I eliminated choices B and C. That left choices A and D. I subtracted 239 from 372 and got 133.	
T: Do you think there could be more than one correct answer?	
Penny: No. If *x* were anything other than 133, the equation wouldn't work.	
T: How could you use manipulatives, like base ten blocks, or a picture to help you solve the problem or prove your answer?	
Penny: Hmm . . . I know, I could use base ten blocks and make 239 in one pile. Then I could add base ten blocks until I got to 372. I would put the blocks I was adding into a separate pile so I could count them to see how many I added. Or I could use a number line and start at 239 and count up until 372, and that would prove my answer.	

Informed Instructional Suggestions

Penny understood how to solve this problem. She is ready to work with more complex problems or in other areas of algebra.

Student Work Sample: Darren

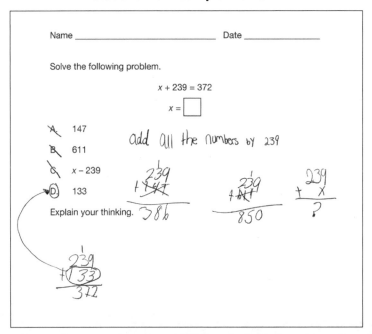

A Conversation with Darren	Teacher Insights
T: Please tell me about your thinking and convince me that it makes sense. **Darren:** I knew one of the answer choices had to be right. So all I had to do was add each one of them to 239. I knew that whatever number I added to 239 had to equal 372. So I added them. When I added 133 to 239, I got 372 so I knew that had to be the answer. I didn't understand choice C, but that was OK because choice D worked. **T:** If there hadn't been four answer choices, what is another strategy you could have used? **Darren:** I'm not too sure. Maybe I could estimate. I know that I have to add at least 100 to 239. That would give me 339. And then if I add 30 more to that, it would be 369. That's 130 I've added so far. If I add 3 more, that would be 372 and a total of 133 that I added. That would work! **T:** Are there any other ways you can think of? **Darren:** No, not really. The answer choices made it easier for me.	**T:** Darren applied a good multiple-choice test-taking strategy as his initial strategy. He tried the choices until he got the correct answer. When I asked him if he could solve the problem without answer choices, he developed a second strategy that involved adding on to 239 until he reached the sum of 372. This is also a useful strategy. In his figuring, Darren showed that he could mentally compute accurately and efficiently.

Informed Instructional Suggestions

In his written and verbal explanations, Darren applied both test-taking strategies and mathematical understanding. He did not apply or indicate awareness that he could use inverse operations to solve this problem. Developing the algebraic skill of using inverse operations would be a good next step for Darren. If we had relied solely on his multiple-choice response, we would have missed an opportunity to more fully develop his skills and understanding.

Student Work Sample: Eduardo

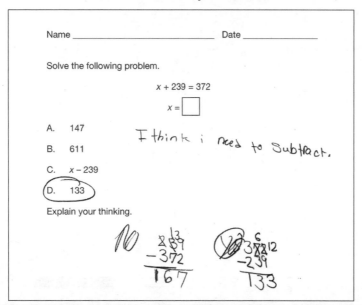

Name _____   Date _____

Solve the following problem.

$$x + 239 = 372$$

$$x = \boxed{}$$

A.   147

B.   611   I think i need to subtract.

C. $x - 239$

D.   133

Explain your thinking.

A Conversation with Eduardo	Teacher Insights
T: What did you do to solve this equation? **Eduardo:** I was pretty sure I needed to subtract to figure out what number is x. I thought that because in second grade, we did problems like $x + 3 = 5$, and all you had to do was subtract 3 from 5, and that would be 2, or the box number. You could check to be sure by adding 2 plus 3, and it was 5. This problem is sort of like that except I wasn't sure if I should do 239 minus 372 or 372 minus 239. I tried 239 minus 372 and got 167. So I tried 372 minus 239 and got 133, and that was one of the answer choices, so it must be right. **T:** Does your answer to your first problem of 167 seem reasonable to you? **Eduardo:** Yes, because that is what I got. Nine minus two is 7, 13 minus 7 is 6, and 2 minus 3 is 1. Yep, that's right.	*T: Eduardo made a nice connection between this problem and problem solving he learned as a younger student. He knew that subtraction was an appropriate solution strategy for this problem. Even knowing this, however, Eduardo ran into difficulties. He wasn't sure of the order of the numbers to subtract. He tried both possibilities and his computation and verbal explanation revealed a weakness that needs to be addressed. He used the subtraction algorithm inappropriately when regrouping. Also, he showed no awareness that when subtracting a larger number from a smaller number, as he did in his first problem, the result will be a negative number.*

Informed Instructional Suggestions

Eduardo marked a correct answer and he had partial understanding of the problem. It would be helpful to provide Eduardo with experiences that would solidify his understanding of why subtraction is a useful strategy for this problem. Also, Eduardo needs activities that will help him develop conceptual understanding of subtraction to enable him to accurately compute.

Student Work Sample: Louie

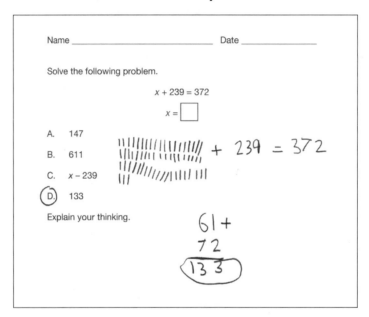

A Conversation with Louie	Teacher Insights
T: Please convince me that your answer makes sense. **Louie:** I know that the equals sign means that there is the same amount on both sides. The side with *x* has to equal up to 372, but so far there are only 239. I have to figure out how many to put with 239 to make 372. I drew 61 tally marks and put it together with 239 to make 300. That means I need 72 more to make 372. I added 61 and 72. That makes 133. One hundred thirty-three is what goes in the box. **T:** When I first saw your paper, I didn't understand why you had sixty-one tally marks or why you added sixty-one and seventy-two. Your verbal explanation helped me understand, and now your thinking makes sense to me. Is there another way you could think of to solve this problem? **Louie:** I can't think of another way now, but maybe there is one. I'm not sure.	**T:** *Louie used the landmark number of 300 to help him solve this question. He used number sense and added on to 239 to find his solution. Louie did not realize during our conversation that he could have used the inverse operation of subtraction. Louie would benefit from similar instructional experiences as Darren to help him understand the benefits of using inverse operations.*

Informed Instructional Suggestions

Louie had access to this problem using a sensible strategy that yielded a correct answer. During the verbal discussion, it became apparent that Louie does not understand how using an inverse operation is a useful tool for problems such as this one. This information will help us provide him with instructional opportunities that should strengthen and broaden his understanding.

Student Work Sample: Lilli

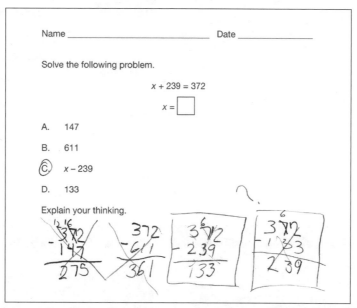

A Conversation with Lilli	Teacher Insights
T: What did you do to solve this problem? **Lilli:** I know that both sides have to be equal, and so I think I have to subtract. I subtracted each of the answer choices from 372. I knew the right answer couldn't be choices A or B. But then I sort of got confused about choices C and D. When I subtracted 133 from 372, I got 239, and that made sense because then if I add 133 to 239, I get 372. But then I looked at choice C again and thought maybe it was *x* minus 239. I chose it because I subtracted.	**T:** *Lilli was on the right track. She had some important understandings about this problem and she demonstrated a useful multiple-choice test-taking strategy when she tried all the answer choices. She then got confused, and because she subtracted, she selected the one answer choice that showed subtraction.*

Informed Instructional Suggestions

Lilli needs to strengthen her understanding of what x represents. It would be helpful for her to understand that when x is substituted with the correct solution, the equation will be true. If she substituted $x - 239$ for x, she would see that she still needed to solve for x before the problem was complete. If she substituted her other answer choice of 133 for x, she would see that the equation was true.

Student Work Sample: Mick

Name _____ Date _____

Solve the following problem.

$$x + 239 = 372$$

$$x = \boxed{}$$

Ⓐ   147

B.   611

C. $x - 239$

D.   133

Explain your thinking.

this is my thinking

Ⓐ 147
~~B 611~~
~~C x 239~~
~~D 133~~

pros ot alinton

$$\begin{array}{r} 1\,4\,7 \\ 2\,3\,9 \\ \hline 3\,8\,6 \end{array}$$

A Conversation with Mick	Teacher Insights
T: Please tell me about your thinking.	**T:** *Mick did his addition correctly, but he indicated little understanding of the problem. He did not demonstrate understanding of the relational nature of the equal sign. He interpreted it as a signal to do something, to take action—in this case to add. The equal sign is a relational symbol indicating that the quantities on either side of it are equivalent. Mick did not realize that the sum he got when he added should have been 372. He seemed to think choice A was correct just because it was the first choice.*
Mick: I decided to eliminate all of the answers but the right one. So I crossed off B, C, and D. Then I added 147 to 239 and got 386.	
T: Tell me in your own words what you think the problem is telling you to do.	
Mick: It is telling me to add. Do you see this addition sign here? [Mick points to the addition sign in the problem.] That means to add. So I added 147 because it was the first choice.	
T: Why is 372 in the problem?	
Mick: Oh, I don't know. Maybe I was really supposed to add 372 with 239? I got the wrong answer if that is what it means.	
T: What does the equal sign tell you?	
Mick: I have to add.	

Informed Instructional Suggestions

Mick needs foundational experiences. He needs to develop understanding of the meaning of the equal sign. Once he understands that an equal sign is a relational symbol indicating both sides of the equation are equivalent, he will benefit from the same activities and instructional experiences as Eduardo and Louie, as well as from learning to consider all answer choices.

Reassessment

1. Use a similar problem at the same level of difficulty.

   Solve the following problem for x.

   $$x + 433 = 624$$

   A. 1,057
   B. 191
   C. 211
   D. $x - 433$

   Explain your thinking.

2. Choose a problem that is similar but slightly more challenging.

   Solve the following problem for x.

   $$35 + x + 213 = 1,000$$

   A. 248
   B. 787
   C. 1,248
   D. 752

   Explain your thinking.

ⓟⓡⓞⓑⓛⓔⓜ ⓢⓘⓧ

Overview

In this question, students must find the correct value of a variable to solve the problem. The twist to the problem is that there are three variables, shown as boxes, and students must remember that the same variable within a problem represents the same number throughout that problem.

Sample Problem

What number, when placed in each box, makes a true equation?

$$24 + \Box + \Box + \Box = 48$$

A. 24
B. 12
C. 6
D. 8

Explain your thinking.

Possible Student Solution Strategies

o   Students correctly solve the problem by finding one number that can be placed into each box to produce the sum of forty-eight and make the equation true.
o   Students use multiplication by three or division by three to figure the correct number to substitute.
o   Students find one or two numbers that when added to twenty-four equal forty-eight.
o   Students find three different numbers that when added to twenty-four equal forty-eight.

Conversation Starters

o   Please put this problem into your own words.
o   What piece of information is important for finding the correct solution to this problem?
o   How could you explain your thinking to another student?
o   Is there more than one way to solve this problem? Is there more than one correct answer? Explain.
o   How do you know your answer is reasonable?

Student Work Samples: Penny, Jordan, and Kylie

Name _____ Date _____

What number, when placed in each box, makes a true equation?

$$24 + \boxed{} + \boxed{} + \boxed{} = 48$$

A. ~~24~~

B. ~~12~~

C. ~~8~~

D. ⑧

Explain your thinking.

The first thing I did was I looked at all of my answer choices.
I eliminated all of the answer choices that didn't make sense.

A. 24 - I know its not 24 because 24+24 = 48 & you have to add it 1 more time so it would be more.

Then I multiplied the #'s 3 times & added it to 24 to see what would equal 48.

Ⓑ.
```
  12
×  3
────
  36
+ 24
────
  60
```

Ⓒ
```
   6
×  3
────
  18
+24
────
  42
```

Ⓓ
```
   8
×  3
────
  24
+ 24
────
  48
```

Thats how I got my answer.

Name _____ Date _____

What number, when placed in each box, makes a true equation?

$$24 + \boxed{} + \boxed{} + \boxed{} = 48$$

A.   24

B.   12

C.   6

Ⓓ 8

Explain your thinking.

Ⓐ
```
  24
×  3
────
  72
+ 24
────
  96
```

Ⓑ
```
  12
×  3
────
  36
+ 24
────
  60
```

Ⓒ
```
   6
×  3
────
  18
+ 24
────
  42
```

☆Ⓓ
```
   8
×  3
────
  24
+ 24
────
☆ 48
```

Name _____ Date _____

What number, when placed in each box, makes a true equation?

$$24 + \boxed{} + \boxed{} + \boxed{} = 48$$

A. 24

B. 12

C. 6

D. 8

$$\begin{array}{r} 48 \\ -24 \\ \hline 24 \end{array} \qquad 24 \div 3 = 8$$

Explain your thinking. I knew that I first subtract 48−24=24. I know there are 3 blocks I need to fill in, so I did 24÷3=8. 8 is the answer.

A Conversation with Penny, Jordan, and Kylie	Teacher Insights
T: Penny, Jordan, and Kylie, all three of you got the same answer, but your written work looks different. Please share your work with each other. Decide how your work is the same and how it is different, and think about whether there is more than one way to solve this problem. **Kylie:** The first thing I did was to figure out the difference between twenty-four and forty-eight. **Jordan:** Yep, I did that too, and it's twenty-four, right? [All three girls nod in agreement.] **Kylie:** Because there are three variables and they are all boxes, I knew the number that went in them had to be the same. So I divided twenty-four by three and got eight. **Penny:** I didn't think of dividing. That's a great idea. I thought of multiplication. I thought in my brain, "Three times what number is twenty-four?" Three times eight is twenty-four. Then I added twenty-four and twenty-four, and it's forty-eight. **Jordan:** That's pretty much what I did too. Penny used more words. **T:** What is similar about how the three of you thought about this problem? **Kylie:** We all knew that the boxes had to equal twenty-four and the number that went into the boxes had to be the same. **Penny:** You said to think about differences too, and one difference was that Kylie figured out the boxes with division and Jordan and I used multiplication. **Jordan:** That means there are at least two ways to solve this problem but both ways get the same answer.	**T:** These three girls have a strong grasp of the concepts and skills involved in this problem. They were also able to effectively share their thinking with one another and appreciate the similarities and differences in their thinking.

Informed Instructional Suggestions

Penny, Jordan, and Kylie are ready to explore similar but more complex problems. To stretch their thinking and develop their skills, they should work on problems with larger numbers, different operations, or different variables.

Student Work Samples: Jerome and Jerry

Name _____ Date _____

What number, when placed in each box, makes a true equation?

$$24 + \boxed{} + \boxed{} + \boxed{} = 48$$

A. 24

B. 12

C. 6

D. 8

Explain your thinking.

$$24 + (8 \times 3) = 48$$

$$\begin{array}{r} 8 \\ \times\ 3 \\ \hline 24 \end{array} \qquad \begin{array}{r} 24 \\ +\ 24 \\ \hline 48 \end{array}$$

Name _____ Date _____

What number, when placed in each box, makes a true equation?

$$24 + \boxed{} + \boxed{} + \boxed{} = 48$$

A. 24

B. 12

C. 6

D. 8

Explain your thinking.

$$24 + \boxed{8} + \boxed{8} + \boxed{8} = 48$$

$$\begin{array}{r} \times\ 24 \\ \times\ 2 \\ \hline \boxed{48} \end{array}$$

A Conversation with Jerome and Jerry	Teacher Insights
T: Jerome and Jerry, you each have clear numeric solutions on your paper. It is easy for me to see your thinking. Please share your solutions with each other. Find out how your solutions are the same and also please discuss what information someone must have before being able to solve the problem.	**T:** *Jerome and Jerry, like Penny, Jordan, and Kylie, have strong understanding.*
Jerry: It looks like we both started our equation with 24. You wrote *8 × 3* and I wrote three boxes and put 8 inside of each one.	
T: How did you both know to use the number eight?	
Jerome: There were three boxes and they are all the same, so it is some number three times.	
Jerry: I know that three eights is twenty-four.	
T: What is one very important piece of information needed for this problem?	
Jerome: I don't know if this is what you are talking about, but one trick of this problem is the boxes. When the variable is the same in a problem, the number has to be the same. So three boxes means three of the same number. I think that's tricky.	
Jerry: So some things that are the same are we both got 8. Jerome wrote it as multiplication but actually I thought of it as 24 divided by 3 because I knew the boxes together equal 24 and there are three boxes, so 24 divided by 3 is 8. And the piece of information we needed to have was that each box in this problem had to represent the same number.	

Informed Instructional Suggestions

Penny, Jordan, Kylie, Jerome, and Jerry all have similar strengths and understandings and would benefit from the same learning opportunities. All five would also benefit from working, learning, and sharing together.

Student Work Sample: Louie

Name _____ Date _____

What number, when placed in each box, makes a true equation?

$$24 + \boxed{} + \boxed{} + \boxed{} = 48$$

A.   24

B.   12

Ⓒ   6

D.   8

Explain your thinking.

$$\begin{array}{r} 24 \\ 6 \\ 6 \\ 6 \\ \hline 48 \end{array}$$

A Conversation with Louie	Teacher Insights
T: How could you explain your thinking to another student? **Louie:** First I know that the boxes have to have the same number. Then I know that together the boxes have to equal 24 because 24 and some number equal 48, and 24 and 24 make 48. I think the boxes are 6 because three 6s make 24. **T:** Louie, please tell me how you figured that three sixes are twenty-four. **Louie:** I can count by sixes: six, twelve—uh-oh, it's eighteen! I goofed. **T:** I agree that three sixes equal eighteen. What number would work? **Louie:** I think eight: eight, sixteen, twenty-four. Yep, that works! I need to practice multiplication some more.	**T:** *Louie has the needed understanding to solve this problem, although he marked an incorrect response. He made an error because he doesn't know the multiplication facts well enough, not because he has weak understanding of variables.*

Informed Instructional Suggestions

Louie does not need remedial instruction in variables. He is ready for the same activities and instruction as the other students. He also should continue to work toward accuracy and fluency with the multiplication facts.

Student Work Sample: Nina

Name _____ Date _____

What number, when placed in each box, makes a true equation?

$$24 + \boxed{} + \boxed{} + \boxed{} = 48$$

A.   24

B.   12

C.   6

D.   8

Explain your thinking.

A Conversation with Nina	Teacher Insights
T: Please put this problem into your own words. **Nina:** I am supposed to figure out what is missing in this equation. Because I see the variables are the same—they are all boxes—I know that the numbers have to all be the same, so I have to figure out four numbers that equal forty-eight. I started with twenty-four and I added that four times. That equaled ninety-six, and that's too big. Then I added twelve four times, and that was just right. Four twelves is forty-eight. I have the answer! **T:** Do all of the numbers have to be the same or just the ones that go into the boxes? **Nina:** All of them have to be the same.	**T:** *Nina has partial understanding. She knows that the same variable in a problem represents the same number. However, she overgeneralized and came to the conclusion that all of the numbers must be the same, not just the ones represented by the same variable.*

Informed Instructional Suggestions

The few moments it took to talk with Nina uncovered a misunderstanding that should be relatively easy to correct. Nina needs to learn that only the numbers represented by the same variable within a problem must be the same, not all numbers in the problem. Once Nina understands this, she'll be ready for the same learning experiences as the other students.

Student Work Sample: Lilli

Name _____ Date _____

What number, when placed in each box, makes a true equation?

$$24 + \boxed{} + \boxed{} + \boxed{} = 48$$

(A.) 24

B. 12

C. 6

D. 8

Explain your thinking.

A Conversation with Lilli	Teacher Insights
T: What is this problem asking you to do?	**T:** *Lilli had some understanding, but she needed some guiding questions to help her find the correct solution. She was ignoring the three variables and treating them as one. Once she realized there were three variables, she was uncertain about whether or not they had to be the same. When this was clarified, she quickly found the correct solution.*
Lilli: I am supposed to figure out a number that added to twenty-four equals forty-eight. I did that. Twenty-four plus twenty-four equals forty-eight.	
T: What do the boxes mean?	
Lilli: They mean that there is a number missing there, and that number is twenty-four.	
I tried all the other answer choices just to make sure and none of them made forty-eight. I even tried multiplying twenty-four times six, and that didn't work either.	
T: I agree with you that twenty-four needs to be added to twenty-four to equal forty-eight, but I see three boxes, not one.	
Lilli: Does that mean that there have to be three numbers? [I nod.] Oh! I bet that since the boxes are the same, the numbers have to be the same. Actually, that's easy! I got it. Eight plus eight plus eight equals twenty-four. Three eights, three boxes!	

Informed Instructional Suggestions

Lilli needs additional practice to reinforce her new understanding. Then she will be ready to work with the other students.

Reassessment

1. Use a similar problem at the same level of difficulty.

    What number, when placed in each box, makes a true equation?

    $$16 + \square + \square + \square + \square = 32$$

    A. 32
    B. 8
    C. 12
    D. 4

    Explain your thinking.

2. Choose a problem that is similar but slightly more challenging.

    What number, when placed in each box, makes a true equation?

    $$36 - \square - \square + \square = 30$$

    A. 2
    B. 6
    C. 12
    D. 3

    Explain your thinking.

Study the pyramid below. How

Geometry

8

6

n your thinking.

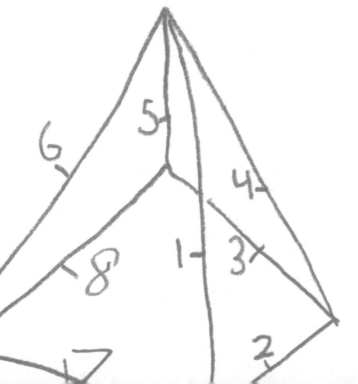

ⓅⓇⓄⒷⓁⒺⓂ ⓄⓃⒺ

Overview

A large part of the geometry curriculum in elementary school revolves around vocabulary—both learning and applying geometric vocabulary. This can be especially challenging for second language learners. One way to help students overcome this difficulty is to provide many conceptual, hands-on experiences along with many opportunities to use the vocabulary of geometry. Labels and vocabulary lists posted around the classroom further support learning this terminology. This question tests students' knowledge and understanding of the vocabulary of angles: *acute*, *obtuse*, and *right*.

Sample Problem

Which group correctly describes the angles inside the pentagon below?

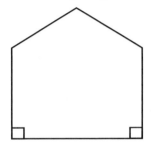

A. 2 right angles, 2 acute angles, and 1 obtuse angle
B. 3 right angles and 2 acute angles
C. 2 right angles and 3 obtuse angles
D. 4 right angles and 1 acute angle

Explain your thinking.

Possible Student Solution Strategies

o   Students know and are able to apply their knowledge of the vocabulary of angles.
o   Students lack the necessary vocabulary to name the angles within the pentagon.

Conversation Starters

o   What knowledge did you need to have to correctly answer this question?
o   How did you think about this problem?
o   What have you seen before that looks like this?
o   How could you explain your thinking to another student?

Student Work Sample: Chrystal

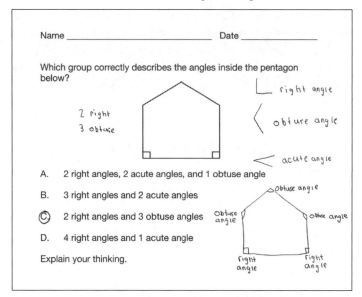

Name _____ Date _____

Which group correctly describes the angles inside the pentagon below?

2 right
3 obtuse

∟ right angle

< obtuse angle

< acute angle

A.   2 right angles, 2 acute angles, and 1 obtuse angle

B.   3 right angles and 2 acute angles

Ⓒ.   2 right angles and 3 obtuse angles

D.   4 right angles and 1 acute angle

Explain your thinking.

Obtuse angle

Obtuse angle   Obtuse angle

right angle   right angle

A Conversation with Chrystal	Teacher Insights
T: What knowledge did you need to have to correctly answer this question?	**T:** *Chrystal understands what right, acute, and obtuse angles are. Both her written and verbal explanations indicated the strength of her understanding.*
Chrystal: I had to know what angles are, and I had to know the three different kinds of angles, like acute, right, and obtuse. I had to know both their names and what they look like.	
T: Where have you seen something like this picture or the angles in the picture?	
Chrystal: The whole picture reminds me of how a little kid draws a house. I see angles everywhere. They are on this paper, they are made from lines on the sidewalk, they are where the panes of glass in the window meet, the top of my desk makes an angle with the side of my desk. They're all over the place!	
T: How could you explain your thinking about this problem to another student?	
Chrystal: I would explain that there are three kinds of angles. The easiest angle is probably the right angle, and it looks like the corner of a piece of paper. If an angle is smaller—that means the sides are closer together than a right angle—then it is an acute angle. If the sides are spread farther apart than a right angle, it is an obtuse angle. The pentagon has two right angles in the lower corners. The rest of the angles are obtuse. You can even use the corners of the page to show that they are wider than a right angle. [Chrystal demonstrates this by bending and twisting her paper to compare each of the obtuse angles with a corner of her paper.]	

Informed Instructional Suggestions

Chrystal's multiple-choice answer was correct and strongly supported by her written and verbal explanations. She is ready to continue to explore angles of pentagons and other polygons. One challenge might be to ask her to draw a polygon with a particular number of acute, obtuse, and right angles. She could also explore what is the greatest number of right angles a pentagon (or other polygon) could have or whether a pentagon (or other polygon) could be made with only acute angles. All of these activities would involve learning and applying the target vocabulary.

Student Work Sample: Jordan

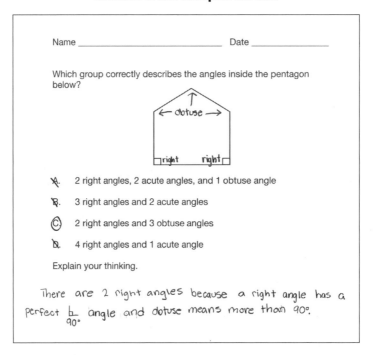

Name _____   Date _____

Which group correctly describes the angles inside the pentagon below?

A. 2 right angles, 2 acute angles, and 1 obtuse angle

B. 3 right angles and 2 acute angles

C. 2 right angles and 3 obtuse angles

D. 4 right angles and 1 acute angle

Explain your thinking.

There are 2 right angles because a right angle has a perfect ∟ angle and obtuse means more than 90°.
90°

A Conversation with Jordan	Teacher Insights
T: Please tell me how you thought about this problem. **Jordan:** Well, I studied the picture of the pentagon and noticed that it had two right angles. I can tell by the little symbol in the bottom two corners. I knew all of the other angles were obtuse. That means they are bigger than right angles. Then I looked at the answer choices. None of the angles were acute, and the only answer choice that doesn't have acute angles is choice C. That's the right answer.	**T:** *Jordan understood this problem and was able to solve it. She knew that the pentagon was made up of right and obtuse angles. She also recognized that three of the four answers involved acute angles, and there were no acute angles in this figure.*

Informed Instructional Suggestions

Jordan is ready to participate in the same types of instructional activities we recommended for Chrystal.

Student Work Sample: Walter

Name _____ Date _____

Which group correctly describes the angles inside the pentagon below?

A.   2 right angles, 2 acute angles, and 1 obtuse angle

B.   3 right angles and 2 acute angles

C.   2 right angles and 3 obtuse angles

D.   4 right angles and 1 acute angle

Explain your thinking.

None of the angles are less than 90° so none of them are acute 2 of the angles are 90° so they are right and 3 of the angles are more than 90° so they are obtuse.

A Conversation with Walter	Teacher Insights
T: You have a very nice written explanation about your thinking. You wrote about 90-degree angles. What is another name for a 90-degree angle?	**T:** *Walter has clear understanding of what he needed to know about angles for this problem.*
Walter: A 90-degree angle is the same as a right angle. Right angles, or 90-degree angles, look like the corners of pages.	
T: Please tell me more about acute and obtuse angles.	
Walter: When angles are less than 90 degrees, their sides are closer together. The number of degrees in these angles is less than 90, and they are called acute angles. When angles are larger than 90 degrees, their sides are wider apart. They have more than 90 degrees and they are called obtuse angles.	

Informed Instructional Suggestions

Walter's needs are similar to those of Chrystal and Jordan. He would benefit from the same instruction.

Student Work Sample: Albert

Name _____ Date _____

Which group correctly describes the angles inside the pentagon below?

A. 2 right angles, 2 acute angles, and 1 obtuse angle

B. 3 right angles and 2 acute angles

C. 2 right angles and 3 obtuse angles

D. 4 right angles and 1 acute angle

Explain your thinking.

A Conversation with Albert	Teacher Insights
T: What do you need to know to solve this problem? **Albert:** I need to know about angles. I am not too sure about angles. It's hard for me to remember the names and which ones are which. That's why I put a question mark on my paper; I don't really know too much. **T:** I noticed that you circled an answer. How did you decide to circle choice C? **Albert:** I think acute angles are little angles and there are no little angles in the picture. Choices A, B, and D all say something about acute angles, but I am pretty sure there are no acute angles in the picture, so I chose choice C because it didn't have anything about acute angles. **T:** What do you know about right and obtuse angles? **Albert:** Not too much.	**T:** *Albert had a hunch about acute angles and used it to make a reasonable guess. His knowledge of angles is limited.*

Informed Instructional Suggestions

Albert's correct answer alone would have masked his needs. He should have conceptual, experience-based opportunities to interact with angles. He needs to draw them, find them in the environment around him, label them, measure them, and so on. Opportunities to speak or write about angles using the appropriate vocabulary would also support his learning.

Student Work Sample: Darren

Name _____ Date _____

Which group correctly describes the angles inside the pentagon below?

A. 2 right angles, 2 acute angles, and 1 obtuse angle

B. 3 right angles and 2 acute angles

C. 2 right angles and 3 obtuse angles

D. 4 right angles and 1 acute angle

Explain your thinking.

If you see the shape, there is 2 boxes. Those 2 boxes are right angle

A Conversation with Darren	Teacher Insights
T: How could you explain your thinking to another student? **Darren:** First, I have to tell the angles in the picture. If you look in the shape, you will see two little boxes in the corners. That means those two angles are right angles. Then I have to figure out the other three. I know the answer isn't choice D because there aren't four little boxes in the shape so there can't be four right angles. I know it can't be choice B because that one says three right angles and there aren't three boxes in the shape so there can't be three right angles. That leaves A and C. Choice A has acute angles. I think acute angles are skinny angles and there are no skinny angles, just fat ones. So that leaves choice C. I am not really sure, but I think I am right.	**T:** *Darren used good reasoning to come to the correct answer. However, he did indicate uncertainty about his knowledge of acute and obtuse angles.*

Informed Instructional Suggestions

Darren marked the correct answer and he does have partial, emerging knowledge of the vocabulary and what it represents. His multiple-choice answer alone would not have provided a complete picture of his needs though. To strengthen his knowledge, Darren needs additional experiences similar to this problem to explore angles and practice using the correct vocabulary to describe angles.

Student Work Sample: Alvin

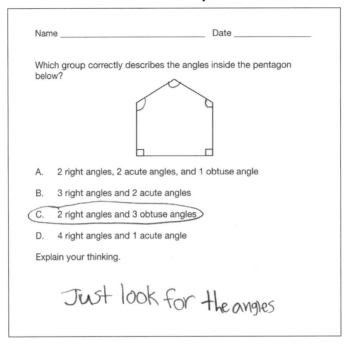

Name _____ Date _____

Which group correctly describes the angles inside the pentagon below?

A.   2 right angles, 2 acute angles, and 1 obtuse angle

B.   3 right angles and 2 acute angles

C.   2 right angles and 3 obtuse angles

D.   4 right angles and 1 acute angle

Explain your thinking.

Just look for the angles

A Conversation with Alvin	Teacher Insights
T: Please tell me how you thought about this problem. I know you wrote that I should just look at the angles, but please tell me what I should look for when I look at the angles. **Alvin:** What I mean is that you should look at the angles and count them. There are five angles. Then look at the answer choices. I saw one that had a 2 and a 3, and I know that adds up to 5, so that must be the answer. **T:** Do any of the other answer choices add up to five? **Alvin:** Probably not. **T:** What do you know about acute, obtuse, and right angles? **Alvin:** Nothing, really. I guess they must all be angles.	*T: Alvin does know the word* angle *and correctly counted that there were five angles in the figure. But that is the extent of his knowledge on this topic. He found one combination of angles that equaled five and assumed it was the correct answer without actually figuring the total angles of the other choices.*

Informed Instructional Suggestions

Alvin's correct answer by itself would have created the impression that he understood the content being assessed. This is not the case, however. His needs are much like those of Albert. He should participate in concrete, hands-on experiences to help him develop his conceptual understanding of angles and their names. Also, Alvin needs to carefully consider the merits of all answer choices.

Student Work Sample: Monty

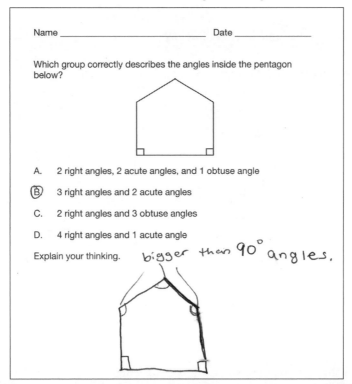

Name _____ Date _____

Which group correctly describes the angles inside the pentagon below?

A.   2 right angles, 2 acute angles, and 1 obtuse angle

Ⓑ   3 right angles and 2 acute angles

C.   2 right angles and 3 obtuse angles

D.   4 right angles and 1 acute angle

Explain your thinking.   *bigger than 90° angles.*

A Conversation with Monty	Teacher Insights
T: What have you seen before that looks like this? **Monty:** It looks like a house or home plate. **T:** Please tell me how you thought about this problem. **Monty:** I know that a right angle is 90 degrees. There are two in the pentagon. You can tell because of the little squares in the bottom corners. The other three angles are larger than 90 degrees. I can't remember if angles greater than 90 degrees are called obtuse or acute. I chose choice B. **T:** Please read aloud choice B. **Monty:** Oh no! It says three right angles. I know there are only two right angles. I should read more carefully. I think maybe the right answer is really choice C.	**T:** *Monty does have some of the knowledge needed for this problem; however, he is not sure of the names used to describe angles greater than or less than 90 degrees.*

Informed Instructional Suggestions

Monty recognizes and understands right angles. He needs experiences to develop and strengthen his understanding of acute and obtuse angles.

Reassessment

1. Use a similar problem at the same level of difficulty.

   Which group correctly describes the angles inside the polygon below?

   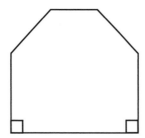

   A. 2 right angles and 3 acute angles
   B. 4 right angles and 2 obtuse angles
   C. 2 right angles, 2 acute angles, and 2 obtuse angles
   D. 2 right angles and 4 obtuse angles

   Explain your thinking.

2. Choose a problem that is similar but slightly more challenging.

   Which group correctly describes the angles inside the polygon below?

   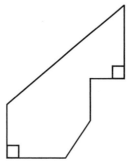

   A. 2 right angles and 5 obtuse angles
   B. 2 right angles, 4 acute angles, and 1 obtuse angle
   C. 3 right angles, 3 obtuse angles, and 1 acute angle
   D. 2 right angles, 4 obtuse angles, and 1 acute angle

   Explain your thinking.

PROBLEM TWO

Overview

This problem tests students' knowledge and application of the vocabulary of geometry and attributes of polygons.

Sample Problem

Which of these is *not* a name for this figure?

A. pentagon
B. quadrilateral
C. square
D. polygon

Explain your thinking.

Possible Student Solution Strategies

o Students effectively apply their knowledge of vocabulary and attributes of polygons.
o Students do not have the knowledge of vocabulary or attributes of polygons to correctly answer the question.

Conversation Starters

o Put the problem into your own words.
o Is there more than one correct answer? Explain.
o Does the figure have more than one name? Explain.
o What are names you could use to describe the figure?
o Convince me that your answer makes sense.
o How did you think about this problem?

Student Work Sample: Sumita

Name _____ Date _____

Which of these is *not* a name for this figure?

A.) pentagon

B. quadrilateral

C. square

D. polygon

Explain your thinking.

I think A. because Penta means 5 sides or angles quad means 4 and tri means 3 a polygon is a close 2-D figure so a pentagon would be ment for a 5 sided polygon.

A Conversation with Sumita	Teacher Insights
T: Please convince me that your answer makes sense. **Sumita:** I think that the picture is a polygon, a square, a quadrilateral, a rectangle, or even a parallelogram. It is not a pentagon. A pentagon has five sides and five angles. The picture has only four sides and four angles. A square is a special kind of rectangle, which is a special kind of quadrilateral. The picture is a polygon because it is 2-D, it has straight sides, and it is closed.	**T:** *Sumita has a good understanding of both the attributes of polygons and the vocabulary used to describe them.*

Informed Instructional Suggestions

Sumita's written and verbal explanations showed the strength of her understanding. Next, she could explore irregular or concave polygons, and then she could move on to working with 3-D shapes, also known as polyhedra.

Student Work Sample: Sophie

Name _____ Date _____

Which of these is *not* a name for this figure?

4

2

4 3

A. pentagon
B. quadrilateral
C. square
D. polygon

Explain your thinking. A Pentagon is a 5 sided and 5 angled shape. A quadr. lateral is a 4 sided and a 4 angled sape. Guadr.laterds have special names and the special name for the shape is a square. Polygon are 2D shapes.

A Conversation with Sophie	Teacher Insights
T: Please tell me how you thought about this problem.	**T:** *Sophie has a clear understanding of the vocabulary appropriate to this problem.*
Sophie: I read the problem and knew I had to find a name that did not match the picture. I looked at the picture, then I looked at each of the choices. It was kind of easy, actually. The picture is of a square. The first answer choice says *pentagon*. Well, a pentagon has five angles and five sides. *Pentagon* is not a name for the picture. I looked at the next choice and it said *quadrilateral*. That's easy. A quadrilateral has four sides and four angles. I numbered the sides and angles on the picture to prove it is a quadrilateral. I looked at the third choice. It says *square*. The picture is a square. It has four right angles and four congruent sides. A square is also a special kind of quadrilateral. There are lots of kinds of quadrilaterals. The last thing I did was look at the last answer, *polygon*. The picture is a polygon because a polygon has three or more straight sides and angles and it is closed and two-dimensional.	
T: Wow, that was a very complete, well-spoken explanation. I can tell you know a lot about polygons, quadrilaterals, and pentagons.	

Informed Instructional Suggestions

Sophie has a strong command of the knowledge tested by this question. She and Sumita could work together on the instructional experiences we suggested for Sumita.

Student Work Sample: Neal

Name _____ Date _____

Which of these is *not* a name for this figure?

(A) pentagon

B. quadrilateral

C. square

D. polygon

Explain your thinking.

Because a pentagon does not have parallel lines like a square.

A Conversation with Neal	Teacher Insights
T: Please tell me more about your thinking about parallel sides in squares and pentagons. **Neal:** A square has two pairs of parallel sides. A pentagon doesn't have any. **T:** Please draw me a picture of a pentagon with no parallel sides. [Neal draws a picture that looks like two mountain peaks.] I agree that you drew a pentagon with no parallel sides. [Note: Had Neal drawn the figure differently, the sides of the mountain peaks could have been parallel.] What about this pentagon? [I draw a pentagon that looks like a house.] **Neal:** Oh, yours does have a pair of parallel lines! But a square always has two pairs of parallel lines and pentagons don't . . . at least I don't think so because pentagons have an odd number of sides and parallel sides come in pairs. **T:** Besides square, what other answer choices describe the picture? **Neal:** A square is a polygon. It is two-dimensional, has straight sides, and is closed. A square is also a quadrilateral. *Quadrilateral* means four sides, and a square has four sides.	*T: Neal understood the content required to answer this question, and during the course of the conversation he discovered that pentagons could have one pair of parallel sides. He also was willing to conjecture about why not all sides in a pentagon could be parallel.*

Informed Instructional Suggestions

Neal is ready for the same next steps as Sumita and Sophie. He would also benefit from further exploring shapes that can have all parallel sides, shapes that have more than one pair but not all parallel sides, and shapes that have no parallel sides.

Student Work Sample: Belinda

Name _____ Date _____

Which of these is *not* a name for this figure?

(A) pentagon

B. quadrilateral

C. square

D. polygon

Explain your thinking.

Because if you use pentagons you have to use only triangles.

A Conversation with Belinda	Teacher Insights
T: Please put this problem in your own words. **Belinda:** One of the answer choices is not a name for the picture. **T:** How would you explain your thinking to another student? **Belinda:** Well I don't really remember what a pentagon is. I do know about triangles. They have three sides and three angles. I know a lot of things can be made from triangles, so I just thought pentagons could be too. **T:** Do you know what any of the answer choices are? **Belinda:** I know square, and the picture is a square. I think maybe a quadrilateral has four sides, or maybe not. I guess if a quadrilateral has four sides, then a square is a quadrilateral. I don't know about the last answer.	**T:** *Belinda has emerging understanding of the material being tested. She does know what squares and triangles are. She indicated a lack of understanding of pentagons and polygons and only fragile understanding of quadrilaterals.*

Informed Instructional Suggestions

Belinda needs hands-on conceptual experiences to become familiar with the attributes of polygons and their names. She needs opportunities to find and name polygons in the real world along with many opportunities to discuss or to write about them and their attributes. She should explore and develop understanding of such ideas as all squares are rectangles but not all rectangles are squares, and all squares are quadrilaterals but not all quadrilaterals are squares.

Student Work Sample: Alma

Name _____   Date _____

Which of these is *not* a name for this figure?

A. pentagon

B. quadrilateral

C. square

D. polygon

Explain your thinking.

Polygon isn't a shape. It's the name of these shapes:
- pentagon
- quadrilateral
- triangles
- hexagons

A Conversation with Alma	Teacher Insights
T: Please tell me how you thought about this problem. **Alma:** I think the right answer is choice D because a polygon isn't the name of just one shape. *Polygon* is a name for a whole bunch of different shapes. I know that a polygon is two-dimensional, it has straight sides, it has at least three sides and three angles, and it's closed up like a fence so that a dog couldn't get out. I wrote on my paper that some polygons are pentagons, quadrilaterals, triangles, and hexagons. **T:** What is a name you could use to label the picture on your paper? **Alma:** I think it is a square. It has four congruent sides and four right angles. **T:** I agree that a square is one name for the shape. What is another? **Alma:** It could be called a rectangle too because a square is a special kind of rectangle. **T:** Please tell me more about that. **Alma:** Squares and rectangles both have four sides and four right angles. A square's sides are all congruent. With a rectangle, the opposite sides are congruent, but if all the sides are congruent, then it is a square. Oh, I remembered one more thing: both squares and rectangles have two pairs of parallel sides. **T:** You know a lot about squares and rectangles. What is another name for the picture? **Alma:** It could also be a parallelogram because of the parallel sides, or a quadrilateral because it has four sides and four angles, and *quad* means four. **T:** Could the shape be a pentagon? How do you know? **Alma:** No, it can't be a pentagon because it doesn't have five angles and five sides. **T:** Could a square be a polygon? **Alma:** Yes, because it is a quadrilateral, and quadrilaterals are four-sided polygons. **T:** You have told me a lot and that has helped me understand what you know. Please reread this problem and the answer choices. **Alma:** Oh, I made a mistake, didn't I? The square is a polygon, but it's not a pentagon!	**T:** *Alma marked the incorrect answer, but she actually had strong understanding about polygons. The few moments it took to engage her in conversation revealed a great deal about what she actually knew and provided the opportunity to guide her to correct a misunderstanding she demonstrated in her written explanation.*

Informed Instructional Suggestions

Alma's incorrect answer was the result of a misconception on her part. But after a few moments of conversation, that misconception was corrected. She showed lots of knowledge and understanding in both her written and verbal explanations that we would have missed with just a multiple-choice response. Alma is ready for the same instructional experiences as Sumita, Sophie, and Neal.

Student Work Sample: Patti

Name _____ Date _____

Which of these is *not* a name for this figure?

A.   pentagon

(B.)   quadrilateral

C.   square

D.   polygon

Explain your thinking.   I think B because a — square isn't a quadrilateral and it is a polygon and a square and is a penigon because a square has 4 congrent sides and angles and a pentigon has 10 congruent sides or angles.

A Conversation with Patti	Teacher Insights
T: Please convince me that your answer makes sense. **Patti:** Actually, I don't really get this. I was just hoping that if I wrote and used the words in the answer choices I might get it right. I do know that the picture is a square. I just don't really know what it isn't because I don't really know what is a quadrilateral or a polygon or a pentagon.	**T:** *Patti is confused. She knows what a square is, and she attempted to answer the question, but both her written work and the discussion reflected her confusion.*

Informed Instructional Suggestions

Patti would benefit greatly from the same materials and instructional activities we recommended for Belinda. She needs lots of opportunities to develop her foundational understanding.

Reassessment

1. Use a similar problem at the same level of difficulty.

   Which of these is *not* a name for this figure?

   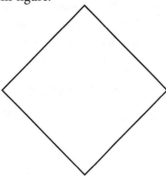

   A. cube
   B. square
   C. rhombus
   D. parallelogram

   Explain your thinking.

2. Choose a problem that is similar but slightly more challenging.

   Which of these is *not* a name for this figure?

   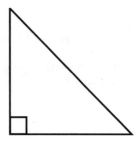

   A. polygon
   B. right triangle
   C. obtuse triangle
   D. isosceles triangle

   Explain your thinking.

ⓟⓡⓞⓑⓛⓔⓜ ⓣⓗⓡⓔⓔ

Overview

This problem involves the language of three-dimensional shapes, otherwise known as polyhedra. Students need to have command of vocabulary such as *face*, *edge*, and *vertex* (*vertices*). The question is designed to determine students' knowledge of these words by asking them to count edges.

Sample Problem

Study the pyramid below. How many edges does the pyramid have?

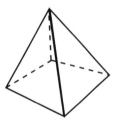

A. 5
B. 4
C. 8
D. 6

Explain how you know.

Possible Student Solution Strategies

o   Students apply their knowledge of the word *edge* and correctly count the number of edges.
o   Students partially count edges but leave some out.
o   Students count faces or vertices rather than edges.

Conversation Starters

o   What do you have to know to answer this question?
o   How could the picture help you solve this problem?
o   Is there more than one possible correct answer to this question? Explain.

Student Work Sample: Lainie

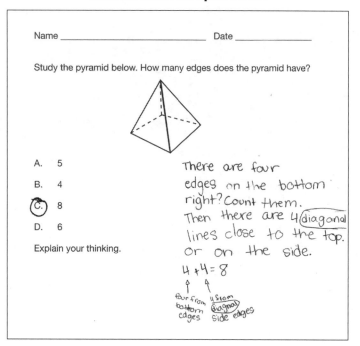

Name _____ Date _____

Study the pyramid below. How many edges does the pyramid have?

A. 5

B. 4

C. 8

D. 6

Explain your thinking.

There are four edges on the bottom right? Count them. Then there are 4 (diagonal) lines close to the top. or on the side.

4 + 4 = 8

four from bottom edges   4 from (diagonal) side edges

A Conversation with Lainie	Teacher Insights
T: What did you need to know to solve this problem? **Lainie:** I had to know what part of the pyramid is the edge. Then I had to count them. I also had to remember that some parts of the pyramid are hidden. That's what the dotted lines show. The dotted lines show hidden edges. **T:** Is there more than one correct answer to the question of how many edges are on this pyramid? How do you know? **Lainie:** No. If you count correctly and count every edge, including the ones that are hidden, you will get eight. There is no other answer. First count the edges on the bottom. There are four. Then count all the edges that go from the bottom up to the top vertex. There are four. Four plus four equals eight. I think all pyramids must have eight edges, right?	**T:** *Lainie had the needed skills to correctly answer this question and discuss it both in writing and verbally.*

Informed Instructional Suggestions

Lainie posed an idea at the end of the discussion. She conjectured that all pyramids have eight edges, but she wasn't sure. A good next step for Lainie would be to investigate her own idea. Then she could find out about the number of faces and vertices on pyramids (such as triangular pyramids) as well as other polyhedra.

Student Work Sample: Sonya

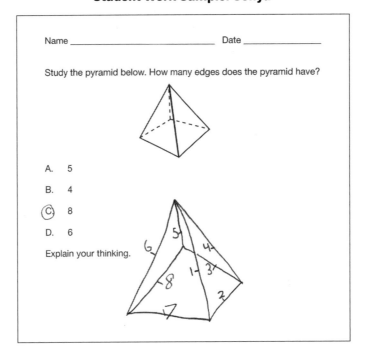

Name _____ Date _____

Study the pyramid below. How many edges does the pyramid have?

A. 5

B. 4

(C.) 8

D. 6

Explain your thinking.

A Conversation with Sonya	Teacher Insights
T: I noticed that you used a picture to help you. Please tell me more about what you did.	**T:** *Like Lainie, Sonya had a strong grasp of the information tested by this question. An additional question allowed me to know that Sonya was also familiar with faces and vertices. She was also confident that all rectangular pyramids have eight edges, a misconception that I need to address.*
Sonya: I just drew the pyramid to help me think about it and then I numbered each one of the edges until they all had a number. The greatest number was eight, and that is how many edges there are. The picture helped me to keep track so that I counted every edge once and didn't skip any.	
T: What knowledge did you have to use to answer this question?	
Sonya: I had to know about edges and that I had to count each one once and only once.	
T: What are the other parts of a pyramid?	
Sonya: The other parts are faces and vertices. The faces are the flat parts of a pyramid and the vertices are the pointy parts.	
T: Do you think all rectangular pyramids have the same number of edges? Why?	
Sonya: They all have to have the same number of edges or they'd be something else.	

Informed Instructional Suggestions

Sonya is ready to continue exploring the attributes of other pyramids, such as triangular pyramids, in addition to other polyhedra. Using solid figures to help her explore faces, vertices, and edges will increase the depth of her understanding. It might also be helpful for Sonya to draw the various polyhedra and then count and label the faces, edges, and vertices.

Student Work Sample: Jasper

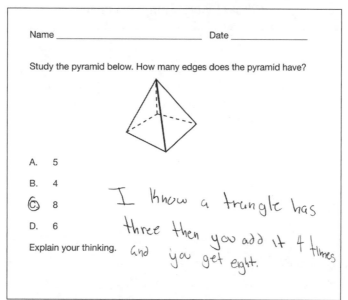

Name _____ Date _____

Study the pyramid below. How many edges does the pyramid have?

A. 5

B. 4

C. 8

D. 6

Explain your thinking.

I know a triangle has three then you add it 4 times and you get eight.

A Conversation with Jasper	Teacher Insights
T: What do you have to know to correctly answer this question? **Jasper:** I knew that a triangle has three sides. In the pyramid there are four triangles, so just add three sides four times and that gives you the answer. **T:** What do you get when you add three four times? **Jasper:** You get twelve, but that wasn't an answer choice, so I picked eight, which is closest. I wrote that it equaled eight because I didn't know what else to write. **T:** Is there another way you could count edges? **Jasper:** Maybe. I guess I could just count the dark and dotted lines in the picture. [Jasper does this.] Oh, I guess there really are eight edges. I wonder why my way didn't work. I see four triangles and I know each triangle has three sides.	[R1]T: *Jasper had partial understanding of what edges are and was eventually able to count them correctly. He was confused about why his thinking about the sides of triangles didn't help him correctly solve this problem. Also, Jasper tended to use the terms* edge *and* side *interchangeably.* Edge *is used to describe where two faces intersect on a polyhedron, while* side *is used to describe the line segments that make up a polygon.*

Informed Instructional Suggestions

Jasper's correct multiple-choice answer covered his gaps in understanding, and without his written and verbal explanations, we would not have had the opportunity to tease out his misunderstandings and help him explore why his thinking didn't work. It would be appropriate for Jasper to investigate why his idea of adding the three sides of the four triangles didn't produce the correct answer. Using actual solid figures would help him more clearly see why his idea didn't work: he counted some edges more than once.

Student Work Sample: Jason

Name _____ Date _____

Study the pyramid below. How many edges does the pyramid have?

A.   5

B.   4

C.   8

D.   6

Explain your thinking.

You count all the lines and you get your answer.

A Conversation with Jason	Teacher Insights
T: What is this problem asking you to do? **Jason:** I have to count the lines. **T:** What word in the problem told you that you needed to count the lines? **Jason:** The problem says how many edges. Edges are the lines in the picture. I counted them and there are eight. On a real pyramid, you wouldn't be able to see them all at the same time, so there are some dotted lines in the picture to show the hidden lines. **T:** Mathematicians refer to the lines you are talking about as *edges*. A clearer way to communicate your ideas would be use the word *edge* or *edges* rather than *line* or *lines*.	**T:** *Jason understands what edges are and used this knowledge to correctly answer the question. The conversation allowed me to help Jason see the benefit of using the correct mathematical language to more clearly communicate his thinking.*

Informed Instructional Suggestions

Jason's needs are similar to those of Lainie and Sonya. Instruction for Jason should also focus on the use of correct mathematical language. Working with Lainie and Sonya would provide all three students the opportunity to discuss their work using the correct language.

Student Work Sample: Suri

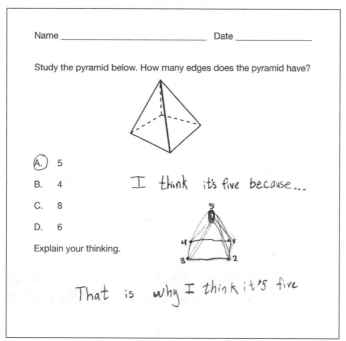

A Conversation with Suri	Teacher Insights
T: What did you need to know to answer this question? **Suri:** I needed to know what edges are. They are the pointy parts. So I counted them and there are five of them. I drew a picture on my paper to show this.	**T:** *Suri demonstrated a lack of understanding of the term* edge. *She confused it with* vertex. *Her picture clearly indicated this confusion.*

Informed Instructional Suggestions

Suri needs concrete experiences to help her learn the language involved. By handling geometric solids, she could see and touch the different parts to help her associate each of the words with the part it represents on a solid figure. Drawing pictures of geometric solids and labeling the parts would also be useful in reinforcing the vocabulary. Once Suri has a command of the vocabulary and can accurately count the edges, faces, and vertices, she will be ready for the same instruction as Lainie and Sonya.

Student Work Sample: Jona

Name _____ Date _____

Study the pyramid below. How many edges does the pyramid have?

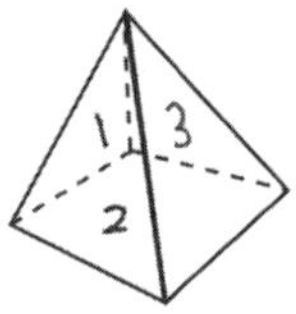

A.   5

B.   4

C.   8

D.   6

Explain your thinking.

I counted all the edges and
while I counted I numbered them
to keep track. when I was finish I
recounted them and got choic B.

A Conversation with Jona	Teacher Insights
T: It looks like you used the picture to help you answer this question. What did you count? **Jona:** I counted the edges. The edges are the flat parts of the pyramid. I numbered each one of them on the picture to help me to keep track of what I had counted. **T:** What are the names of the other parts of the pyramid? **Jona:** I think the points are called *angles* and the lines are *sides*. I am not too sure.	**T:** *Jona has not mastered the vocabulary needed to correctly answer this question. She counted the faces as if they were edges. She also used incorrect vocabulary to describe edges and vertices.*

Informed Instructional Suggestions

Like Suri, Jona needs additional experiences designed to develop her knowledge of the needed vocabulary. The suggestions for Suri also would be appropriate for Jona. The girls could work together, which would provide authentic opportunities for them to use the vocabulary.

Reassessment

1. Use a similar problem at the same level of difficulty.

   Study the pyramid below. How many faces does the pyramid have?

   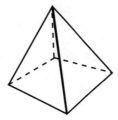

   A. 5
   B. 4
   C. 8
   D. 6

   Explain your thinking.

2. Choose a problem that is similar but slightly more challenging.

   Study the cube below. How many vertices does the cube have?

   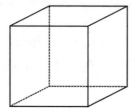

   A. 6
   B. 8
   C. 12
   D. 4

   Explain your thinking.

ⓅⓇⓄⒷⓁⒺⓜ ⒻⓄⓊⓇ

Overview

Students' knowledge of the attributes of trapezoids is tested by this question. Students must understand geometric terms such as *trapezoid*, *parallel sides*, and *right angles*.

Sample Problem

Which of these attributes does a trapezoid *always* have?

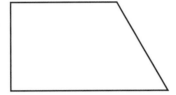

A. at least 1 pair of parallel sides
B. 4 equal sides and 4 right angles
C. 4 parallel sides
D. opposite sides that are equal and parallel

Explain your thinking.

Possible Student Solution Strategies

o   Students are able to apply their knowledge and understanding of the attributes of trapezoids to correctly answer the question.
o   Students misunderstand the meaning of *parallel*.

Conversation Starters

o   How can you prove your answer?
o   How do you know your answer is reasonable?
o   How did using a picture help you?
o   What do you know about this problem? What do you need to find out?

Student Work Sample: Arnie

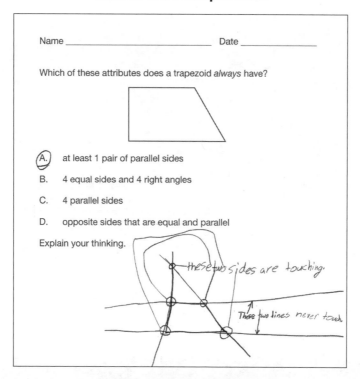

Name _____ Date _____

Which of these attributes does a trapezoid *always* have?

A. at least 1 pair of parallel sides

B. 4 equal sides and 4 right angles

C. 4 parallel sides

D. opposite sides that are equal and parallel

Explain your thinking.

these two sides are touching.

These two lines never touch.

A Conversation with Arnie	Teacher Insights
T: Please explain your picture and how it helped you. **Arnie:** It helped me a lot because my thinking was hard to explain using words. I drew a trapezoid and then I made all of the sides longer to see if they would meet. Two of the opposite sides did meet, the ones on the sides of the trapezoid. The top and bottom sides don't meet. The ones that don't meet are parallel. Choice A says a trapezoid has at least one pair of parallel sides, and this one does—like all trapezoids. **T:** What can you tell me about the other answer choices? **Arnie:** Choice B is incorrect because the sides are not equal and there are only two right angles. Choice C is wrong because there are not four parallel sides. Choice D is wrong because opposite sides are not equal and they are not all parallel. Only two sides are parallel.	**T:** *Arnie's understanding of the vocabulary and concepts is strong. He used the vocabulary correctly to explain his answer choice as well as why each of the other three was incorrect.*

Informed Instructional Suggestions

Arnie is ready to explore the attributes of other quadrilaterals and, later, other polygons. Once Arnie has developed a strong understanding of the attributes of polygons, he can move on to investigating polyhedra.

Student Work Sample: Carmen

Name _____ Date _____

Which of these attributes does a trapezoid *always* have?

A. at least 1 pair of parallel sides

B. 4 equal sides and 4 right angles

C. 4 parallel sides

D. opposite sides that are equal and parallel

Explain your thinking.

top and bottom gose like this

side and side gose like this if you keep on going

A Conversation with Carmen	Teacher Insights
T: What do you know about this problem and what do you need to find out? **Carmen:** I know that a trapezoid is a quadrilateral. I know that it has at least one pair of parallel sides. Parallel sides are opposite sides that can go on forever and never meet. What I have to do in this problem is figure out which answer is best for the trapezoid. **T:** How can you prove your answer? **Carmen:** Choice A says a trapezoid has at least one pair of parallel sides and this one does. I said that a minute ago and I showed that on my paper. Choice B is silly because the sides are not equal. Choice C is silly too because there are not four parallel sides, there are only two. Choice D is wrong because opposite sides are not equal and only one pair of opposite sides is parallel. **T:** Which of your pictures shows parallel sides? **Carmen:** The first one shows parallel sides and the other one proves that the other pair of sides is not parallel because they meet.	**T:** *Carmen understands the content being tested. She proved this in both her written and her verbal explanations.*

Informed Instructional Suggestions

Carmen and Arnie have similar needs and would benefit from the same instruction and activities. Carmen could further clarify her written work by using labels, such as identifying which of her drawings showed parallel sides in this case.

Student Work Sample: Sumita

Name _____ Date _____

Which of these attributes does a trapezoid *always* have?

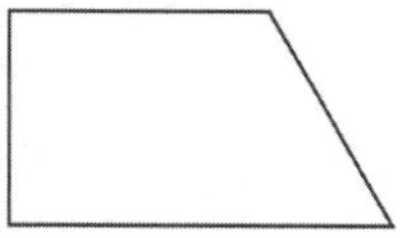

(A)   at least 1 pair of parallel sides

B.   4 equal sides and 4 right angles

C.   4 parallel sides

D.   opposite sides that are equal and parallel

Explain your thinking.

> I think A. because it does have at least one pair of parallel sides, I will prove it.

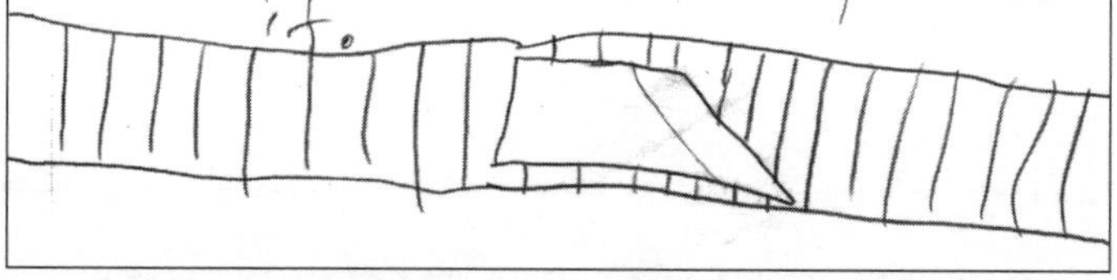

A Conversation with Sumita	Teacher Insights
T: I see you used a picture to help you explain your thinking. I am not certain of what you are trying to show. Please tell me more about it. **Sumita:** I think choice A is right because the trapezoid has at least one pair of parallel sides. Parallel sides are like train tracks, the rails go on and on and on and never, ever meet. If the rails met, the train would fall off and that would be a problem. So I drew train tracks and put the trapezoid inside of it to show that the bottom and top of the trapezoid are like train tracks.	**T:** *Although Sumita's picture initially was not clear to me, her verbal explanation showed a understanding of parallel lines and a nice connection between the question and a real-world use of parallel.*

Informed Instructional Suggestions

Sumita would benefit from the same activities, explorations, and instruction as Arnie and Carmen.

Student Work Sample: Neal

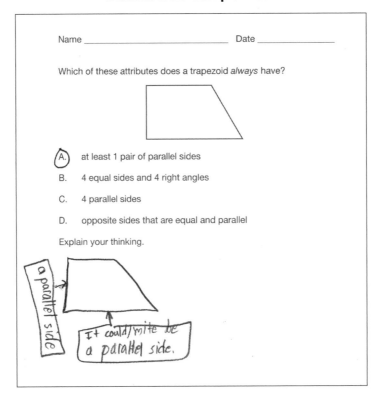

Name _____ Date _____

Which of these attributes does a trapezoid *always* have?

A. at least 1 pair of parallel sides

B. 4 equal sides and 4 right angles

C. 4 parallel sides

D. opposite sides that are equal and parallel

Explain your thinking.

a parallel side

It could/mite be a parallel side.

A Conversation with Neal	Teacher Insights
T: I see that you used a picture. Please tell me more about it.	**T:** *Neal circled the correct answer, but his picture indicated that he did not understand what parallel sides are. He labeled two intersecting sides as parallel. He most likely confused* parallel *and* perpendicular.
Neal: I just drew a picture of a trapezoid and then labeled the two sides that I thought were parallel. Then I circled choice A because there is one pair of parallel sides and the other answers had something wrong with them.	

Informed Instructional Suggestions

Neal's correct answer masked his lack of understanding of the term *parallel*. He needs concrete, hands-on experiences to help him understand what parallel lines are. Finding parallel lines in the real world as well as drawing and labeling parallel sides would be useful activities for Neal. Also, it would benefit him to explore intersecting and perpendicular lines.

Student Work Sample: Cherisse

Name _____ Date _____

Which of these attributes does a trapezoid *always* have?

(A) at least 1 pair of parallel sides

B. 4 equal sides and 4 right angles

C. 4 parallel sides

D. opposite sides that are equal and parallel

Explain your thinking. The answer is A because the top of the trapezoid and the bottom are both horizontal

A Conversation with Cherisse	Teacher Insights
T: Please share with me what you know about parallel lines. **Cherisse:** They are lines that never meet and they have to be horizontal. I drew the lines in the picture longer to show that they would not meet. **T:** You said on your paper that the top and bottom lines are horizontal and you said that they are also parallel. What if I rotate the paper—will they still be parallel? [I rotate the paper 90 degrees.] **Cherisse:** Yes, but now the top and bottom are the sides. **T:** Are the lines horizontal now that I have rotated the paper? **Cherisse:** They are horizontal because they are parallel and parallel lines are horizontal. They're like synonyms; they're the same thing.	**T:** *Cherisse's written and verbal explanations uncovered some confusion that needs to be clarified. She believes that* parallel *and* horizontal *are synonyms.*

Informed Instructional Suggestions

Cherisse's correct answer alone would not have revealed an important flaw in her vocabulary. Cherisse needs additional opportunities to explore different kinds of lines, specifically parallel, perpendicular, intersecting, vertical, and horizontal lines. She also needs experiences to help her understand that position in space does not define some attributes of lines, such as parallelism, while it does define others, such as horizontality. These experiences should be concrete, with opportunities to find examples of the five types of lines in the real world.

Student Work Sample: Haily

Name _____ Date _____

Which of these attributes does a trapezoid *always* have?

A.   at least 1 pair of parallel sides

B.   4 equal sides and 4 right angles

C.   4 parallel sides

(D.)   opposite sides that are equal and parallel

Explain your thinking.

I think the answer is D because A, B and C say four equal sides and there are not 4 equal sides. Thats how I got my answer.

A Conversation with Haily	Teacher Insights
T: Please reread the answer choices and tell me using your own words what each of them says.	**T:** *Haily's written work and incorrect multiple-choice response implied she had little understanding of the concepts being tested. That is not the case. She was able to explain her correct thinking clearly in her verbal explanation. She also used the correct language. She did not read carefully and as a result chose the wrong answer.*
Haily: [Reads the choices quietly.] Choice A says one pair of parallel sides. Choice B says four equal sides and four right angles. Choice C says four parallel sides.	
T: Thank you, Haily. On your paper you wrote that Choices A, B, and C all say equal sides. Do you still think that?	
Haily: No. I didn't read carefully. Only choice B says anything about equal sides, and it says all the sides are equal. Not all of the sides in the picture are equal.	
T: Do you think any of the sides are equal?	
Haily: No, actually I don't think any of them are equal. I think choice D is wrong too. I think the real right answer is actually choice A. The trapezoid can have at least one pair of parallel sides. I already explained why choice B is wrong. Choice C says all the sides are parallel, and they are not; just the top and bottom are parallel. Choice D is wrong because opposite sides are not equal and only one pair of sides is parallel. Boy, did I mess up! I didn't read as carefully as I should have.	

Informed Instructional Suggestions

Haily's incorrect multiple-choice response did not provide an accurate picture of her knowledge. She does not need remediation and in fact has good understanding. The few moments it took to discuss her thinking revealed her strengths and provided sound direction for next instructional steps. Haily's needs are similar to those of Arnie and Carmen.

Student Work Sample: Jona

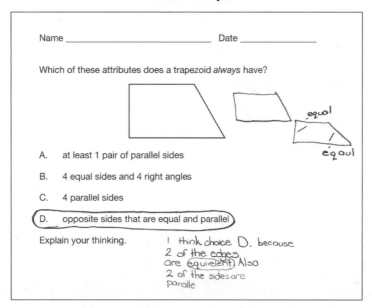

A Conversation with Jona	Teacher Insights
T: Please tell me more about your thinking. **Jona:** I studied the trapezoid and then I looked at each of the answer choices. I knew that choices B and C were wrong. There aren't four parallel sides like choice C says, and there aren't four equal sides and four right angles like choice B says. That left choices A and D. I wasn't really too sure which one is correct. Choice A says one pair of parallel sides and there is one pair of parallel sides, and choice D says opposite sides that are equal and parallel. I drew a picture to show that there were two equal sides. The left and right sides are equal. I also know that the top and bottom are parallel. I decided on choice D. **T:** How did you measure the left and right sides to be sure they were equivalent? **Jona:** I just looked. Maybe I should have used a ruler. [Jona reaches for a ruler and measures the two lines.] Uh-oh! They looked equivalent, but the diagonal one was actually longer. That must mean that choice A is correct since none of the lines are equivalent like choice D says.	**T:** *Jona marked the incorrect answer but she has partial understanding. She used some good thinking to eliminate two of the incorrect answers. Jona's understanding of the phrase in choice D seemed to cause her some difficulty; she did not realize that it referred to one pair of sides being both equal and parallel. She also assumed by looking that two of the sides were equal. After a few moments of discussion, however, she was able to correctly reason her way to choice A.*

Informed Instructional Suggestions

Jona needs the opportunity to engage with other problems similar to this one to help her strengthen her comprehension skills. Because her mathematical knowledge is strong, she is also ready to do additional explorations like those we suggested for Arnie and Carmen, but with a focus on comprehension. She also needs experiences that require her to measure in order to check for equal sides rather than just looking.

Reassessment

1. Use a similar problem at the same level of difficulty.

   Which of these attributes does a parallelogram *always* have?

   A. no parallel sides
   B. 4 equal sides and 4 right angles
   C. opposite sides that are equal and parallel
   D. exactly 1 pair of parallel sides

   Explain your thinking.

2. Choose a problem that is similar but slightly more challenging.

   Which of these attributes does a rectangle *always* have?

   A. 4 right angles and opposite sides that are parallel and congruent
   B. 4 sides and no right angles
   C. 4 right angles and no parallel sides
   D. no congruent sides and no right angles

   Explain your thinking.

PROBLEM FIVE

Overview

This question provides students with the opportunity to apply their understanding of angles to correctly identify and count obtuse angles in the quadrilateral pictured.

Sample Problem

How many obtuse angles does this quadrilateral have?

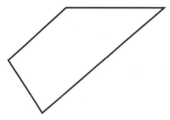

A. 2
B. 3
C. 1
D. 4

Explain your thinking.

Possible Student Solution Strategies

o   Students correctly apply their knowledge of the vocabulary to find the number of obtuse angles.
o   Students count all the angles rather than just the obtuse angles.
o   Students don't understand the vocabulary and are unable to correctly count the number of obtuse angles.

Conversation Starters

o   How could you explain your thinking to another student?
o   How is this problem like others you have done?
o   How did you think about this problem?
o   Besides obtuse angles, what other kinds of angles are in this quadrilateral?

Student Work Sample: Kylie

Name _____ Date _____

How many obtuse angles does this quadrilateral have?

A. 2

B. 3

C. 1

D. 4

Explain your thinking.

I know that a right angle looks like this ∟, so I just look for the one that's more than the right angle, like this

A Conversation with Kylie	Teacher Insights
T: Please tell me how you could explain your thinking to another student. **Kylie:** I know what a right angle is. It is like the corner of a page. An obtuse angle is larger; the sides are more spread out than a right angle. I drew a picture to show. The problem wants to know how many obtuse angles are in the quadrilateral, so I looked for angles greater than a right angle. I circled them on the picture to show you I know. **T:** What is the name of angles less than a right triangle? **Kylie:** Those are acute angles and there are two of them in the quadrilateral just like there are two obtuse angles. It seems to me that if there are 360 degrees in a quadrilateral and two of the angles are greater than 90 degrees, the other two angles have to be less than 90 degrees. I wonder if that's true.	**T:** *Kylie knows the information needed for this question. She raised a very interesting question: If two angles of a quadrilateral are greater than 90 degrees, do both the other angles have to be less than 90 degrees?*

Informed Instructional Suggestions

Kylie is ready to explore other ideas. She could start by investigating the question she raised. She could draw a variety of quadrilaterals with two angles greater than 90 degrees and then measure the remaining angles.

Student Work Sample: Jordan

Name _____ Date _____

How many obtuse angles does this quadrilateral have?

(A.) 2

B. 3

C. 1

D. 4

Explain your thinking.

The answer is 2 because a quadrilateral has 4 angles and 2 of these are acute so the other 2 have to be obtuse or right. You can tell they are obtuse because obtuse looks like this ∠ and right looks like ∟.

A Conversation with Jordan	Teacher Insights
T: Please explain to me why your answer makes sense. **Jordan:** There are four angles in a quadrilateral. I can tell by looking at this quadrilateral that two of them are acute because they are less than a right angle. I labeled the acute angles. If two of the angles are acute, I am thinking the other two must be obtuse. Hmm, maybe there could be two acute angles, a right angle, and an obtuse angle. I am not sure, but I could tell from the picture that there were two acute angles in the quadrilateral. I could also tell that there were two obtuse angles. I drew a picture to show how I know, and I labeled all the angles to show my thinking.	**T:** *Jordan has ideas very similar to Kylie's and has good foundational understanding.*

Informed Instructional Suggestions

Jordan and Kylie should work together to explore their similar ideas. Their slightly different perspectives would make for enriching discussion and learning.

Student Work Sample: Leah

Name _____ Date _____

How many obtuse angles does this quadrilateral have?

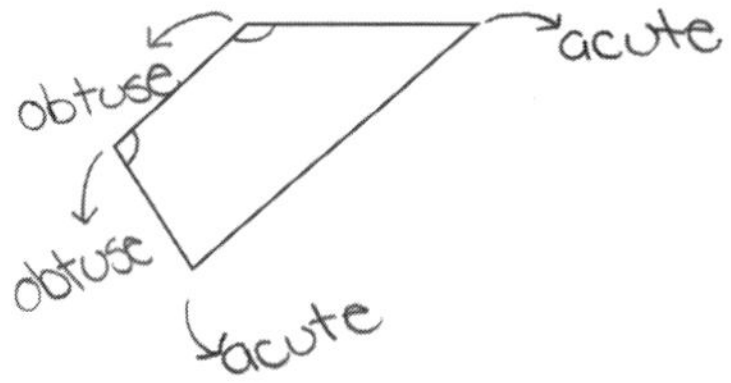

A. 2
B. 3
C. 1
D. 4

Explain your thinking.

I chose A because this quadrilateral has 2 obtuse angles and 2 acute angles.

A Conversation with Leah	Teacher Insights
T: How is this problem like others that you have seen? **Leah:** We have had problems before where we had to count different kinds of angles in triangles, squares, rectangles, pentagons, and stuff like that. This problem is like one of those. **T:** Please tell me more about how you thought about this problem. **Leah:** I just looked at each of the angles and labeled them. Then I counted the obtuse angles and there were two, so I chose two as my answer.	**T:** *Like Kylie, Leah has a good understanding of angles and was able to correctly answer this question.*

Informed Instructional Suggestions

It would be beneficial for Leah to collaborate with Kylie and Jordan as they explore their ideas. Working together would strengthen each girl's understanding, communication skills, and ability to cooperate.

Student Work Sample: Caren

Name _____ Date _____

How many obtuse angles does this quadrilateral have?

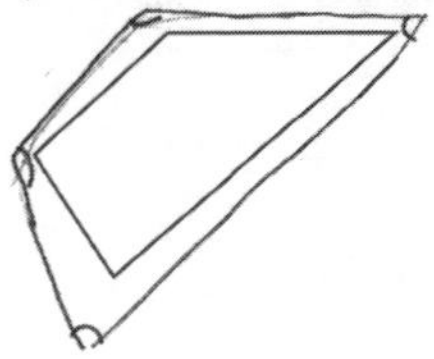

(A) 2

B. 3

C. 1

D. 4

Explain your thinking.

trace the same shape around the shape
and put a rainbow in every corner.
Ya'll see what angles are obtuse and
acute.

A Conversation with Caren	Teacher Insights
T: Please tell me more about your thinking. I see your wrote about rainbows. I am interested in how this helped you. **Caren:** Well, pretty much if you get bigger rainbows, it means bigger angles, and smaller rainbows mean smaller angles. I got two big rainbows and two little rainbows, so the answer must be two. **T:** How can you tell which angles are obtuse and which are acute? **Caren:** I'm not too sure, but there are two of each.	*T: Caren has minimal understanding. She has developed a rainbow analogy, but she is not sure whether the larger rainbows measure obtuse or acute angles.*

Informed Instructional Suggestions

Caren's correct answer alone would have masked her weak understanding. She needs opportunities to explore, draw, and label different kinds of angles, such as acute, right, and obtuse angles. She also needs to find examples of these angles in the real world.

Student Work Sample: Eddie

Name _____ Date _____

How many obtuse angles does this quadrilateral have?

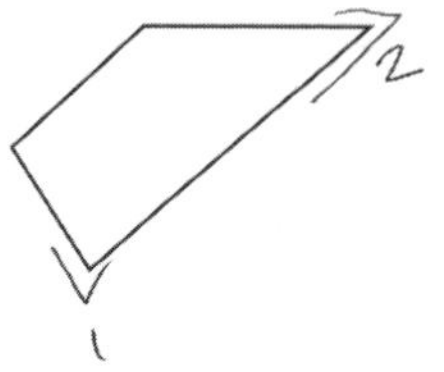

A. 2

B. 3

C. 1

D. 4

Explain your thinking.

A Conversation with Eddie	Teacher Insights
T: It looks like you used the picture to help you. Please tell me more about your thinking. **Eddie:** Well, I have to count obtuse angles. They are less than 90 degrees. So I noticed that the bottom angles were less than 90 degrees. I put a *1* and a *2* in the angles to show the angles I was counting. Then I circled my answer choice.	**T:** *Eddie has confused obtuse and acute angles. He mistakenly counted the acute angles to solve the problem.*

Informed Instructional Suggestions

Eddie's needs are similar to Caren's. Like Caren, he could use a variety of hands-on, conceptual experiences to help him understand obtuse and acute angles.

Student Work Sample: Aubrey

Name _____ Date _____

How many obtuse angles does this quadrilateral have?

A. 2

B. 3

C. 1

D. 4

Explain your thinking.

A Conversation with Aubrey	Teacher Insights
T: What did you have to know to answer this question? **Aubrey:** I had to know what angles were. I know what angles are. That is the place where two sides come together. I just counted up all of the corners. There are four, so I circled choice D because it says 4. **T:** Does the problem ask you for any angles or for a certain type of angle? **Aubrey:** Oh, it says obtuse angles. I counted all of the angles. Obtuse angles are greater than 90 degrees. The top two angles in the quadrilateral are obtuse. The bottom two are acute. The correct answer is choice A because there are two obtuse angles. I should have reread the problem before answering it to make sure I understood it.	**T:** *Aubrey selected an incorrect answer, but her verbal explanation showed she has the understanding necessary to correctly answer this question.*

Informed Instructional Suggestions

Although Aubrey marked an incorrect answer, she understands and can apply the skills being tested by this question. She does not need reteaching, as her incorrect multiple-choice response alone would have indicated. She needs the same instructional opportunities as Kylie, Jordan, and Leah, as well as reminders to read questions more carefully.

Student Work Sample: Kristen

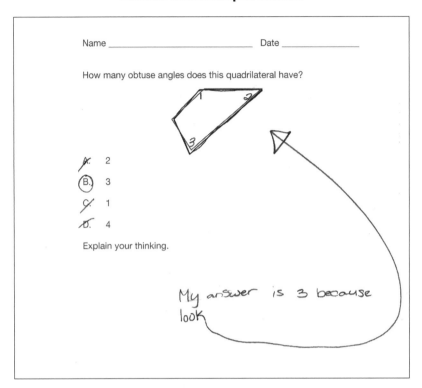

Name _____ Date _____

How many obtuse angles does this quadrilateral have?

A. 2

(B.) 3

C. 1

D. 4

Explain your thinking.

My answer is 3 because look

A Conversation with Kristen	Teacher Insights
T: How could you explain your thinking to a younger student? **Kristen:** The problem says to count the obtuse angles. I don't really know what those are, so I just counted some of the angles. I numbered the ones I counted. Then I saw the 3 for an answer choice and I circled it.	**T:** *Kristen essentially guessed. She stated she didn't understand, and her explanations verified this.*

Informed Instructional Suggestions

Like Caren, Kristen needs many conceptual experiences to build her knowledge about angles.

Reassessment

1. Use a similar problem at the same level of difficulty.

    How many acute angles does this polygon have?

    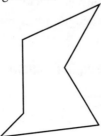

    A. 4
    B. 6
    C. 2
    D. 3

    Explain your thinking.

2. Choose a problem that is similar but slightly more challenging.

    How many obtuse and acute angles does this polygon have?

    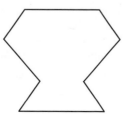

    A. 2 obtuse and 6 acute angles
    B. 4 obtuse and 4 acute angles
    C. 6 obtuse and 2 acute angles
    D. 8 obtuse and 0 acute angles

    Explain your thinking.

 PROBLEM SIX

Overview

To successfully answer this question, students must be able to identify parallel lines. It is helpful to also know about intersecting lines and perpendicular lines and how these three types of lines vary from each other.

Sample Problem

Which two pairs of lines are parallel?

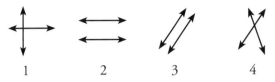

    1   2   3   4

A. 1 and 4
B. 2 and 4
C. 2 and 3
D. 1 and 3

Explain your thinking.

Possible Student Solution Strategies

o Students apply their knowledge of parallel lines to successfully answer the question.
o Students apply an incorrect meaning of *parallel lines*.
o Students focus on whether the lines are congruent rather than their position relative to each other.
o Students confuse *parallel* with *perpendicular* or *intersecting*.

Conversation Starters

o Please explain why your answer makes sense.
o What do you know about lines?
o What makes lines parallel? What other pairs of lines are there?
o Is there more than one possible correct answer? How do you know?

Student Work Sample: Brent

Name _____ Date _____

Which two pairs of lines are parallel?

    1   2   3   4

A.   1 and 4

B.   2 and 4

C.   2 and 3   Parel iel means never ever ever ever ever
                     touch ⟨yes⟩   so never do
D.   1 and 3   ⟨no X⟩
                                            this X do this So thats my
Explain your thinking.   Explainshon

A Conversation with Brent	Teacher Insights
T: Please tell me what makes lines parallel. **Brent:** Lines that are parallel never touch. Even if you made them go on forever, they wouldn't touch. **T:** What is the name we use for lines that do touch or meet? **Brent:** Lines that touch could be perpendicular lines or intersecting lines. **T:** Please tell me more about this. **Brent:** Intersecting lines are lines that touch, meet, or cross each other. Perpendicular lines are special intersecting lines because where they intersect, they make right angles. **T:** Thank you for sharing your clear understanding of lines.	**T:** *Brent knew and applied the information assessed by this question. By engaging him in a brief conversation, I learned that he understood not only parallel lines but also intersecting lines and perpendicular lines.*

Informed Instructional Suggestions

Brent's clear verbal explanation indicated he knows what he needs to know about lines. If Brent has not already had the opportunity to do so, he needs to find examples of parallel, perpendicular, and intersecting lines in the world around him. Also, he may be interested in creating pictures or structures with straws or other materials that involve the use of parallel, perpendicular, and intersecting lines. He could investigate questions such as *How do parallel, perpendicular, and intersecting lines influence structural strength?*

Student Work Sample: Rocky

Name _____ Date _____

Which two pairs of lines are parallel?

1   2   3   4

A.   1 and 4

B.   2 and 4

C.   2 and 3

D.   1 and 3

Explain your thinking. *Because one is perpendicular and four is intersecting lines.*

A Conversation with Rocky	Teacher Insights
T: I see that you used the words *perpendicular* and *intersecting* in the explanation you wrote on your paper. Please tell me more about what you know about perpendicular and intersecting lines. **Rocky:** Intersecting lines are lines that cross or meet. Picture 4 shows intersecting lines. Perpendicular lines intersect too, but in a special way. When perpendicular lines meet, they have to form right angles; otherwise they are just intersecting lines. And of course the question wants to know about parallel lines, and parallel lines never, ever meet, touch, cross, or intersect. I guess that all pairs of lines that aren't parallel are intersecting, but some are special because of the 90-degree angles they form so they have a special name of *perpendicular*, but they are still intersecting too. It's sort of like squares and rectangles. A square is also a rectangle, but a special rectangle because its sides are all congruent. Yep! That's what I think.	**T:** *Rocky's multiple-choice response alone would not have revealed the depth of his knowledge, nor would it have encouraged him to make the connections he did during his verbal explanation. Rocky demonstrated mastery of the concepts being measured by this question.*

Informed Instructional Suggestions

Rocky would benefit from enriching his knowledge much in the same way as we suggested for Brent. The boys could work together to learn from each other's perspectives as well.

Student Work Sample: Patti

Name _____ Date _____

Which two pairs of lines are parallel?

A. 1 and 4

B. 2 and 4

C. (2 and 3)

D. 1 and 3

Explain your thinking.

I chose 2 & 3 because you can see that they are never going to meet they are like train tracks becaus they never meet if they did it wouldn't be so good.

Train track are alike pallel lines.

A Conversation with Patti	Teacher Insights
T: What else do you know about lines besides what you already wrote about parallel lines? **Patti:** Well, there are parallel lines that never meet, like train tracks. Then there are lines that meet. Those are intersecting lines. Then there are lines that meet at right angles. I think those are perpendicular lines. I used to get parallel and perpendicular all mixed up, but I discovered something. If you look at the word parallel, there is a pair of *parallel* lines in the word *parallel*. **T:** Picture 1 shows what type of lines? **Patti:** Those are perpendicular lines. Picture 2 and picture 3 are parallel lines. Picture 4 shows intersecting lines.	**T:** *It was clear from the brief conversation and Patti's written explanation that Patti not only understood the concept being tested but knew much more about pairs of lines.*

Informed Instructional Suggestions

Patti would benefit from the same activities as Brent and Rocky. Also, Patti could share her tip about how train tracks are a real-life example of parallel lines.

Student Work Sample: Jason

Name _____ Date _____

Which two pairs of lines are parallel?

    1   **2**   **3**   **4**

A.   1 and 4

B.   2 and 4

C.   2 and 3

D.   1 and 3

Explain your thinking.

Because parallel means straight and 2,3 are straight.

A Conversation with Jason	Teacher Insights
T: Please share with me what you know about lines. **Jason:** Like I said on my paper, I know that parallel lines are straight. **T:** Are the lines in all of the pictures straight? **Jason:** Yes, but some of them meet. Parallel lines are straight and they never meet. When I said parallel lines were straight, I meant that they don't cross each other. They stay the same amount of space apart. **T:** I see. Your explanation helps me understand your thinking. What is the name for lines that cross? **Jason:** I forget. I just know parallel. I like to parallel ski, and that means I have to keep my skis straight and not let them cross.	**T:** *Jason's last comment gave me important insight into his written explanation. He most likely wrote it based on his experience with skiing. Jason does understand parallel, but he needs additional experiences to help him learn the vocabulary of* intersecting lines *and* perpendicular lines.

Informed Instructional Suggestions

Jason's correct multiple-choice answer accurately indicated that he knew about parallel lines, but the brief discussion gave a more complete picture, revealing that he needs to learn about intersecting and perpendicular lines. This learning could be linked to his interest in skiing. For example, when his skis cross, they are intersecting. If they intersect at right angles, then they are perpendicular, and he is in trouble!

Student Work Sample: Tony

Name _____ Date _____

Which two pairs of lines are parallel?

     1   **2**   **3**   **4**

A.   1 and 4

B.   2 and 4

C.   2 and 3

D.   1 and 3

Explain your thinking.

I think it is 2 and 3 because I mesured them and 2 were both 2cm. and 3 were both 2cm.

A Conversation with Tony	Teacher Insights
T: Please tell me more about what you think makes lines parallel. **Tony:** Lines are parallel if they are the same length. I used my ruler and I measured the lines in pictures 2 and 3. They were all 2 centimeters so they are parallel. **T:** Did you also measure the lines in pictures 1 and 4? **Tony:** No. They didn't look like they would be the same length. In picture 1 the line going up and down looks shorter and in picture 4 they look different too. **T:** When two things are exactly the same size and shape, we say that they are *congruent*. I think maybe you might have gotten *congruent* and *parallel* confused. **Tony:** Oh! So then parallel doesn't mean that they are the same length. I think I don't know what *parallel* is. **T:** What else do you know about lines? **Tony:** Not very much. **T:** Parallel lines are lines that never meet. **Tony:** Oh, that's right. Parallel lines are like the yardage lines on football fields. They never meet. They are always exactly 5 yards apart. The top and bottom of my paper are parallel. They'll never meet. I get it!	**T:** *Tony marked the correct answer but had no understanding of parallel lines. He confused congruent and parallel. After I provided a brief explanation, he was able to give an example of parallel lines in the real world.*

Informed Instructional Suggestions

After asking Tony a few questions and listening carefully to his responses, it was easy to quickly guide him to an understanding of parallel lines and establish that he didn't have much knowledge of lines in general. Tony's correct answer alone would have covered up his true needs, and, had it been the only indicator of his knowledge, important opportunities for learning would have been lost. Tony needs more experiences to build his conceptual understanding of lines. Because Tony immediately made the connection between parallel lines and yardage lines on a football field, finding examples of other types of lines in real life would be a beneficial and interesting activity for Tony.

Student Work Sample: Boz

Name _____ Date _____

Which two pairs of lines are parallel?

1   2   3   4

A. 1 and 4

B. 2 and 4

C. 2 and 3

D. 1 and 3

Explain your thinking.

parallel lines must in a million years cross if the lines continus.

A Conversation with Boz	Teacher Insights
T: Boz, please tell me what it is that you think makes lines parallel. **Boz:** I know that they never meet. But I don't know if I believe that. It seems like they must meet in a million years, don't you think? One of the lines has got to bend just a little so that after a million years, they'd touch. A million years is before people as we know them existed on Earth. In a million years, the lines have got to meet. **T:** Your thinking is very interesting to me, Boz. You are correct. The definition of parallel lines says that they never meet. Once they meet they are no longer considered to be parallel lines. Do you know the names of lines that meet? **Boz:** Yes, they are intersecting lines. They touch or cross each other. There are perpendicular lines too. They meet at right angles. **T:** Where are the intersecting and perpendicular lines on the paper? **Boz:** Picture 1 is probably perpendicular because the angles look like right angles, pictures 2 and 3 are parallel, and picture 4 is intersecting. Also on the paper, the top and bottom are parallel and the left side of the paper and the bottom are perpendicular. I still think that in a million years the lines will cross, especially if they start out close to each other.	**T:** *Boz is skeptical about the existence of parallel lines. His thinking is creative, probing, and interesting. He was able to explain his understanding of parallel, perpendicular, and intersecting lines.*

Informed Instructional Suggestions

Boz is ready for the same types of instructional activities as Brent and Rocky. Perhaps he could devise a way to investigate his theory about parallel lines further. Giving him the opportunity to explore his hypothesis would place value on his ideas and willingness to think deeply.

Student Work Sample: Scott

Name _____ Date _____

Which two pairs of lines are parallel?

1   2   3   4

A.   1 and 4
B.   2 and 4
C.   2 and 3
D.   1 and 3

Explain your thinking.

I think tht is 2 and 4 because there both the same.

A Conversation with Scott	Teacher Insights
T: Please tell me about how you thought about this problem. **Scott:** I don't know my lines. The lines in picture 2 and the lines in picture 4 look like they are the same lines, just turned. That's why I wrote that they were the same.	**T:** *Scott is confused. He made his best attempt, but his explanations revealed that he doesn't know about different types of lines.*

Informed Instructional Suggestions

Scott needs a variety of learning experiences that will help him develop conceptual understanding of parallel, perpendicular, and intersecting lines. Hands-on activities, drawing lines, and searching for examples of different types of lines are all good ways to help him. He needs opportunities to use the terms both orally and in writing to reinforce his understanding.

Reassessment

1. Use a similar problem at the same level of difficulty.

   Which two pairs of lines are intersecting?

   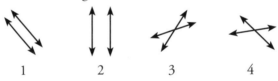

   A. 1 and 2
   B. 3 and 4
   C. 1 and 3
   D. 2 and 4

   Explain your thinking.

2. Choose a problem that is similar but slightly more challenging.

   Which two lines in the quadrilateral below are perpendicular?

   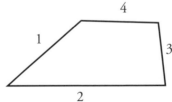

   A. 1 and 2
   B. 2 and 3
   C. 1 and 4
   D. 2 and 4

   Explain your thinking.

Date

Probability

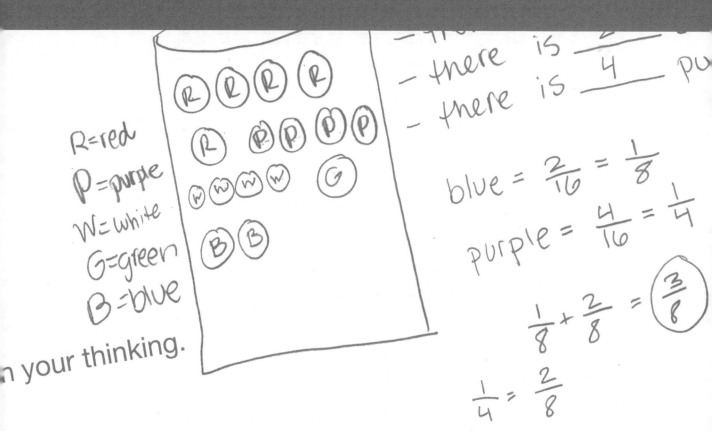

R=red
P=purple
W=white
G=green
B=blue

n your thinking.

- there is ___ ___
- there is __4__ pu

blue = $\frac{2}{16}$ = $\frac{1}{8}$

purple = $\frac{4}{16}$ = $\frac{1}{4}$

$\frac{1}{8}$ + $\frac{2}{8}$ = $\boxed{\frac{3}{8}}$

$\frac{1}{4}$ = $\frac{2}{8}$

PROBLEM ONE

Overview

This question asks students to use their skills at reading pictographs. Each symbol represents five objects rather than one. Also, students must find the difference between two amounts shown on the graph.

Sample Problem

This graph shows the number of cans collected during a food drive. Use the graph to answer the following question.

Cans Collected During Food Drive

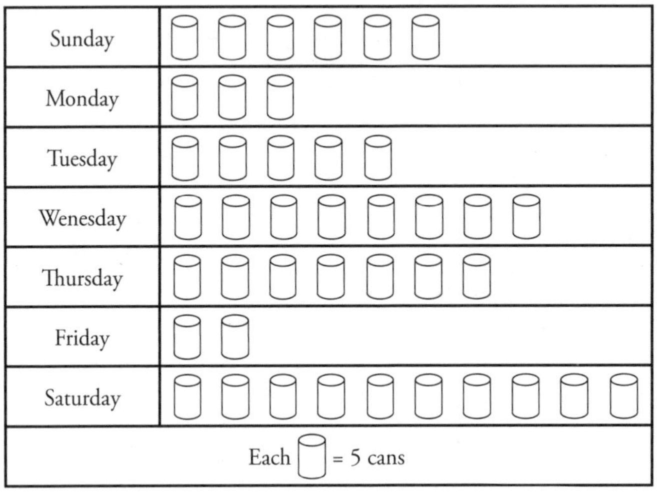

Sunday	⬚ ⬚ ⬚ ⬚ ⬚ ⬚
Monday	⬚ ⬚ ⬚
Tuesday	⬚ ⬚ ⬚ ⬚
Wenesday	⬚ ⬚ ⬚ ⬚ ⬚ ⬚ ⬚ ⬚
Thursday	⬚ ⬚ ⬚ ⬚ ⬚ ⬚ ⬚
Friday	⬚ ⬚
Saturday	⬚ ⬚ ⬚ ⬚ ⬚ ⬚ ⬚ ⬚ ⬚ ⬚

Each ⬚ = 5 cans

What is the difference between the number of food cans collected on Monday and the number of food cans collected on Wednesday?

A. 45 cans
B. 25 cans
C. 5 cans
D. 20 cans

Explain your thinking.

Possible Student Solution Strategies

o   Students correctly find the solution using a variety of strategies, including multiplication, repeated addition, and subtraction.
o   Students use an incorrect solution strategy such as finding the sum rather than the difference when comparing the number of cans collected on two days.
o   Students fail to recognize that each pictured can on the graph represents five cans of collected food.

Conversation Starters

o What do you know about this problem? What do you need to find out?
o How did you reach your answer?
o Does your strategy always work? How do you know?
o What did you do to check your answer?

Student Work Sample: Kitty

Name _____ Date _____

This graph shows the number of cans collected during a food drive.
Use the graph to answer the following question.

Cans Collected During Food Drive

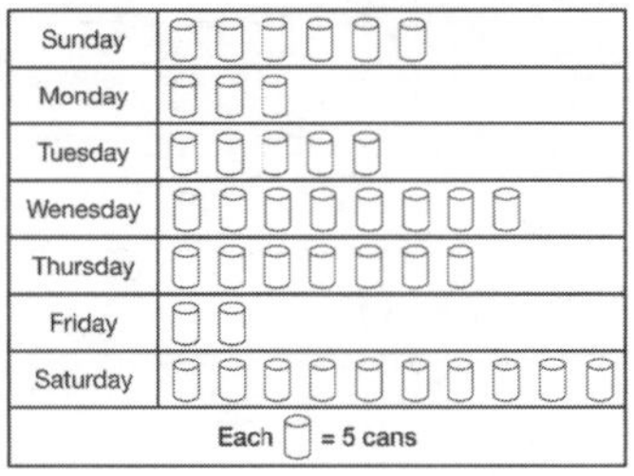

Sunday		
Monday		
Tuesday		
Wenesday		
Thursday		
Friday		
Saturday		

Each = 5 cans

Handwritten: Monday = 15 cans
Wednesday = 40 cans

$$\begin{array}{r} 3^{10} \\ \cancel{40} \\ -15 \\ \hline 25 \end{array}$$

What is the difference between the number of food cans collected on
Monday and the number of food cans collected on Wednesday?

A. 45 cans

B. 25 cans *(circled)*

C. 5 cans

D. 20 cans

Explain your thinking.

Handwritten: What I do is read the question it says what is the difference... the key word is difference, wich means subtract. There are 15 cans for Monday and 40 cans for Wednesday so I subtract 15 from 40. The answer is 25.

A Conversation with Kitty	Teacher Insights
T: Please tell me about your strategy. **Kitty:** First, I read the question. There is an important word in the problem that tells me what to do. The important word is *difference*. I know I have to subtract something. There are fifteen cans on Monday because there are three cans in the picture and each can means five cans. Three times five equals fifteen. There are forty cans on Wednesday because there are eight cans shown, so eight times five is forty. I subtracted fifteen from forty, which is twenty-five. That's my answer. **T:** Does your clearly explained strategy always work for problems likes this? **Kitty:** So far it has. The only time it wouldn't work is if we didn't have to compare but had to do something else and that's a really different problem.	**T:** *Kitty has developed a clear and efficient strategy for solving problems such as this one. She applied multiplication and subtraction skills where appropriate and was able to identify situations when her strategy wouldn't work.*

Informed Instructional Suggestions

Kitty is ready to investigate and consider more complex problems similar to this. She would also benefit from opportunities to create and share problems such as this one. Creating questions that could be answered using the information on this graph and others like it would also be a worthwhile challenge for Kitty.

Student Work Sample: Suri

Name _____ Date _____

This graph shows the number of cans collected during a food drive. Use the graph to answer the following question.

Cans Collected During Food Drive

Sunday	🥫🥫🥫🥫🥫
Monday	🥫🥫🥫
Tuesday	🥫🥫🥫🥫
Wenesday	🥫🥫🥫🥫🥫🥫🥫🥫
Thursday	🥫🥫🥫🥫🥫🥫🥫
Friday	🥫🥫
Saturday	🥫🥫🥫🥫🥫🥫🥫🥫🥫🥫

Each 🥫 = 5 cans

What is the difference between the number of food cans collected on Monday and the number of food cans collected on Wednesday?

A. 45 cans   Note: ☐=5 cans

Ⓑ 25 cans   Monday = ☐☐☐   3×5=15

C. 5 cans   Wednesday=☐☐☐☐☐☐☐☐ 8×5=40

D. 20 cans

Explain your thinking.   40
                           -15
                           25 cans

A Conversation with Suri	Teacher Insights
T: Please tell me what you know about this problem and what you need to find out. **Suri:** I know that each can represents five cans. So all I had to do is to multiply the number of cans pictured by five and I would know how many cans were collected each day. Then I had to subtract Monday from Wednesday to find out how many more cans were collected on Wednesday than Monday. Twenty-five more cans were collected on Wednesday than Monday.	**T:** *Suri successfully applied skills of multiplication, subtraction, and graph interpretation to solve this problem. Her written and verbal explanations were clear.*

Informed Instructional Suggestions

Suri would benefit from the same activities as Kitty. Providing both students with the opportunity to discuss their ideas would strengthen and enhance their learning.

Student Work Sample: Ellen

Name _____ Date _____

This graph shows the number of cans collected during a food drive. Use the graph to answer the following question.

Cans Collected During Food Drive

Sunday	🥫🥫🥫🥫🥫🥫	30
Monday	🥫🥫🥫	15
Tuesday	🥫🥫🥫🥫🥫	25
Wenesday	🥫🥫🥫🥫🥫🥫🥫🥫	40
Thursday	🥫🥫🥫🥫🥫🥫🥫	35
Friday	🥫🥫	10
Saturday	🥫🥫🥫🥫🥫🥫🥫🥫🥫🥫	50

Each 🥫 = 5 cans

$$\begin{array}{r}15\\-40\\\hline \boxed{35}\end{array}$$

What is the difference between the number of food cans collected on Monday and the number of food cans collected on Wednesday?

A.   45 cans

B.   25 cans

C.   5 cans

D.   20 cans

Explain your thinking.

15 — mon.
+40 — wed.

$$\begin{array}{r}15\\+25\\\hline 40\end{array}$$

A Conversation with Ellen	Teacher Insights
T: Please tell me how you reached your answer. **Ellen:** First I saw that each can means five cans. So I counted the cans for each day by five and wrote that down. Then I added Monday and Wednesday because the problem asks about them and I got fifty-five. It wasn't a choice, so I crossed it out. Then I subtracted fifteen minus forty, and that's thirty-five. That choice isn't there either. Finally I looked again and saw that if I put Monday and Tuesday together, it would be about the same as Wednesday. Tuesday has twenty-five cans, and that's an answer choice, so I chose it. Am I right?	**T:** *Ellen showed several areas of concern in both her written and verbal explanations. She added Monday and Wednesday to find a combined total when the problem was asking her to compare the cans collected on those two days. When she did subtract, she did not regroup correctly and found an incorrect answer. In both of these cases, she used the answer choices to determine that her thinking was incorrect. There was little evidence of understanding thus far. Finally, Ellen noticed that the cans collected on Monday and Tuesday were equivalent to the cans collected on Wednesday and used this information to find her answer. After her verbal explanation, she indicated doubt when she asked, "Am I right?" I decided to have Ellen reread the problem aloud to establish what Ellen understood about the problem and obtain better guidance for how to help her.*
T: Please reread the problem aloud, and as you do this, think about how to explain the problem in your own words. **Ellen:** [Reads the problem aloud.] I know I need to find the difference between Monday and Wednesday, and I did that right here [pointing to her subtraction problem]. But that answer isn't there. So I don't get it!	**T:** *Ellen stated that she did not understand. She didn't understand due to her error in regrouping, which generated an answer that was not an answer choice.*

Informed Instructional Suggestions

Ellen's correct answer alone would not have revealed some basic misunderstandings that must be dealt with. Ellen's comprehension of the problem was fragile and she was unable to subtract correctly. She needs additional experiences with story problems that involve subtraction so that she can more easily recognize these situations. She misapplied the standard subtraction algorithm. Ellen needs strategies to use for subtraction. An open number line would be beneficial. It would also be helpful to encourage her to use her number sense to recognize that her answer of thirty-five made no sense within the context of this problem.

Student Work Sample: Jasmine

Name _____ Date _____

This graph shows the number of cans collected during a food drive. Use the graph to answer the following question.

Cans Collected During Food Drive

Sunday	🥫🥫🥫🥫🥫
Monday	🥫🥫🥫
Tuesday	🥫🥫🥫🥫
Wenesday	🥫🥫🥫🥫🥫🥫🥫🥫
Thursday	🥫🥫🥫🥫🥫🥫
Friday	🥫🥫
Saturday	🥫🥫🥫🥫🥫🥫🥫🥫🥫🥫

Each 🥫 = 5 cans

What is the difference between the number of food cans collected on Monday and the number of food cans collected on Wednesday?

A. 45 cans

B. 25 cans

C. 5 cans

D. 20 cans

Explain your thinking.

8 = Wednesday
3 = Monday

$$-\frac{\begin{array}{r}8\,cans\\3\,cans\end{array}}{5\,cans}$$

A Conversation with Jasmine	Teacher Insights
T: Please tell me about your thinking and what you did to check your answer.	**T:** *Jasmine knows how to solve a problem like this. She did not see and consider the fact that each can represented five cans in her initial attempt to solve this problem. Once she recognized this, she immediately found the correct answer.*
Jasmine: Well, it was an easy problem. There are three cans for Monday and eight cans for Wednesday, so eight minus three is five. Easy! I checked it by counting the cans twice, and eight minus five is a basic fact.	
T: Check the graph again to see if there is something on it that tells you what each can represents.	
Jasmine: Ohh! I didn't see that picture that says each can represents 5 cans. I missed it. And it was an easy problem too. All I have to do is multiply the difference of 5 by 5, because each of those 5 cans is really equal to 5 cans, so 5 times 5 is 25 cans.	

Informed Instructional Suggestions

Jasmine's incorrect multiple-choice response would have implied that she needed intervention. In fact, Jasmine had a clear command of how to solve this problem correctly and was immediately able to do so once she realized her error. Jasmine is ready for the same next steps we recommended for Kitty. It would also be helpful to offer her practice with reading graphs and paying attention to all the information in them.

Student Work Sample: Annie

Name _____ Date _____

This graph shows the number of cans collected during a food drive. Use the graph to answer the following question.

Cans Collected During Food Drive

Each ☐ = 5 cans

What is the difference between the number of food cans collected on Monday and the number of food cans collected on Wednesday?

(A.) 45 cans

B. 25 cans

C. 5 cans

D. 20 cans

Explain your thinking.

I picked 45 is because I counted by 5 and together it was 45 cause 45 was the close to 55 thats why I picked 45 cans.

A Conversation with Annie	Teacher Insights
T: Please tell me about your solution.	**T:** *Annie was initially confused by what the problem was asking her to do. Once that was clarified, she had difficulty with subtraction.*
Annie: I know that each can is worth five. I counted the cans on Monday and that's fifteen. I counted the cans on Wednesday and that's forty. Forty plus fifteen is fifty-five. But that wasn't a choice, but forty-five was there and that's close. I picked it. I'm done.	
T: What is this problem asking you to find out?	
Annie: How many cans were collected altogether on Monday and Wednesday.	
T: Please reread the problem and show me where it tells you that.	
Annie: Ohh! I think maybe I should have subtracted because it says to find the difference. Oopsie! Forty minus fifteen is thirty-five. Hmm . . . that's not a choice either. I don't get this.	

Informed Instructional Suggestions

Annie needs more experience with this type of problem in addition to needing instruction in subtraction. Her needs in subtraction are similar to those of Ellen, and she would benefit from the same activities and experiences. Annie would also benefit from more situations involving mental subtraction.

Reassessment

1. Use a similar problem at the same level of difficulty.

   This graph shows the number of cans collected during a food drive. Use the graph to answer the following question.

Cans Collected During Food Drive

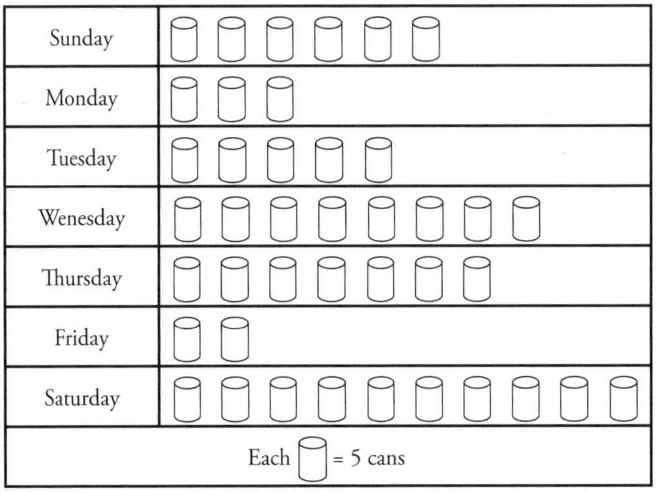

What is the difference between the number of food cans collected on Tuesday and the number of cans collected on Saturday?

A. 75 cans
B. 35 cans
C. 25 cans
D. 5 cans

Explain your thinking.

2. Choose a problem that is similar but slightly more challenging.

This graph shows the number of cans collected during a food drive. Use the graph to answer the following question.

Cans Collected During Food Drive

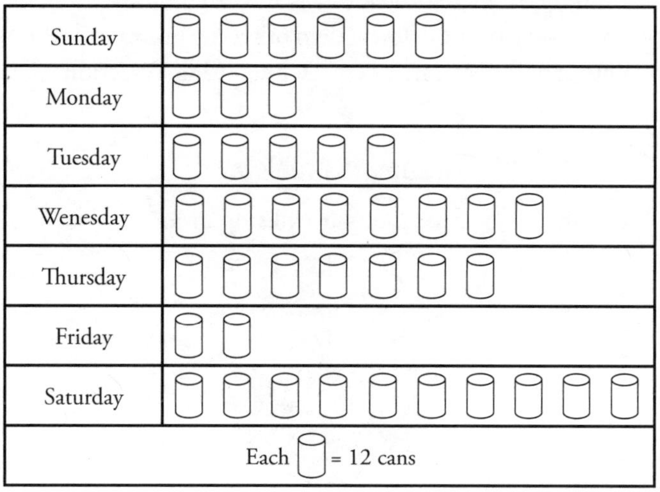

Sunday	
Monday	
Tuesday	
Wenesday	
Thursday	
Friday	
Saturday	

Each [can] = 12 cans

What is the difference between the number of food cans collected on Monday and the number of food cans collected on Saturday?

A. 7 cans
B. 84 cans
C. 116 cans
D. 156 cans

Explain your thinking.

P R O B L E M   T W O

Overview

This problem asks students to apply their probability knowledge to answer a question about a spinner. Understanding that some events may be more likely than others is important. Also, students must recognize that outcomes in a probability experiment can be represented using a fraction.

Sample Problem

If you spin the spinner once, what is the probability it will stop on A?

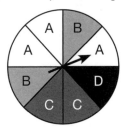

A. $\frac{1}{8}$

B. $\frac{2}{6}$

C. $\frac{1}{6}$

D. $\frac{3}{8}$

Explain your thinking.

Possible Student Solution Strategies

o   Students successfully apply their understanding of chance and fractions to correctly solve the problem.

o   Students misinterpret the problem, which may or may not lead to a correct response.

o   Students fail to consider the context of the problem and focus only on the location of the spinner pointer.

Conversation Starters

o   Put the problem into your own words.

o   Why does your solution (or answer) make sense?

o   How did you think about this problem?

o   How could you explain your thinking to a younger student?

Student Work Sample: Josiah

Name _____ Date _____

If you spin the spinner once, what is the probability it will stop on A?

A. $\frac{1}{8}$

B. $\frac{2}{6}$

C. $\frac{1}{6}$

(D) $\frac{3}{8}$

Explain your thinking.

I counted how many sections there were: 8. That becomes the denominator. Then I counted how many A's there were in all: 3. That becomes the numerator. The probability to have the arrow stop on a is a $\frac{3}{8}$ chance.

A Conversation with Josiah	Teacher Insights
T: How could you explain your thinking to a younger student? **Josiah:** I would tell him that you have to know how many things are possible. There are eight sections on the spinner, so there are eight places where the spinner could land. Then you have to figure out how many As there are because the question is asking about As. There are three, so you would write that as three out of eight. The top number, called the numerator, tells how many As there are on the spinner, and the bottom number, the denominator, tells how many sections altogether.	**T:** *Josiah's written and verbal explanations showed clarity and understanding.*

Informed Instructional Suggestions

Josiah is ready for more complex challenges involving spinners. One good activity for Josiah would be to design a spinner and a game to go along with it. This would tap into his skills, perhaps even stretching them, and allow him to use mathematics in a creative endeavor.

Student Work Sample: Suri

Name _____ Date _____

If you spin the spinner once, what is the probability it will stop on A?

A. $\frac{1}{8}$ There are 3 As, 2 Bs, 2Cs, and 1 D.
B. $\frac{2}{6}$ The probability it will stop on A is:

C. $\frac{1}{6}$

(D.) $\frac{3}{8}$ There are eight sections. Three are A. So.... $\frac{3}{8}$

Explain your thinking.

A Conversation with Suri	Teacher Insights
T: Why does your solution make sense?	**T:** *Like Josiah, Suri had clear understanding of the skills needed to correctly solve this problem.*
Suri: Well, I chose the answer of three-eighths, which in probability means three out of eight. I did that because the question wants to know the probability of spinning the letter A. There are three sections with A on the spinner and there are eight sections in all. So there are three ways to get an A out of eight possibilities. That's my thinking.	
T: What is another question that could be answered by this spinner?	
Suri: What is the probability of getting B, C, or D?	
T: What do you think the answer is to your question?	
Suri: It would be five-eighths because there are two Bs, two Cs, and one D. Two plus two plus one is five. The other three sections are As.	

Informed Instructional Suggestions

Josiah and Suri have similar needs and could work well together or independently, depending on their interests.

Student Work Sample: Annie

Name _____ Date _____

If you spin the spinner once, what is the probability it will stop on A?

A. $\dfrac{1}{8}$

B. $\dfrac{2}{6}$

C. $\dfrac{1}{6}$

D. $\dfrac{3}{8}$

Explain your thinking.

I was thinke of those three shaded D,C, and C. And I counted all of them and got $\frac{3}{8}$

A Conversation with Annie	Teacher Insights
T: Please tell me how you thought about this problem. **Annie:** Well, I saw the spinner and it had some shaded areas. You always count the shaded areas on the spinner. There were three areas shaded and eight areas altogether, so the answer has to be three-eighths. **T:** Please reread the question aloud. [Annie reads.] Please tell me what you are supposed to find out. **Annie:** It says to count the As, but they're not shaded. You always count the shaded parts. [Annie pauses.] I notice that there are three As and three shaded parts. It's the same answer. That's weird!	**T:** *Annie has some issues that need to be corrected. Textbooks and worksheets do often ask students to focus on shaded parts. This is what Annie did. This misunderstanding coincidentally led to a correct answer although Annie's thinking was incorrect.*

Informed Instructional Suggestions

Annie's multiple-choice response alone would have indicated understanding; however, after reading her written response and listening to her verbal explanation, we realized she needed help. Annie needs opportunities to solve problems with spinners that do not have shaded sections.

Student Work Sample: Cassidy

Name _____ Date _____

If you spin the spinner once, what is the probability it will stop on A?

A. $\frac{1}{8}$

B. $\frac{2}{6}$

C. $\frac{1}{6}$

(D.) $\frac{3}{8}$

Explain your thinking.

It is D because there are 3 A's and there is only one 3.

A Conversation with Cassidy	Teacher Insights
T: Please tell me more about your thinking. **Cassidy:** There are three As on the spinner where the spinner could stop. I know the top number means how many As. Choice D is the only choice that has a 3 on the top, so it is the only one that could be right. **T:** What does the bottom number mean? **Cassidy:** There are eight chances, so the bottom means chances. **T:** Please explain what you mean by "chances." **Cassidy:** Chances means the number of sections where the spinner could stop.	**T:** *Cassidy was using good test sense when she selected her answer. The evidence on her paper indicated only a partial understanding. Her verbal explanation revealed that she understood the skills tested by this question.*

Informed Instructional Suggestions

Cassidy's needs are similar to those of Josiah and Suri. She would benefit from the same experiences as those two students. She should also work on writing more clear, complete explanations.

Student Work Sample: Maya

Name _____ Date _____

If you spin the spinner once, what is the probability it will stop on A?

A. $\frac{1}{8}$

B. $\frac{2}{6}$

C. $\frac{1}{6}$

D. $\frac{3}{8}$

Explain your thinking.

I picked $\frac{1}{8}$ because the pointer landed on A and there are eight pieces.

A Conversation with Maya	Teacher Insights
T: Why does your solution make sense to you? **Maya:** The pointer is pointing at A, the question is asking about A, and there are eight sections altogether. So, the answer is one-eighth—one out of eight things could be A. **T:** Please read to me what each of the sections says. **Maya:** D, C, C, B, A, A, B, and A. Hmm . . . there is more than one A, huh? Was I supposed to count the two As where the spinner is not pointing? [Maya pauses as she thinks about this. I wait for her quietly.] Oh, I think maybe I should have counted all three As because the question really said the probability it will stop on A and there are three ways it could stop on A. Maybe choice D is a better answer.	**T:** *Maya has an emerging understanding that would not have been revealed by her multiple-choice response alone. Her confusion was in part the result of how the spinner was drawn. She considered only where it was pointing and did not consider any of the other sections.*

Informed Instructional Suggestions

Maya needs additional spinner experiences that will help her consider all possibilities and outcomes. Then she will be ready for activities such as those we suggested for Josiah.

Reassessment

1. Use a similar problem at the same level of difficulty.

    If you spin the spinner once, what is the probability it will land on B?

    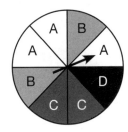

    A. $\frac{3}{8}$

    B. $\frac{2}{6}$

    C. $\frac{2}{8}$

    D. $\frac{1}{8}$

    Explain your thinking.

2. Choose a problem that is similar but slightly more challenging.

    If you spin the spinner three times, what is the probability it will land on D?

    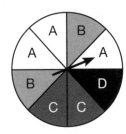

    A. $\frac{3}{8}$

    B. $\frac{1}{6}$

    C. $\frac{1}{8}$

    D. $\frac{3}{5}$

    Explain your thinking.

PROBLEM THREE

Overview

This question involves ideas of central tendency. Range, median, mean, and mode fall into this category of ideas about statistics. Students are asked to identify the mode of a list of distances that a family rode on their bikes each day.

Sample Problem

During a vacation, Blaise's family went on a bike trip. These are the number of miles that his family biked each day.

26   23   33   25   31   30   23

What is the mode of these miles?

A. 7 miles
B. 23 miles
C. 26 miles
D. 10 miles

Explain your thinking.

Possible Student Solution Strategies

o   Students apply their understanding of mode to correctly solve the problem.
o   Students confuse other measures of central tendency, such as mean, range, or median, with mode.

Conversation Starters

o   What do you know about this problem?
o   How did you reach your answer?
o   Convince me that your idea makes sense.

Student Work Sample: Jasmine

Name _____ Date _____

During a vacation, Blaise's family went on a bike trip. These are the number of miles that his family biked each day.

26   23   33   25   31   30   23

What is the mode of these miles?

A.   7 miles

(B.) 23 miles

C.   26 miles

D.   10 miles

Explain your thinking.

23, 23, 25, 26, 30, 31, 33

First, I put the numbers from least to greatest. Then I noticed that 23 showed up twice. No other number showed up twice besides 23. So 23 is the answer.

A Conversation with Jasmine	Teacher Insights
T: Please convince me that your idea makes sense. **Jasmine:** Mode means the thing that happens the most times. So I know I have to find the thing that happens the most times. I put the numbers in order from least to greatest. The number 23 happened twice, which is more than any of the other numbers, so 23 is the mode.	**T:** *Jasmine used an effective strategy to help her solve this problem. She reorganized the numbers and was able to determine which one occurred the most frequently. Jasmine clearly understood the definition of mode.*

Informed Instructional Suggestions

Jasmine is ready to move on to new areas of statistics. She is also capable of stretching her learning and understanding of mode through more complex problems, or she could write and solve her own problems about mode. To give mode context, Jasmine could research real-world events, for example, *What is the most common color (mode) of cars that pass the school in a fifteen-minute period?* or *What snack is most often eaten at recess?*

Student Work Sample: Teddy

Name _____ Date _____

During a vacation, Blaise's family went on a bike trip. These are the number of miles that his family biked each day.

26   23   33   25   31   30   23

What is the mode of these miles?

A.   7 miles

B.   23 miles

C.   26 miles

D.   10 miles

Explain your thinking.

```
       #
    26 |
    23 ||
    33 |
    25 |
    31 |
    30 |
```

A Conversation with Teddy	Teacher Insights
T: Please tell me what you know about this problem. **Teddy:** I have to find the mode on this list of numbers. Mode means the one that happens the most often. I made a chart to help me. Twenty-three has two tallies, the rest have one, so 23 happened the most times. **T:** What if I added two more 26s to the list? What would be the mode then? Would it still be 23? **Teddy:** The mode would be 26 because there would be three of them and only two of the 23s.	*T: Teddy's understanding and application of mode were strong. He was able to demonstrate this both in writing and in his verbal discussion.*

Informed Instructional Suggestions

Teddy and Jasmine have similar needs and could work together on the same instructional activities and investigations.

Student Work Sample: Haily

Name _____ Date _____

During a vacation, Blaise's family went on a bike trip. These are the number of miles that his family biked each day.

26 23 33 25 31 30 23

mode *Median*

What is the mode of these miles?

A. 7 miles

B. 23 miles

C. 26 miles

D. 10 miles

23 23 25 (26) 30 31 33

mode *median* *outlier*

Explain your thinking.

I think it's B. because I put them in order found the median, outlier, and then the mode. Thats how I got my answer

A Conversation with Haily	Teacher Insights
T: I noticed that you used some statistical terms in your explanation. You used the terms *median* and *outlier*. Please tell me more about what you think a median is. **Haily:** A median is the number in the middle. First you have to put the list in order from least to greatest. That's why I rewrote the list. Then you find the middle and that's the median. **T:** Please tell me more about what an outlier is. **Haily:** That's easy. It's the one at the end. That's 33 because it is at the end of the list. Twenty-three happens first, so it's the mode. See? I labeled them all on my paper.	**T:** *Haily was correct about which number represented the median. She misunderstood the meanings of* mode *and* outlier. *The question did not ask Haily for information about the median or outliers, but her writing provided good information to guide instructional decisions. Haily marked the correct answer but applied an incorrect meaning of mode. She believes the* mode *is the first number in a sequential list of numbers rather than an event that occurs most frequently.*

Informed Instructional Suggestions

Haily needs additional experiences using measures of central tendency to develop her understanding of the terms *mode* and *outlier*. A real-world context would make the experiences more powerful and useful. For example, Haily could collect data about the number of times her classmates can jump during one minute and then find the mode.

Student Work Sample: Damon

Name _____ Date _____

During a vacation, Blaise's family went on a bike trip. These are the number of miles that his family biked each day.

26   23   33   25   31   30   23

What is the mode of these miles?

A.   7 miles

B.   23 miles   *My teacher said some tricks and one is Mode and most is the most number that appers the most.*

C.   26 miles

D.   10 miles

Explain your thinking.

26 (23) 33 25 31 30 (23)
Mode!

A Conversation with Damon	Teacher Insights
T: Please convince me that your answer makes sense. I see that you said the mode is the most and is the answer. When I look at the list of numbers, I notice that 33 is the most. Please help me understand your thinking.	**T:** *Damon showed good understanding of the mode when he was challenged to think and explain more clearly.*
Damon: I know that it's not necessarily the highest or largest number. Mode means the one that happens the most often. Twenty-three happened twice and the other numbers happened only once.	
T: Why do you think that *mode* and *most* is a trick?	
Damon: They sound the same, so the mode is the most.	
T: In this case, 33 is the most according to your definition. Can you help me with that?	
Damon: Most can be the greatest, but that's not what mode is. It means the one that happens the most. I guess I should put that in my writing so you know what I mean. Damon quickly revised his work to more clearly show his thinking.	

Informed Instructional Suggestions

Damon understands the concepts involved. He needs to be more precise in his writing and his verbal explanations. The conversation helped Damon see the value of using more specific language. Damon is ready for the same activities as Jasmine and Teddy.

Student Work Sample: Ellen

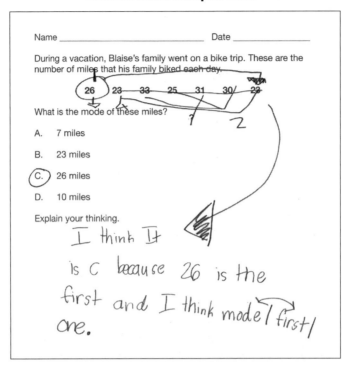

Name _____ Date _____

During a vacation, Blaise's family went on a bike trip. These are the number of miles that his family biked each day.

26   23   33   25   31   30   23

What is the mode of these miles?

A.   7 miles

B.   23 miles

C.   26 miles

D.   10 miles

Explain your thinking.

I think It is C because 26 is the first and I think mode | first| one.

A Conversation with Ellen	Teacher Insights
T: Please tell me about your thinking. **Ellen:** *Mode* means the *first* one. Twenty-six is the first one on the list so the mode must be 26. I showed using an arrow in my writing how I think mode and first are the same thing. Am I right? **T:** I notice you have a 2 and a 1 written underneath the list of numbers. What are those numbers for? **Ellen:** There are two 23s and one of each of the other numbers. So I wrote that.	*T: Ellen has a significant misconception about mode. The mode is not the first number in a list, as Ellen believes. However, her written count of the number of times each of the numbers appeared is a good beginning point upon which to build the conceptual understanding she needs about mode.*

Informed Instructional Suggestions

Ellen and Haily have similar misconceptions and would benefit from the same instructional activities.

Student Work Sample: Lainie

Name _____ Date _____

During a vacation, Blaise's family went on a bike trip. These are the number of miles that his family biked each day.

26   23   33   25   31   30   23

What is the mode of these miles?

A.   7 miles

B.   23 miles

C.   26 miles

(D.)   10 miles

Mode means the highest and the lowest number out of a group of numbers subtrackted.

Explain your thinking.

$$\begin{array}{r} 33 \\ -23 \\ \hline \end{array}$$

23 ____ 10+ ____ 33

A Conversation with Lainie	Teacher Insights
T: How did you reach your answer? **Lainie:** I took the lowest number and the highest number on the list and subtracted them to find the mode. I used a number line to show my subtraction. **T:** You found the correct answer to a different question. You found the range of the numbers. The *range* is exactly what you said: it's the difference between the least and greatest numbers. The mode is the one that occurs the most often. Knowing that, can you find the mode now? **Lainie:** Ohh, I got confused. The mode is 23 because it happens twice and the others only happen once. Darn! **T:** What numbers could we add to the list to change the mode from 23 to another number? **Lainie:** Hmm, that's interesting. If I added three 24s to the list, then 24 would be the mode. I don't think that would change the range either. If I wanted to change the range, I would have to make the smallest number smaller or the largest number larger. That's kind of cool.	**T:** *Lainie's misconception about mode and range was easily and quickly corrected through a brief conversation, as her conjectures at the end of our talk showed.*

Informed Instructional Suggestions

After this discussion, Lainie is ready for the same instruction as Jasmine and Teddy.

Reassessment

1. Use a similar problem at the same level of difficulty.

   During summer vacation, Scott's family drove to many fun tourist spots. These are some of the distances in miles that his family traveled each day.

   $$35 \quad 27 \quad 28 \quad 36 \quad 28 \quad 27 \quad 31 \quad 27$$

   What is the mode of these miles?

   A. 28 miles
   B. 9 miles
   C. 27 miles
   D. 8 miles

   Explain your thinking.

2. Choose a problem that is similar but slightly more challenging.

   In a jumping jack contest, students jumped the following number of jumping jacks in one minute.

   $$36 \quad 29 \quad 34 \quad 28 \quad 29 \quad 36 \quad 34 \quad 29 \quad 35$$

   What is the mode of these numbers of jumping jacks?

   A. 34
   B. 29
   C. 8
   D. 9

   Explain your thinking.

PROBLEM FOUR

Overview

In this problem, students use their understanding of chance to determine the likelihood of events occurring when rolling a cube. Students must also use their knowledge of how to represent the likelihood of outcomes as a fraction.

Sample Problem

The faces of this cube are labeled A, B, B, B, C, and D. What is the probability of rolling a B?

A. $\frac{1}{4}$

B. $\frac{3}{6}$

C. $\frac{1}{3}$

D. $\frac{6}{3}$

Explain your thinking.

Possible Student Solution Strategies

o Students apply their knowledge of probability to correctly figure the likelihood of rolling the letter B.
o Students misapply their knowledge of the likelihood of events.
o Students misapply their knowledge of how to represent outcomes as fractions.

Conversation Starters

o Why does your solution make sense?
o What have you seen before that reminds you of this problem?
o Is there more than one possible correct answer? Explain.
o How did you think about this problem?
o How could you explain your thinking to another student?

Student Work Sample: Kylie

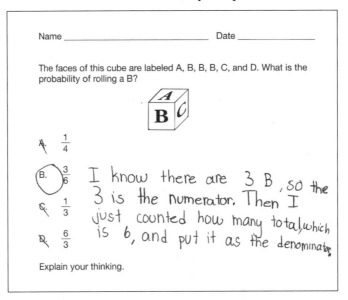

Name _____ Date _____

The faces of this cube are labeled A, B, B, B, C, and D. What is the probability of rolling a B?

A. $\frac{1}{4}$

B. $\frac{3}{6}$ I know there are 3 B, so the 3 is the numerator. Then I just counted how many total, which is 6, and put it as the denominator.

C. $\frac{1}{3}$

D. $\frac{6}{3}$

Explain your thinking.

A Conversation with Kylie	Teacher Insights
T: How did you think about this problem? **Kylie:** Well, there are six faces on a cube and there were six letters that could happen because there would be one letter on each face. Three faces are B out of the six faces. So B is likely to happen three out of six rolls. Three is the numerator because that tells how many ways to get B, and 6 is the denominator because there are six faces that could be rolled. **T:** What have you seen before that reminds you of this problem? **Kylie:** Hmm . . . let me think about that for a minute. It sort of reminds me of that spinner experiment we did only instead of faces on a cube, we were looking at sections on a spinner. **T:** Suppose the spinner had six sections labeled A, B, B, B, C, and D, and the cube's faces were labeled A, B, B, B, C, and D. Do you think the data would be similar or different? **Kylie:** I am not too sure. Maybe the same.	**T:** *Kylie had a strong understanding of the question and underlying mathematics. She was also able to make a connection between probability activities—the cube and the spinner. However, she was uncertain whether the cube and the spinner would generate similar results if the likelihood of events was the same on each.*

Informed Instructional Suggestions

Kylie is ready to explore other ideas such as the one from our discussion. She needs to participate in probability experiments to discover for herself that the answer to the question posed to her is yes, a spinner and a cube with the outcomes distributed in the same way should generate similar results. One way to do this is to spin a spinner with six equal sections numbered 1 to 6, and record the data for several spins. Repeat this process using a number cube. Then compare the results to determine whether they are similar. Kylie can continue to do this over several days to see the effect of sample size on expected outcomes.

Student Work Sample: Yolanda

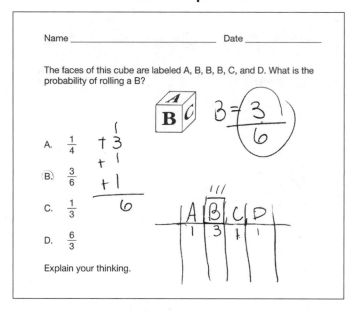

Name _____ Date _____

The faces of this cube are labeled A, B, B, B, C, and D. What is the probability of rolling a B?

A. $\frac{1}{4}$

B. $\frac{3}{6}$

C. $\frac{1}{3}$

D. $\frac{6}{3}$

Explain your thinking.

A Conversation with Yolanda	Teacher Insights
T: Please explain why your solution makes sense. **Yolanda:** I made a chart. I wrote on the chart the letters that were on the cube and how many times each letter was on the cube. There is one letter A, three letter Bs, one letter C, and one letter D. That's six letters total, which is the same number of faces on the cube. The question asked me what was the probability of rolling a B. There are three Bs out of six, so the probability is three out of six. It's likely I'll roll a B, but not for positive! **T:** Do you think that there is more than one possible correct answer? **Yolanda:** Yep, I think another correct answer is one-half. There are three ways to roll a B out of six ways; three is half of six, so one-half is another correct answer. In fractions one-half and three-sixths are equivalent—that means the same amount. **T:** What is the likelihood of not rolling a B? **Yolanda:** That would be three-sixths or one-half too because there are three out of six ways not to roll a B.	**T:** *Yolanda has a firm understanding of the skills addressed by this question.*

Informed Instructional Suggestions

Like Kylie, Yolanda showed strong understanding and the ability to stretch her thinking. Yolanda and Kylie have similar needs and Yolanda would benefit from the same activities as Kylie.

Student Work Sample: Steve

Name _____ Date _____

The faces of this cube are labeled A, B, B, B, C, and D. What is the probability of rolling a B?

A. $\frac{1}{4}$

B. $\frac{3}{6}$

C. $\frac{1}{3}$

D. $\frac{6}{3}$

Explain your thinking.

I picked the fraction that was closest to $\frac{1}{2}$ then I compared it to the dice

A Conversation with Steve	Teacher Insights
T: Please tell me why your solution makes sense.	*T: Steve's written explanation did not clearly indicate his level of understanding. During the brief conversation, however, his knowledge became apparent.*
Steve: There are six faces on the cube. Three of them are the letter B. That's one-half. One-half was not a choice, but one-half is the same as three-sixths, and that was a choice, so that's the one I picked.	
T: How could you explain your idea about this problem to another student?	
Steve: I think I would draw a picture of all six faces of the cube and label them. That would be six boxes labeled A, B, B, B, C, and D. Then I'd cut the boxes apart so I had six. I would put all the Bs together in one group, then I'd put the As, Cs, and Ds together in one group. The two groups would be equal, and that's a way to show halves.	
T: Thanks for sharing. That is a nice way to explain your thinking.	

Informed Instructional Suggestions

The instructional activities that would benefit Kylie and Yolanda would also be appropriate for Steve. He should also work on writing more detailed, clear explanations.

Student Work Sample: Eddie

Name _____ Date _____

The faces of this cube are labeled A, B, B, B, C, and D. What is the probability of rolling a B?

A. $\frac{1}{4}$

(B.) $\frac{3}{6}$

C. $\frac{1}{3}$

D. $\frac{6}{3}$

Explain your thinking.

BBB   ACD

V   V

3   3

$\frac{3}{6}$

$\frac{1}{3}$

A Conversation with Eddie	Teacher Insights
T: Eddie, please explain how you thought about this problem. **Eddie:** First I wrote the letters and how many times they happened. There were three letter Bs, one A, one C, and one D. That's three too. So I added three plus three and that's six, so I put 6 on the bottom. Then I put 3 on the top because both groups had three. There are three Bs, so the chance of getting a B is one out of three. Oh, I made a mistake. I should have circled one-third instead of three-sixths. Can I change my answer?	**T:** *Eddie marked the correct answer, but his explanations revealed uncertainty and confusion.*

Informed Instructional Suggestions

Eddie needs the opportunity to interact with ideas of probability, specifically, considering outcomes and their likelihood. Steve has a higher level of understanding, and asking Steve to share his thinking with Eddie would deepen Steve's comprehension while giving Eddie access to new ideas. Eddie also needs to conduct probability experiments and record the data correctly. Finally, Eddie would benefit from additional opportunities to label chance using fractional notation.

Student Work Sample: Amy

Name _____ Date _____

The faces of this cube are labeled A, B, B, B, C, and D. What is the probability of rolling a B?

A. $\frac{1}{4}$

Ⓑ $\frac{3}{6} = \frac{1}{2}$

C. $\frac{1}{3}$

D. $\frac{6}{3}$

Explain your thinking.

Total Sides: $\frac{6}{3} = \frac{2}{1} = \frac{1}{2}$
B cubes: 3

A Conversation with Amy	Teacher Insights
T: Please tell me about your thinking. **Amy:** There are six sides on the cube so I wrote that down. There are three B sides. I wrote that down and got the fraction six-thirds, which is equal to two ones, which equals one-half. I know because I can just flip the numbers. I did that because I also know that three-sixths equals one-half and so I have to make two ones equal one-half. **T:** I see that choice D is six-thirds, just like you wrote. Why didn't you choose that one? **Amy:** Well, aren't they the same? Isn't three-sixths the same as six-thirds?	**T:** Amy showed a lack of conceptual understanding of fractions and what each of the numbers in a fraction represents. Although this was a probability question, her difficulties with fractions were interfering with her ability to clearly communicate her understanding about probability in a meaningful way. She did understand that there were six faces on the cube and thus there were six possible outcomes. She also indicated understanding that the letter B could be rolled three ways because there were three Bs on the cube.

Informed Instructional Suggestions

Amy did select the right answer, but for reasons that made little sense. Amy needs basic conceptual development with fractions and what the numerator and denominator represent. Once she has developed this understanding, she needs experiences to help her clearly connect how fractions can be used to represent probability outcomes.

Student Work Sample: Nina

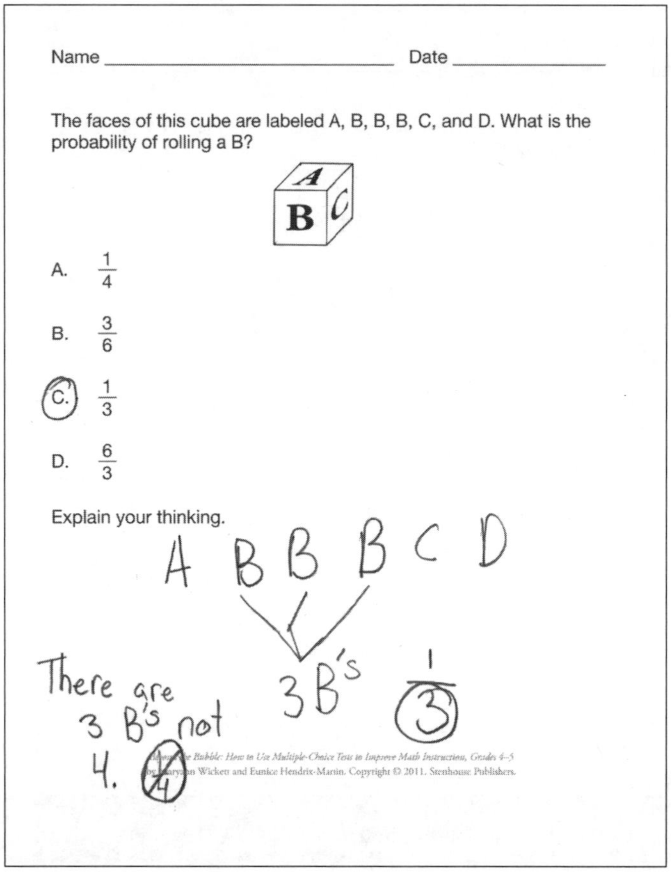

Name _____ Date _____

The faces of this cube are labeled A, B, B, B, C, and D. What is the probability of rolling a B?

A. $\frac{1}{4}$

B. $\frac{3}{6}$

C. $\frac{1}{3}$ (circled)

D. $\frac{6}{3}$

Explain your thinking.

A B B B C D

There are 3 B's not 4. ④   3 B's $\frac{1}{3}$ (circled)

A Conversation with Nina	Teacher Insights
T: How did you think about this problem? **Nina:** I noticed that there were three letter Bs. So when I roll the cube I could get a B one out of three times. That's one-third. I didn't choose one-fourth because there are only three Bs, not four. If there had been four Bs, then the answer would be one-fourth.	**T:** *Nina's understanding at this point was somewhat misguided. She was looking only at rolling the letter B rather than at all possible outcomes of this particular cube. She was correct that the fact that there were three Bs was important, but she needed to consider this information within the context of all possible outcomes.*

Informed Instructional Suggestions

Nina needs to engage in generating and collecting data with guidance about appropriate ways to represent the outcomes.

Student Work Sample: Amalia

Name _____ Date _____

The faces of this cube are labeled A, B, B, B, C, and D. What is the probability of rolling a B?

A. $\frac{1}{4}$ *(circled)*

B. $\frac{3}{6}$

C. $\frac{1}{3}$

D. $\frac{6}{3}$

Explain your thinking. → if you roll the cube that had A B BBCD on it you probly will get B it would be a ¼ chance to get B.

A Conversation with Amalia	Teacher Insights
T: Please tell me why your solution makes sense.	**T:** *Amalia's understanding is emerging, as indicated by her observation that perhaps more Bs would increases the likelihood of rolling a B.*
Amalia: There are four letters: A, B, C, and D. If I roll the cube there is a one-in-four chance of getting a B because B is one of the four letters.	
T: Do all of the letters appear on the cube the same number of times?	
Amalia: No, there are three Bs, one A, one C, and one D. I didn't think about that before. Maybe you would get B more because there are more Bs, but I don't know for sure.	

Informed Instructional Suggestions

Amalia needs concrete experiences to help her solidify her beginning understanding. She needs to roll dice, spin spinners, and draw tiles from a bag and record all the data as she does so. This will further develop her comprehension of outcomes, their predictability, and why predictions can be made.

Reassessment

1. Use a similar problem at the same level of difficulty.

   The faces of this cube are labeled A, B, B, B, C, and D. What is the probability of rolling a D?

   A. $\frac{3}{6}$

   B. $\frac{1}{4}$

   C. $\frac{2}{4}$

   D. $\frac{1}{6}$

   Explain your thinking.

2. Choose a problem that is similar but slightly more challenging.

   The faces of this cube are labeled A, A, B, B, C, and C. What is the probability of *not* rolling a C?

   A. $\frac{4}{6}$

   B. $\frac{2}{6}$

   C. $\frac{1}{2}$

   D. $\frac{1}{3}$

   Explain your thinking.

PROBLEM FIVE

Overview

Students must be able to read and interpret a graph to answer this question. Students need to recognize that each tree symbol represents one hundred trees and they must be able to use computational skills to determine the appropriate number of missing tree symbols.

Sample Problem

This graph shows the number of trees planted in a national forest during a certain period. Use the graph to answer the following question.

Trees Planted

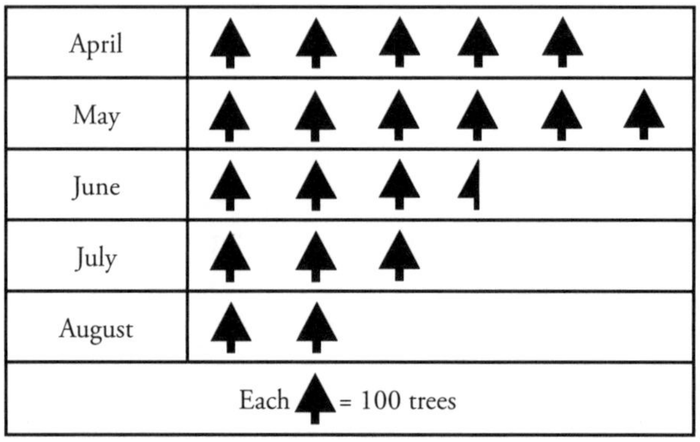

April	🌲 🌲 🌲 🌲 🌲
May	🌲 🌲 🌲 🌲 🌲 🌲
June	🌲 🌲 🌲 ⸦
July	🌲 🌲 🌲
August	🌲 🌲
Each 🌲 = 100 trees	

In July, 500 trees were planted. How many more trees should be added to the graph for July to be correct?

A. 3 trees
B. 300 trees
C. 2 trees
D. 200 trees

Explain your thinking.

Possible Student Solution Strategies

o   Students are able to read and interpret the graph to find a correct solution.
o   Students misinterpret the meaning of the graph and arrive at an incorrect solution.

Conversation Starters

o   Put the problem in your own words.
o   What do you know about this problem? What do you need to find out?
o   Is there more than one possible correct answer for this question? Explain.
o   Convince me that your idea makes sense.

Student Work Sample: Penny

Name _____ Date _____

This graph shows the number of trees planted in a national forest during a certain period. Use the graph to answer the following question.

Trees Planted

April	▲ ▲ ▲ ▲ ▲
May	▲ ▲ ▲ ▲ ▲ ▲
June	▲ ▲ ▲ ◀
July	▲ ▲ ▲
August	▲ ▲

Each ▲ = 100 trees

In July, 500 trees were planted. How many more trees should be added to the graph for July to be correct?

A. 3 trees

B. 300 trees

Ⓒ 2 trees

D. 200 trees

Explain your thinking.

$300 + ? = 500$

$300 + 200 = 500$

each tree $= 100$

$3 + 2 = 5$

(300) (200) (500)

A Conversation with Penny	Teacher Insights
T: What do you know about this problem? **Penny:** An interesting thing about this problem is that every tree stands for one hundred trees. I had to remember that and it was a little tricky. **T:** What do you have to find out? **Penny:** I had to find out how many more single trees to add to the graph to show that there were five hundred trees planted in July. The graph shows that so far three hundred trees were planted, which means two hundred more need to be added. But I don't add two hundred pictures of trees. Instead I add only two pictures of trees because each picture equals one hundred trees. But the answer choices give both two and two hundred, and that's tricky because I need two hundred trees but only two trees go on the graph. So the answer is actually two.	**T:** *Penny showed clear understanding of the skills needed for this problem in both her written and oral explanations.*

Informed Instructional Suggestions

Penny would benefit from creating her own graphs similar to this one. She should also generate questions that can be answered by the data represented on her graph. Exchanging graphs and answering questions from other students would be an interesting and challenging activity for those involved. For an additional challenge, Penny could write questions based on another student's graph.

Student Work Sample: Addison

Name _____ Date _____

This graph shows the number of trees planted in a national forest during a certain period. Use the graph to answer the following question.

Trees Planted

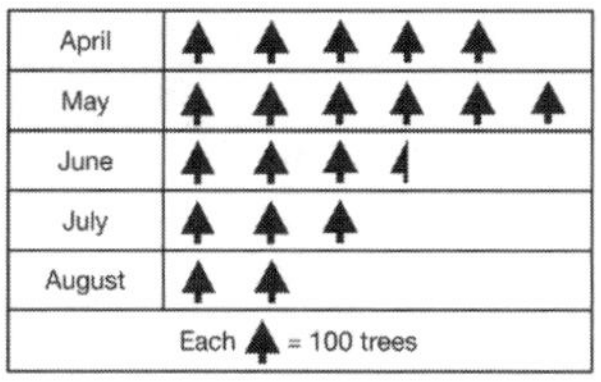

April	🌲 🌲 🌲 🌲 🌲
May	🌲 🌲 🌲 🌲 🌲 🌲
June	🌲 🌲 🌲 ˧
July	🌲 🌲 🌲
August	🌲 🌲

Each 🌲 = 100 trees

In July, 500 trees were planted. How many more trees should be added to the graph for July to be correct?

A.   3 trees

B.   300 trees

Ⓒ   2 trees

D.   200 trees

Explain your thinking.

$$July = \frac{-500}{-388}$$
$$\boxed{2\,\cancel{00}}$$

A Conversation with Addison	Teacher Insights
T: Convince me that your idea makes sense. **Addison:** The question is about hundreds of trees, but the answer isn't given in hundreds at all because each tree represents one hundred so one tree isn't one tree but one hundred trees. I have to figure out how many more trees to add to the graph for July. I just turned everything into hundreds. Five hundred trees minus three hundred trees equals two hundred trees. Then I crossed out the zeros to tell me how many trees to add. I have to add two trees to show that two hundred more were needed.	**T:** *Addison was able to successfully apply his understanding to correctly answer this question and explain his thinking.*

Informed Instructional Suggestions

Addison and Penny have similar needs and would benefit from working together.

Student Work Sample: Amy

Name _____ Date _____

This graph shows the number of trees planted in a national forest during a certain period. Use the graph to answer the following question.

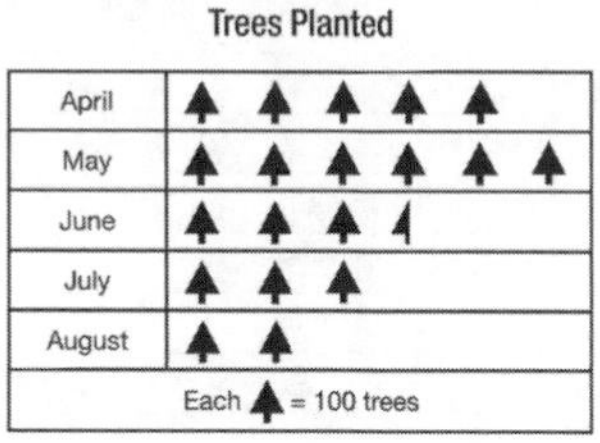

Trees Planted

April	🌲 🌲 🌲 🌲 🌲
May	🌲 🌲 🌲 🌲 🌲 🌲
June	🌲 🌲 🌲 🌲
July	🌲 🌲 🌲
August	🌲 🌲

Each 🌲 = 100 trees

In July, 500 trees were planted. How many more trees should be added to the graph for July to be correct?

A.   3 trees

B.   300 trees

C.   2 trees   *(circled)*

D.   200 trees

Explain your thinking.

$$\begin{array}{r} 500 \\ -300 \\ \hline 200 \end{array}$$

🌲 = 100

$$100\overline{)200} \quad \begin{array}{r}2\\200\\\hline 0\end{array}$$

A Conversation with Amy	Teacher Insights
T: I notice that you used division to help you solve this problem. Please tell me more about that. **Amy:** Well, first I had to figure out how many more trees were needed for July. I did that by subtracting five hundred minus three hundred, which is two hundred. I noticed before that each tree equals one hundred. I need two hundred trees so, I divided two hundred by one hundred to prove I need to add two trees to the chart. **T:** Thank you for sharing how you thought about this problem.	*T: Amy was able to communicate her thinking and understanding well.*

Informed Instructional Suggestions

Amy's needs are similar to those of Penny and Addison. The suggestions for Penny would also be effective for Amy.

Student Work Sample: Abbie

Name _____ Date _____

This graph shows the number of trees planted in a national forest during a certain period. Use the graph to answer the following question.

Trees Planted

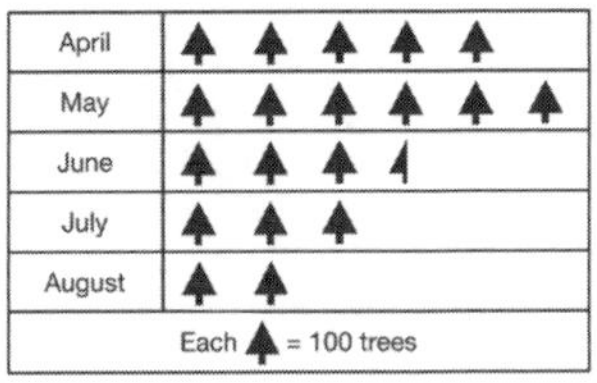

April	▲ ▲ ▲ ▲ ▲
May	▲ ▲ ▲ ▲ ▲ ▲
June	▲ ▲ ▲ ▲
July	▲ ▲ ▲
August	▲ ▲

Each ▲ = 100 trees

In July, 500 trees were planted. How many more trees should be added to the graph for July to be correct?

A. 3 trees

B. 300 trees

(C.) 2 trees

D. 200 trees

Explain your thinking. There are only 3 trees planted whitch = 300 trees. If I added 3 trees, that would = 300 trees + 300 more trees = 3,300 tree − 200 trees = 2,300.

A Conversation with Abbie	Teacher Insights
T: Convince me that your idea makes sense. Please reread your writing. **Abbie:** [Abbie reads her paper aloud.] I circled two but I don't know why. I think I don't get this problem at all. **T:** Please reread the problem and question. **Abbie:** [Abbie reads.] I know that in July there were three hundred trees planted. I can tell because there are three trees on the graph and each tree means one hundred trees. I have to add some more trees to make five hundred. That's the part I really don't get. I looked at Maria's paper and she circled choice C, so I did too.	**T:** *Abbie circled the correct answer but had only minimal understanding of the problem and no good method for finding the correct response.*

Informed Instructional Suggestions

Abbie needs experiences with simpler graphs. When she is comfortable and able to explain her reasoning in a logical way, she can move on to more complex graphs, such as this one.

Student Work Sample: Andrew

Name _____ Date _____

This graph shows the number of trees planted in a national forest during a certain period. Use the graph to answer the following question.

Trees Planted

April	♠ ♠ ♠ ♠ ♠
May	♠ ♠ ♠ ♠ ♠ ♠
June	♠ ♠ ♠ ⌀
July	♠ ♠ ♠
August	♠ ♠

Each ♠ = 100 trees

In July, 500 trees were planted. How many more trees should be added to the graph for July to be correct?

A.   3 trees

B.   300 trees   *300 because each tree is 100, so to finish the chart you need 3 more trees.*

C.   2 trees

D.   200 trees

Explain your thinking.   *3 x 100 = 300*

A Conversation with Andrew	Teacher Insights
T: Please put the problem in your own words.	**T:** *Andrew had two issues initially. The first was he misread the graph and figured his solution based on the information for August rather than July. He was able to catch this error himself. The second issue was his lack of understanding of the value of each tree shown on the graph. Even with some gentle guiding questions, he was not able to correct himself on this point.*
Andrew: There is this graph and you have to answer a question about it. The graph has trees on it. The question is about how many more trees have to be added to the graph to show that there were five hundred trees planted in July. I looked and there were just two trees on the graph. I know that three more trees have to be added to make five trees. I multiplied three times one hundred to show this and that's three hundred. Then I looked at the answers and there was three hundred, so I chose it.	
T: Please show me on the graph where the trees are for July.	
Andrew: Uh-oh! I think I looked at August. I thought there were only two trees for July, but there are three. Bummer! My answer should actually be two hundred, not three hundred.	
T: Do you need to actually add two hundred more trees to the graph?	
Andrew: Yes, and that is really going to take a long, long time.	

Informed Instructional Suggestions

Andrew would benefit from the same types of instructional activities we recommended for Abbie.

Student Work Sample: Jeremiah

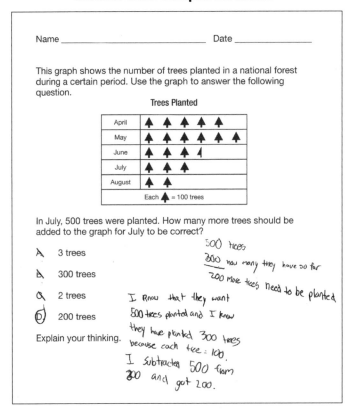

Name _____   Date _____

This graph shows the number of trees planted in a national forest during a certain period. Use the graph to answer the following question.

Trees Planted

April	▲ ▲ ▲ ▲ ▲
May	▲ ▲ ▲ ▲ ▲ ▲
June	▲ ▲ ▲ ⟋
July	▲ ▲ ▲
August	▲ ▲

Each ▲ = 100 trees

In July, 500 trees were planted. How many more trees should be added to the graph for July to be correct?

A.   3 trees

B.   300 trees

C.   2 trees

(D.)   200 trees

Explain your thinking.

500 trees
300 how many they have so far
200 more trees need to be planted

I know that they want 500 trees planted and I know they have planted 300 trees because each tree = 100. I subtracted 500 from 300 and got 200.

A Conversation with Jeremiah	Teacher Insights
T: I appreciate your clear and detailed written explanation. Please study the graph once more to make sure you have considered all necessary information. **Jeremiah:** [Looks over the graph.] You know, I noticed something I didn't see before. I think I did it wrong because each tree really means one hundred trees. I didn't figure it out that way. The correct answer should really be two, not two hundred. It's true, two hundred more trees are needed, but on the graph that would be shown as two trees, not two hundred. I guess I should make sure to know all the necessary information, huh?	**T:** *Jeremiah solved the problem incorrectly but actually does have the knowledge needed to solve it correctly. Asking him to study the graph one more time was all it took for him to find his error and determine the correct solution.*

Informed Instructional Suggestions

Jeremiah's incorrect answer without his verbal explanation would have indicated he needed remediation with these skills. This is not the case, and providing him with remediation would have been a poor use of energy and instructional time. Taking a few minutes to talk with him and listen to him was a more efficient way to meet his needs. He is ready for the same types of activities and experiences as Penny and Addison.

Reassessment

1. Use a similar problem at the same level of difficulty.

    This graph shows the number of trees planted in a national forest during a certain period. Use the graph to answer the following the question.

    Trees Planted

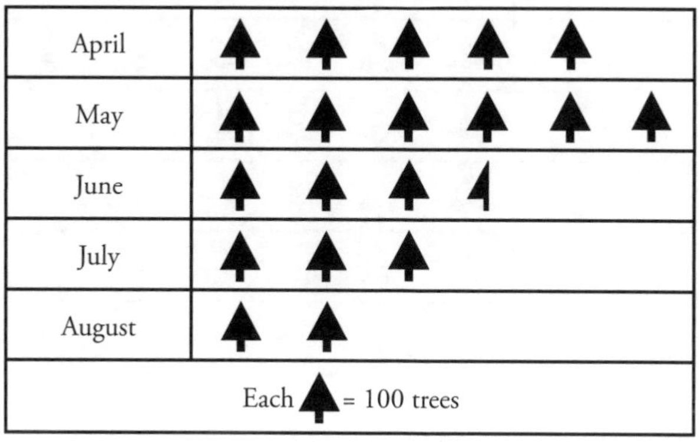

April	🌲 🌲 🌲 🌲 🌲
May	🌲 🌲 🌲 🌲 🌲 🌲
June	🌲 🌲 🌲 ⼁
July	🌲 🌲 🌲
August	🌲 🌲

    Each 🌲 = 100 trees

    In August, 600 trees were planted. How many more trees should be added to the graph for August to be correct?

    A. 400 trees
    B. 3 trees
    C. 4 trees
    D. 300 trees

    Explain your thinking.

2. Choose a problem that is similar but slightly more challenging.

This graph shows the number of trees planted in a national forest during a certain period. Use the graph to answer the following the question.

Trees Planted

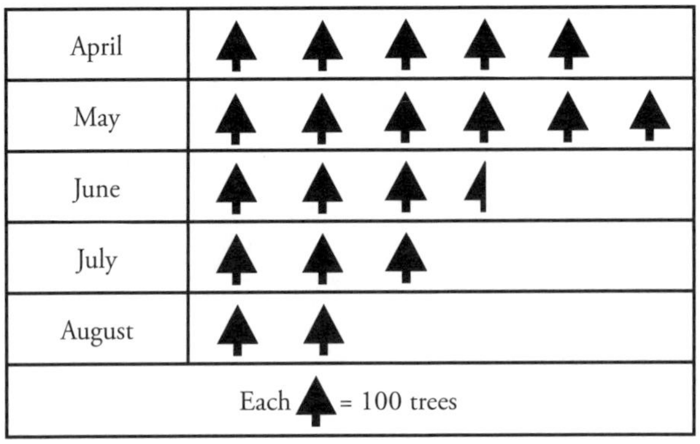

April	🌲 🌲 🌲 🌲 🌲
May	🌲 🌲 🌲 🌲 🌲 🌲
June	🌲 🌲 🌲 🌲
July	🌲 🌲 🌲
August	🌲 🌲
Each 🌲 = 100 trees	

In August, 650 trees were planted. How many more trees should be added to the graph for August to be correct?

A. 450 trees

B. 4 trees

C. $4\frac{1}{2}$ trees

D. $5\frac{1}{2}$ trees

Explain your thinking.

PROBLEM SIX

Overview

To correctly solve this problem, students must understand and apply ideas about sampling, outcomes, and equivalent fractions. Students must also recognize that this question asks them to combine outcomes to answer the question. They need to be able to make sense of complex data in a way that allows them to interpret it accurately.

Sample Problem

There are 16 marbles in Mr. Chen's jar. There are 5 red, 4 purple, 4 white, 1 green, and 2 blue marbles. If Mr. Chen takes out one marble without looking, what is the probability that he will choose a purple *or* blue marble?

A. $\frac{1}{4}$

B. $\frac{1}{8}$

C. $\frac{3}{8}$

D. 1

Explain your thinking.

Possible Student Solution Strategies

o   Students are able to use their knowledge of probability and equivalent fractions to correctly solve this problem.
o   Students may use strategies involving words, pictures, or numbers.
o   Students do not fully understand the question, resulting in an incorrect or partial solution to the problem.

Conversation Starters

o   How did you use words and pictures to help you solve this problem?
o   What is alike and what is different about your solution and those of others?
o   How did you reach your answer?
o   What do you know about this problem? What are you trying to find out?

Student Work Samples: Penny, Rachel, and Jeremiah

Name _____ Date _____

There are 16 marbles in Mr. Chen's jar. There are 5 red, 4 purple, 4 white, 1 green, and 2 blue marbles. If Mr. Chen takes out one marble without looking, what is the probability that he will choose a purple *or* blue marble?

$\cancel{A}$ $\frac{1}{4}$

$\cancel{B}$ $\frac{1}{8}$

C. $\frac{3}{8}$

$\cancel{D}$ 1

Explain your thinking.

Mr. Chen's Marble Jar

R=red
P=purple
W=white
G=green
B=blue

— there is __16__ marbles
— there is __2__ blue
— there is __4__ purple

blue $= \frac{2}{16} = \frac{1}{8}$

purple $= \frac{4}{16} = \frac{1}{4}$

$\frac{1}{8} + \frac{2}{8} = \boxed{\frac{3}{8}}$

$\frac{1}{4} = \frac{2}{8}$

Name _____ Date _____

There are 16 marbles in Mr. Chen's jar. There are 5 red, 4 purple, 4 white, 1 green, and 2 blue marbles. If Mr. Chen takes out one marble without looking, what is the probability that he will choose a purple *or* blue marble?

red   Purple   white

A. $\frac{1}{4}$

B. $\frac{1}{8}$

C $\frac{3}{8}$

green   blue

D.   1

$\begin{array}{r} 4 \\ + 2 \\ \hline \end{array}$

Explain your thinking.

$\frac{6}{16} = \frac{3}{8}$

I got C because purple was 4 and blue was 2, if you put those together you get $\frac{6}{16}$ is equal to $\frac{3}{8}$.

Name _____ Date _____

There are 16 marbles in Mr. Chen's jar. There are 5 red, 4 purple, 4 white, 1 green, and 2 blue marbles. If Mr. Chen takes out one marble without looking, what is the probability that he will choose a purple *or* blue marble?

~~a.~~ $\frac{1}{4}$

~~b.~~ $\frac{1}{8}$ I got my answer by adding $\frac{2}{16}$ & $\frac{4}{16}$

~~c.~~ $\frac{3}{8}$ and go $\frac{6}{16}$ and reduced $\frac{6}{16} = \frac{3}{8}$ = my answer

~~d.~~ 1

Explain your thinking.

$\frac{2}{16} = \frac{1}{8}$ = blue ★

$\frac{4}{16} = \frac{1}{4}$ = purple ★

$\frac{5}{16}$ = red

$\frac{4}{16}$ = white

$\frac{1}{16}$ = green

A Conversation with Penny, Rachel, and Jeremiah	Teacher Insights
T: Please share your work with each other. As you are sharing and listening to each other, consider what is alike and what is different about your solution and those of the others.	**T:** *Rachel, Jeremiah, and Penny all showed strong understanding and were able to communicate their thinking with one another. They were all able to listen to and evaluate the thinking of others as well.*
Rachel: I drew a picture of the marbles. I put them in groups by their color. I counted them to find that there were sixteen marbles in all.	
Penny: I did the same thing as you, Rachel, only I drew the marbles in rows in a jar.	
Jeremiah: I got sixteen marbles, but I didn't draw a picture. Instead I just added up all the marbles and then wrote a fraction for each color to tell how many marbles for that color. Besides, the problem tells us there are sixteen marbles.	
Rachel: The tricky part was knowing to add the purple and blue. At first I thought it might be just blue or just purple but that really didn't make too much sense. So, all I had to do was find out how many blue and purple marbles there were and that would be the probability of choosing a blue or purple. There were six altogether.	
Jeremiah: I think another tricky part was we had to simplify because the answer of six-sixteenths wasn't a choice.	
Penny: Well, it wasn't that hard because the blue is $\frac{2}{16}$, which is the same amount as $\frac{1}{8}$, and purple was $\frac{4}{16}$, which is $\frac{1}{4}$, but $\frac{1}{4}$ is the same as $\frac{2}{8}$. One-eighth plus $\frac{2}{8}$ equals $\frac{3}{8}$, and that's the probability of picking a blue or purple marble.	
Rachel: I knew that each marble is equal to one-sixteenth so I just counted all of the blue and purple marbles and that was six-sixteenths. That wasn't an answer and I already knew that six-sixteenths is equivalent to three-eighths.	
Jeremiah: We did three different ways, but we all got the same answer! That's pretty cool!	

Informed Instructional Suggestions

Penny, Rachel, and Jeremiah are ready for more complex problems. They should also create their own problems, share them, and solve each other's problems. Another challenge for these students would be to solve a similar problem using a different strategy.

Student Work Sample: Nisa

Name _____ Date _____

There are 16 marbles in Mr. Chen's jar. There are 5 red, 4 purple, 4 white, 1 green, and 2 blue marbles. If Mr. Chen takes out one marble without looking, what is the probability that he will choose a purple *or* blue marble?

A. $\frac{1}{4}$

B. $\frac{1}{8}$

C. $\frac{3}{8}$

D. 1

16 marbles
4 Purple
2 blue

Explain your thinking.

Thiers more purple that you could probobility get.

A Conversation with Nisa	Teacher Insights
T: How did you reach your answer? **Nisa:** Well, I counted up all of the colors of the marbles and there were 16 marbles. There were 4 purple and 2 blue. That means you could get more purple. I chose $\frac{3}{8}$ for my answer because the 3 was halfway between the 2 and the 4, and 8 is half of 16. The answer is $\frac{3}{8}$.	*T: Nisa had a starting strategy. However, her correct answer masked some significant misunderstandings about outcomes and fractions.*

Informed Instructional Suggestions

Nisa's correct answer alone would have caused her to miss out on needed intervention. She needs experiences that will require her to find and understand equivalent fractions. She also needs probability experiences that involve combining outcomes. Essentially, Nisa took the average of the numbers two and four to get her answer of three. This is not what combined outcomes represent.

Student Work Sample: Kelly

Name _____ Date _____

There are 16 marbles in Mr. Chen's jar. There are 5 red, 4 purple, 4 white, 1 green, and 2 blue marbles. If Mr. Chen takes out one marble without looking, what is the probability that he will choose a purple *or* blue marble?

A. $\frac{1}{4}$

B. $\frac{1}{8}$

C. $\frac{3}{8}$ *(circled)*

D. 1

C is the the best answeR Because $\frac{1}{4}$ is to small because there are 4 porple and 2 Blue and $\frac{1}{8}$ is to small so is 1

Explain your thinking.

Red
(rows of circles crossed out)
Porple

(Red)
○○○○○

White
○ ○○○

(Porple)
○○○○

green

Blue
○○

A Conversation with Kelly	Teacher Insights
T: What do you know about this problem? What are you trying to find out? **Kelly:** I know that there are some marbles in a jar. I have to figure out what the chances are of drawing a purple or blue marble from the jar. I drew a picture of the marbles and labeled it. Then I looked at the answers. There are six marbles that are blue or purple. That tells me that all of the answers with one in them are too small. That means one-fourth, one-eighth, and one won't work because of the one. That leaves three-eighths. That must be the answer.	**T:** *Kelly marked the correct answer but has some significant gaps in her understanding of fractions. She was able to find the total number of marbles in the jar. However, her misunderstandings about fractions are significant and need careful, thoughtful intervention. Because of these issues, it is hard to know for sure what she understands about representing outcomes using fractions.*

Informed Instructional Suggestions

Kelly marked the correct answer and that alone would have masked her serious misconceptions. She needs hands-on, concrete experiences to develop basic fraction ideas. Fraction bars, fraction circles, and fraction kits would all be appropriate to support her conceptual development. Kelly should use these materials to discover for herself that the greater the denominator, the smaller the fractional pieces; that a proper fraction is less than one; and what the numerator and denominator represent in common fractions. Kelly needs to do additional, similar probability experiments to reinforce ideas of probability and how they are represented with fractions. She could even put her own marbles in a jar and write about the probability of selecting each type using fractions.

Student Work Sample: Chrystal

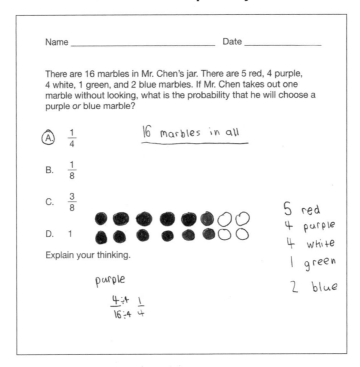

Name _____ Date _____

There are 16 marbles in Mr. Chen's jar. There are 5 red, 4 purple, 4 white, 1 green, and 2 blue marbles. If Mr. Chen takes out one marble without looking, what is the probability that he will choose a purple *or* blue marble?

Ⓐ $\frac{1}{4}$ 16 marbles in all

B. $\frac{1}{8}$

C. $\frac{3}{8}$

D. 1

Explain your thinking.

purple

$\frac{4 \div 4}{16 \div 4} = \frac{1}{4}$

5 red
4 purple
4 white
1 green
2 blue

A Conversation with Chrystal	Teacher Insights
T: You drew a very nice picture. How did that help you think about this problem? **Chrystal:** Drawing a picture always helps me to think about a problem. It helps me to see the information like the marbles and how many of each color there are and how many there are altogether. **T:** What was the problem asking you to find out? **Chrystal:** I am supposed to find out the probability for drawing a purple or a blue marble. I chose purple. There are sixteen marbles. Four of them are purple, so that means the probability of purple is four-sixteenths, or one-fourth. **T:** In this problem, the word *or* actually means something closer to the word *and*. The problem is asking you to consider the chance in one draw of choosing a purple or a blue marble. **Chrystal:** Oh, so that means there is a four-sixteenths chance of choosing a purple and a two-sixteenths chance of choosing a blue. So if I put those together, it would be six-sixteenths, right? That means the best answer choice would be three-eighths because six-sixteenths is equivalent to three-eighths. I see now!	**T:** *Chrystal misunderstood what the problem was asking her to do. This is not an uncommon error because many words have a different meaning in mathematics than in everyday usage. In this case, Chrystal interpreted the word* or *as giving her a choice when in fact the word* or *was being used inclusively to incorporate the possibilities of drawing either a blue or a purple marble.*

Informed Instructional Suggestions

Although Chrystal selected the wrong answer, she possesses a great deal of understanding. A few carefully chosen questions got her on the right track and she was able to quickly correct her error. Chrystal needs to experience a few more activities similar to this one to cement her understanding. Then she will be ready for activities and experiences such as those suggested for Penny, Rachel, and Jeremiah.

Student Work Sample: Albert

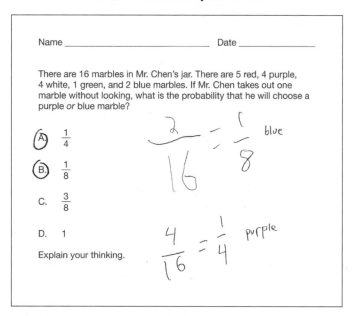

Name _____ Date _____

There are 16 marbles in Mr. Chen's jar. There are 5 red, 4 purple, 4 white, 1 green, and 2 blue marbles. If Mr. Chen takes out one marble without looking, what is the probability that he will choose a purple *or* blue marble?

A. $\frac{1}{4}$

B. $\frac{1}{8}$

C. $\frac{3}{8}$

D. 1

Explain your thinking.

$$\frac{2}{16} = \frac{1}{8} \quad \text{blue}$$

$$\frac{4}{16} = \frac{1}{4} \quad \text{purple}$$

A Conversation with Albert	Teacher Insights
T: What do you know about this problem? **Albert:** The problem told me there were sixteen marbles in a jar. There were two blue and four purples. Then it asked me to figure out the probability of drawing a blue marble and a purple marble. Two-sixteenths of the marbles were blue and that simplifies to one-eighth, and so that's the answer for blue. I circled it. There are four out of sixteen marbles that are purple; that's one-fourth, and I circled that for purple. I thought it was really weird that on a multiple-choice test there were two correct answers, but there they are! Strange!	**T:** *Albert is able to determine the probability of outcomes. His difficulty was similar to Chrystal's: he misunderstood the word* or *in this problem.*

Informed Instructional Suggestions

Albert's needs are very similar to Chrystal's and he would benefit from the same instructional decisions and activities.

Reassessment

1. Use a similar problem at the same level of difficulty.

   There are 18 marbles in Ms. Ramirez's jar. There are 6 red, 5 purple, 4 white, 1 brown, and 2 yellow marbles. If Ms. Ramirez takes out one marble without looking, what is the probability that she will choose a red *or* a white marble?

   A. $\frac{2}{9}$

   B. $\frac{1}{3}$

   C. 1

   D. $\frac{5}{9}$

   Explain your thinking.

2. Choose a problem that is similar but slightly more challenging.

   There are 24 marbles in Mr. Jackson's jar. There are 4 yellow, 8 green, 8 blue, 2 red, and 2 black marbles. If Mr. Jackson takes out one marble without looking, what is the probability he will choose a green, blue, *or* black marble?

   A. $\frac{2}{3}$

   B. $\frac{3}{4}$

   C. $\frac{1}{3}$

   D. $\frac{3}{24}$

   Explain your thinking.

Appendix A: Generic Conversation Starters

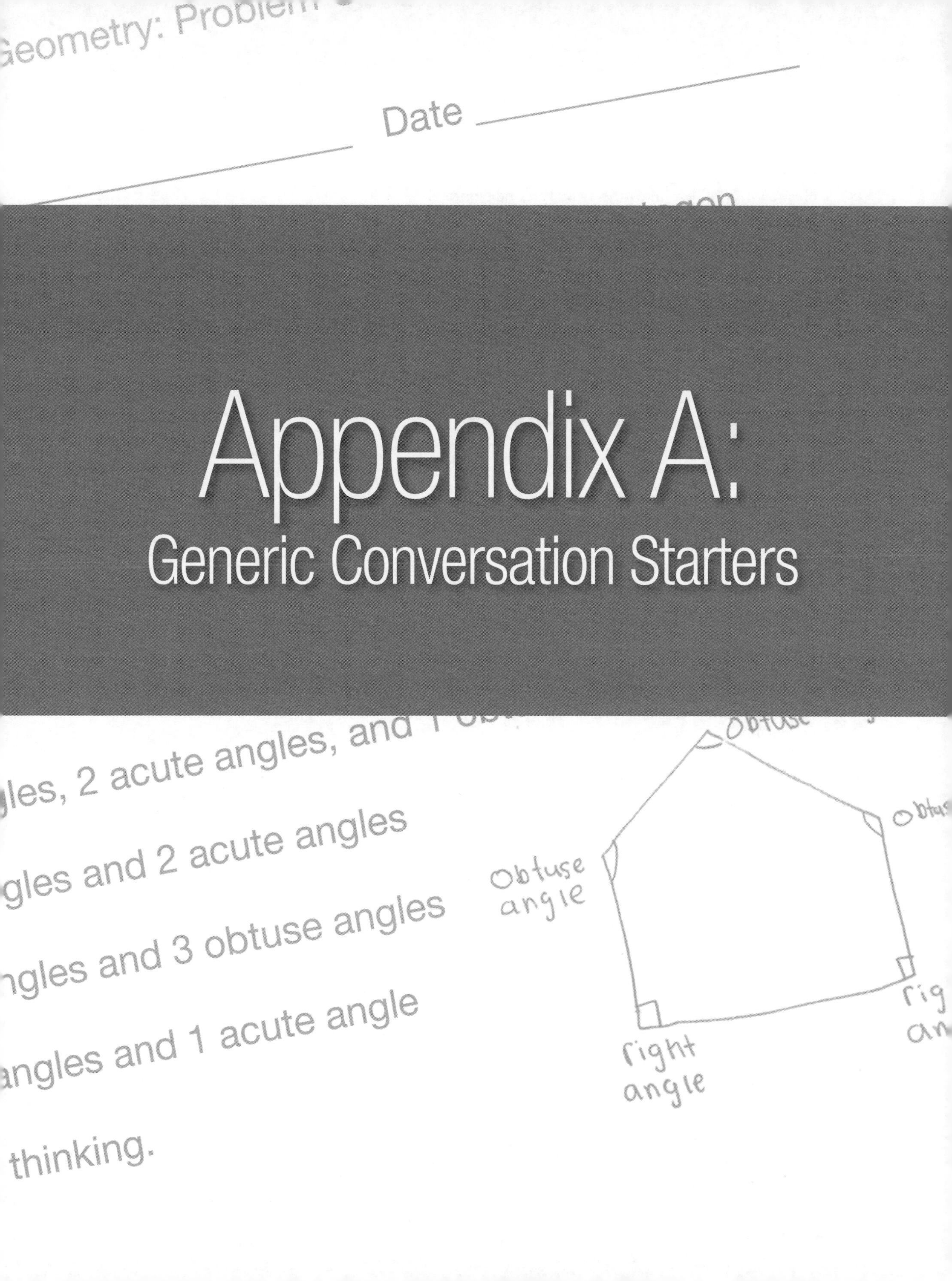

Geometry: Problem
Date
gles, 2 acute angles, and 1 ob
gles and 2 acute angles
ngles and 3 obtuse angles
angles and 1 acute angle
thinking.
Obtuse
Obtuse angle
right angle

o   Restate the problem in your own words.

o   How is this problem like others you've done before?

o   What do you know about this problem? What do you need to find out?

o   How would you use manipulatives or pictures to help you solve this problem?

o   How could a table, chart, or diagram help you solve this problem?

o   Why does your solution [or answer] make sense?

o   How did you reach your answer?

o   What have you seen before that looks like this?

o   How would an estimate help you decide if your answer makes sense?

o   Is there more than one possible correct answer? Explain.

o   Is there more than one way to solve this problem? Show it.

o   How do you know your answer is reasonable?

o   Does your strategy always work? How do you know?

o   How can you prove your answer?

o   What did you do to check your answer?

o   How can you solve this problem in another way?

o   Do you see a pattern that can help you solve this problem? Describe it.

o   How did you think about this problem?

o   Does anyone have a different answer or way to solve the problem?

o   What is alike and what is different about your solution and those of others?

o   Convince me that your idea makes sense.

o   How could you explain your thinking to younger students?

Beyond the Bubble: How to Use Multiple-Choice Tests to Improve Math Instruction, Grades 4–5
by Maryann Wickett and Eunice Hendrix-Martin. Copyright © 2011. Stenhouse Publishers.

Algebra: Problem Four

Appendix B:
Reproducible Problems

PEMDAS

( ) 4^2 x ÷ + -

our thinking.

emdas to answer my qustion in th
ndas told me to,

Number: Problem One

Name _____ Date _____

In which box on the number line does the number 190 belong?

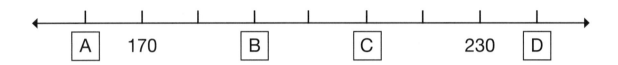

A.   Box A

B.   Box B

C.   Box C

D.   Box D

Explain your thinking.

Number: Problem Two

Name _____ Date _____

Sarah collected 337 baseball cards. Tamika collected fewer baseball cards than Sarah. Which number sentence shows a possible comparison between the number of baseball cards that Sarah collected and the number that Tamika collected?

A. $337 < 325$

B. $340 < 337$

C. $301 < 337$

D. $337 > 350$

Explain your thinking.

Number: Problem Three

Name _____ Date _____

Tyler added 6 tenths and 3 hundredths to 26.78. What was the sum?

A. 27.41

B. 26.89

C. 27.68

D. 386.78

Explain your thinking.

Number: Problem Four

Name _____ Date _____

When the ages of two sisters are added, the sum is 16. When the ages are multiplied, the product is 63. What are their ages?

A.   11 and 5

B.   9 and 6

C.   10 and 6

D.   7 and 9

Explain your thinking.

Number: Problem Five

Name _____ Date _____

Juan ran $2\frac{1}{2}$ kilometers on Tuesday, $3\frac{1}{4}$ kilometers on Wednesday, and 3 kilometers on Thursday. How many kilometers did he run in those three days?

A. $5\frac{3}{4}$ kilometers

B.   7 kilometers

C. $8\frac{3}{4}$ kilometers

D.   8 kilometers

Explain your thinking.

Number: Problem Six

Name _____ Date _____

Which of the following has the same value as 10 nickels?

A. $\frac{1}{10}$ of a dollar

B. $\frac{1}{5}$ of a dollar

C. $\frac{1}{2}$ of a dollar

D. $\frac{1}{4}$ of a dollar

Explain your thinking.

Measurement: Problem One

Name _____ Date _____

Four friends counted their change. Study their coins. Then answer the question below.

Marci had 7 dimes.
Sam had 3 quarters and 2 nickels.
Kyle had 1 quarter and 5 dimes.
Monte had 16 nickels.

Which friend had the most money?

A.   Marci

B.   Sam

C.   Kyle

D.   Monte

Explain your thinking.

Measurement: Problem Two

Name _____ Date _____

If one square unit equals 6 square feet, what is the area of the shaded figure?

☐ = 6 square feet

A.   7 square feet

B.   48 square feet

C.   36 square feet

D.   42 square feet

Explain your thinking.

Measurement: Problem Three

Name _____ Date _____

Sam arrived at the bus station at 11:15 p.m. but found out that his bus had left at 10:35 p.m. By how many minutes did he miss his bus?

A.   50 minutes

B.   20 minutes

C.   30 minutes

D.   40 minutes

Explain your thinking.

Measurement: Problem Four

Name _____ Date _____

What is the measure of ∠C?

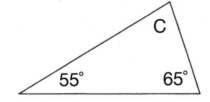

A.   120°

B.   60°

C.   70°

D.   100°

Explain your thinking.

Measurement: Problem Five

Name _____ Date _____

Tony has a piece of rope that is 27 inches long. How much less than a yard is the rope?

A.   12 inches

B.   72 inches

C.   9 inches

D.   36 inches

Explain your thinking.

Measurement: Problem Six

Name _____ Date _____

How many 1-inch cubes could be stored in this box?

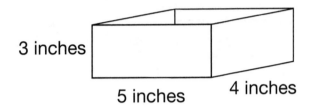

3 inches

5 inches   4 inches

A.   30

B.   60

C.   12

D.   24

Explain your thinking.

Algebra: Problem One

Name _____ Date _____

Choose the number that goes into each box to make this number sentence true.

$$\boxed{} + \boxed{} > 334$$

A.   132

B.   157

C.   169

D.   92

Explain your thinking. Then choose an answer that doesn't work and explain why.

Algebra: Problem Two

Name _____ Date _____

What is the value of the expression below if $y = 7$?

$$34 - (y \times 2) = \boxed{}$$

A.   32

B.   20

C. $y + 20$

D.   14

Explain your thinking.

Algebra: Problem Three

Name _____ Date _____

What is the equation for the rule in this chart?

x	y
1	2
4	8
8	16
12	24

A. $x = 2y$

B. $x + 1 = y$

C. $x + 4 = y$

D. $2x = y$

Explain your thinking.

Algebra: Problem Four

Name _____ Date _____

Solve the following problem using the correct order of operations.

$$3 \times 12 - 10 \div 2 \times 4 =$$

A.   24

B.   16

C.   0

D.   52

Explain your thinking.

Algebra: Problem Five

Name _____ Date _____

Solve the following problem.

$$x + 239 = 372$$

$$x = \boxed{}$$

A. 147

B. 611

C. $x - 239$

D. 133

Explain your thinking.

Algebra: Problem Six

Name _____ Date _____

What number, when placed in each box, makes a true equation?

$$24 + \boxed{} + \boxed{} + \boxed{} = 48$$

A. 24

B. 12

C. 6

D. 8

Explain your thinking.

Geometry: Problem One

Name _____ Date _____

Which group correctly describes the angles inside the pentagon below?

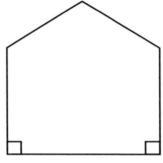

A.   2 right angles, 2 acute angles, and 1 obtuse angle

B.   3 right angles and 2 acute angles

C.   2 right angles and 3 obtuse angles

D.   4 right angles and 1 acute angle

Explain your thinking.

Geometry: Problem Two

Name _____ Date _____

Which of these is *not* a name for this figure?

A.   pentagon

B.   quadrilateral

C.   square

D.   polygon

Explain your thinking.

Geometry: Problem Three

Name _____   Date _____

Study the pyramid below. How many edges does the pyramid have?

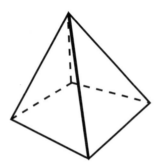

A.   5

B.   4

C.   8

D.   6

Explain your thinking.

Geometry: Problem Four

Name _____ Date _____

Which of these attributes does a trapezoid *always* have?

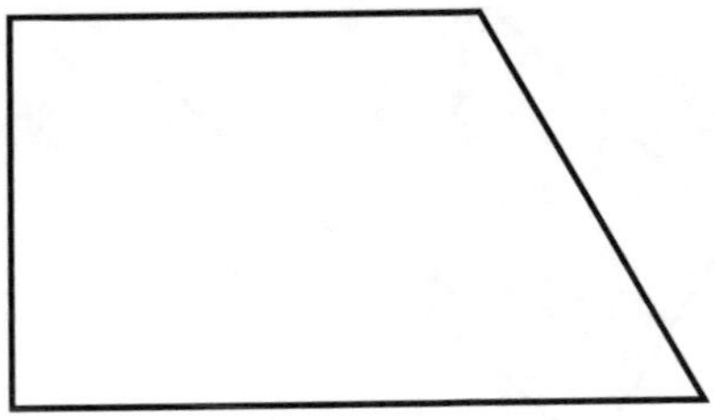

A.   at least 1 pair of parallel sides

B.   4 equal sides and 4 right angles

C.   4 parallel sides

D.   opposite sides that are equal and parallel

Explain your thinking.

Geometry: Problem Five

Name _____ Date _____

How many obtuse angles does this quadrilateral have?

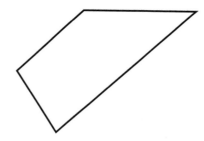

A.   2

B.   3

C.   1

D.   4

Explain your thinking.

Geometry: Problem Six

Name _____ Date _____

Which two pairs of lines are parallel?

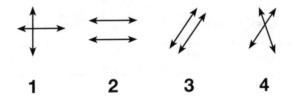

1   **2**   **3**   **4**

A.   1 and 4

B.   2 and 4

C.   2 and 3

D.   1 and 3

Explain your thinking.

Probability: Problem One

Name _____ Date _____

This graph shows the number of cans collected during a food drive. Use the graph to answer the following question.

Cans Collected During Food Drive

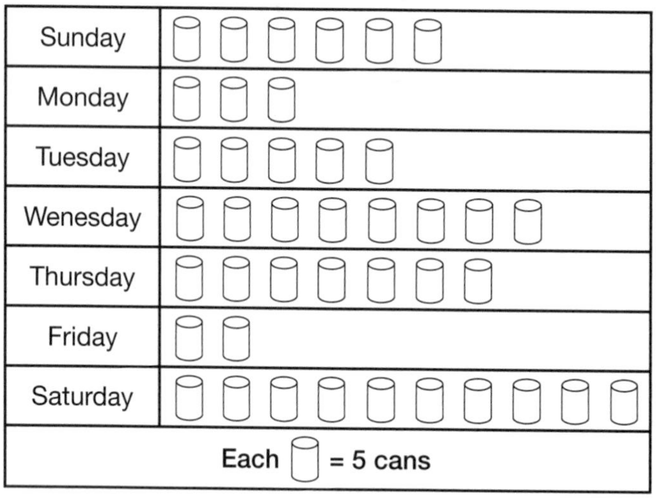

Sunday	🥫🥫🥫🥫🥫🥫
Monday	🥫🥫🥫
Tuesday	🥫🥫🥫🥫🥫
Wenesday	🥫🥫🥫🥫🥫🥫🥫🥫
Thursday	🥫🥫🥫🥫🥫🥫🥫
Friday	🥫🥫
Saturday	🥫🥫🥫🥫🥫🥫🥫🥫🥫🥫

Each 🥫 = 5 cans

What is the difference between the number of food cans collected on Monday and the number of food cans collected on Wednesday?

A.   45 cans

B.   25 cans

C.   5 cans

D.   20 cans

Explain your thinking.

Beyond the Bubble: How to Use Multiple-Choice Tests to Improve Math Instruction, Grades 4–5
by Maryann Wickett and Eunice Hendrix-Martin. Copyright © 2011. Stenhouse Publishers.

Probability: Problem Two

Name _____ Date _____

If you spin the spinner once, what is the probability it will stop on A?

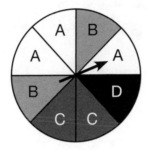

A. $\dfrac{1}{8}$

B. $\dfrac{2}{6}$

C. $\dfrac{1}{6}$

D. $\dfrac{3}{8}$

Explain your thinking.

Probability: Problem Three

Name _____   Date _____

During a vacation, Blaise's family went on a bike trip. These are the number of miles that his family biked each day.

26   23   33   25   31   30   23

What is the mode of these miles?

A.   7 miles

B.   23 miles

C.   26 miles

D.   10 miles

Explain your thinking.

Beyond the Bubble: How to Use Multiple-Choice Tests to Improve Math Instruction, Grades 4–5
by Maryann Wickett and Eunice Hendrix-Martin. Copyright © 2011. Stenhouse Publishers.

Probability: Problem Four

Name _____ Date _____

The faces of this cube are labeled A, B, B, B, C, and D. What is the probability of rolling a B?

A. $\dfrac{1}{4}$

B. $\dfrac{3}{6}$

C. $\dfrac{1}{3}$

D. $\dfrac{6}{3}$

Explain your thinking.

Probability: Problem Five

Name _____ Date _____

This graph shows the number of trees planted in a national forest during a certain period. Use the graph to answer the following question.

Trees Planted

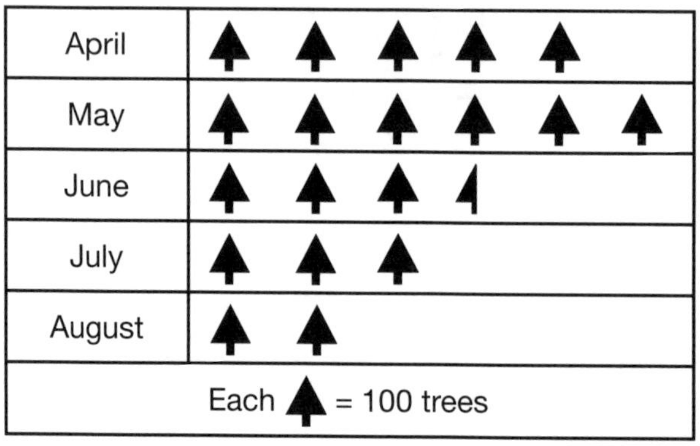

April	🌲 🌲 🌲 🌲 🌲
May	🌲 🌲 🌲 🌲 🌲 🌲
June	🌲 🌲 🌲 🌲
July	🌲 🌲 🌲
August	🌲 🌲
	Each 🌲 = 100 trees

In July, 500 trees were planted. How many more trees should be added to the graph for July to be correct?

A.   3 trees

B.   300 trees

C.   2 trees

D.   200 trees

Explain your thinking.

Beyond the Bubble: How to Use Multiple-Choice Tests to Improve Math Instruction, Grades 4–5
by Maryann Wickett and Eunice Hendrix-Martin. Copyright © 2011. Stenhouse Publishers.

Probability: Problem Six

Name _____ Date _____

There are 16 marbles in Mr. Chen's jar. There are 5 red, 4 purple, 4 white, 1 green, and 2 blue marbles. If Mr. Chen takes out one marble without looking, what is the probability that he will choose a purple *or* blue marble?

A. $\dfrac{1}{4}$

B. $\dfrac{1}{8}$

C. $\dfrac{3}{8}$

D. 1

Explain your thinking.

General Resources

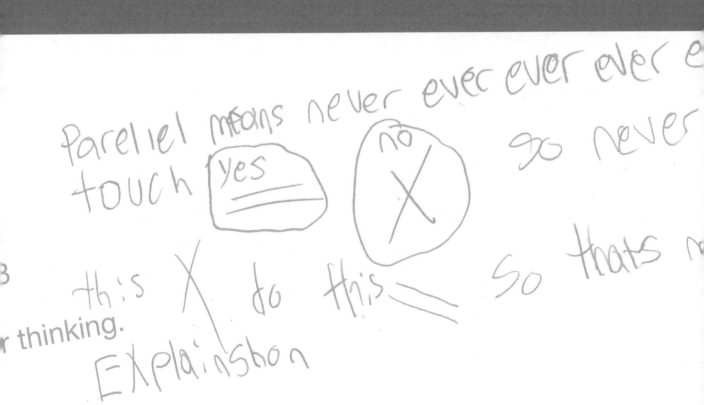

Pareliel means never ever ever ever ever e

touch [yes]   (no X)   so never

B   this X do this ____ so thats

r thinking.

Explainshon

Burns, Marilyn. 1995. *Math By All Means: Probability, Grades 3–4*. Sausalito, CA: Math Solutions.

———. 2001. *Teaching Arithmetic: Lessons for Introducing Fractions, Grades 4–5*. Sausalito, CA: Math Solutions.

———. 2007. *About Teaching Mathematics: A K–8 Resource*. 3rd ed. Sausalito, CA: Math Solutions.

Carpenter, Thomas P., Megan Loef Franke, and Linda Levi. 2003. *Thinking Mathematically: Integrating Arithmetic and Algebra in Elementary School*. Portsmouth, NH: Heinemann.

Chapin, Suzanne H., Catherine O'Connor, and Nancy Canavan Anderson. 2009. *Classroom Discussions: Using Math Talk to Help Students Learn, Grades K–6*. 2nd ed. Sausalito, CA: Math Solutions.

Common Core State Standards. 2010. www.corestandards.org.

Confer, Chris. 2007. *Sizing Up Measurement: Activities for Grades 3–5 Classrooms*. Sausalito, CA: Math Solutions.

Cuevas, Gilbert J., and Karol Yeatts. 2001. *Navigating Through Algebra in Grades 3–5*. Reston, VA: National Council of Teachers of Mathematics.

Dacey, Linda, and Anne Collins. 2010a. *Zeroing in on Number and Operations: Key Ideas and Common Misconceptions, Grades 3–4*. Portland, ME: Stenhouse.

———. 2010b. *Zeroing in on Number and Operations: Key Ideas and Common Misconceptions, Grades 5–6*. Portland, ME: Stenhouse.

Fosnot, Catherine Twomey, and Maarten Dolk. 2001a. *Young Mathematicians at Work: Constructing Multiplication and Division*. Portsmouth, NH: Heinemann.

———. 2001b. *Young Mathematicians at Work: Constructing Number Sense, Addition, and Subtraction*. Portsmouth, NH: Heinemann.

Litton, Nancy, and Maryann Wickett. 2009. *This Is Only a Test: Teaching for Mathematical Understanding in an Age of Standardized Testing*. Sausalito, CA: Math Solutions.

National Council of Teachers of Mathematics (NCTM). 2006. *Curriculum Focal Points for Prekindergarten Through Grade 8 Mathematics: A Quest for Coherence*. Reston, VA: NCTM.

Schuster, Lainie. 2009. *A Month-to-Month Guide: Fourth-Grade Math*. Sausalito, CA: Math Solutions.

Van de Walle, John. 2010. *Elementary and Middle School Mathematics: Teaching Developmentally*. 7th ed. Boston: Pearson/Allyn and Bacon.

Wickett, Maryann, and Marilyn Burns. 2001. *Teaching Arithmetic: Lessons for Extending Multiplication, Grades 4–5*. Sausalito, CA: Math Solutions.

Wickett, Maryann, Katharine Kharas, and Marilyn Burns. 2002. *Lessons for Algebraic Thinking, Grades 3–5*. Sausalito, CA: Math Solutions.